Social Welfare and Social Value

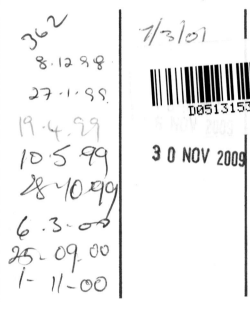

**This book is to be returned on or before
the last date stamped below.**

Also by Richard Hugman

POWER IN CARING PROFESSIONS*
AGEING AND THE CARE OF OLDER PEOPLE
IN EUROPE*
ETHICAL ISSUES IN SOCIAL WORK
(*co-editor David Smith*)
CONCEPTS OF CARE
(*co-editors Moira Peelo and Keith Soothill*)

* Also published by Macmillan

Social Welfare and Social Value

The Role of Caring Professions

Richard Hugman

*Professor of Social Work, Curtin University
of Technology, Perth, Australia*

Consultant Editor: Jo Campling

MACMILLAN

First published 1998 by
MACMILLAN PRESS LTD
Houndmills, Basingstoke, Hampshire RG21 6XS
and London
Companies and representatives throughout the world

ISBN 0–333–64573–1   hardcover
ISBN 0–333–64574–X   paperback

A catalogue record for this book is available from the British Library.

This book is printed on paper suitable for recycling and made from fully
managed and sustained forest sources.

10 9 8 7 6 5 4 3 2 1
07 06 05 04 03 02 01 00 99 98

Printed in Hong Kong

'The cynic knows the cost of everything and the value of nothing.'

– Oscar Wilde

Contents

Preface and Acknowledgements

Across the globe major shifts have taken place in the world of social welfare. The era of 'welfarism' has given way to that of 'economic rationalism' (experienced diversely as Reaganomics, Thatcherism and so on). These changes have affected all aspects of social welfare, including policy, organisation and practice. Large-scale rapid reductions in the scope of public welfare provision have been accompanied by a reshaping of the ways in which social welfare service are delivered. New approaches to structures and practices in social welfare institutions have been generated by the need to respond to changed social and political values attached to health and welfare services.

The impact on the caring professions of nursing, the remedial therapies and social work has been profound. (The connections between this range of occupations is discussed in Chapter 1; for an extended definition of 'caring profession' see Hugman, 1991, Chapter 1.) The organisation, the values and the practices of these occupations have been recast from the mode of 'service' to the mode of '(industrial) production'. The very notion of industry has replaced that of profession in some quarters. The scope of the adaptation to new circumstances which has been required thus goes beyond the development of novel techniques or re-ordering of priorities, to struggles over the meaning of social welfare as a whole.

This book therefore brings together a discussion of the ways in which thinking about social welfare policy and practice has developed, with an examination of the role of caring professions in contemporary society. These two objects of inquiry are seen as facets of the same concern, namely the future of welfare as a *social* issue. In particular, that debates around these questions are political in this sense has to be accepted as inevitable, because the central concern is with the definition of 'well-being' and so is open to difference of interpretation according to the perspective from which it is examined. Caring professions cannot escape the contested nature of their work. The professional is the political. As a consequence, the type of caring professions and their relationship with the wider society which we choose to develop is bound up with the very type of society that we want. Recent arguments that such matters are beyond the remit of the professions are themselves a device for achieving specific outcomes in these debates: they are statements based on quite specific social values.

This book seeks to challenge such an interpretation of social welfare and the role of the caring professions. In particular, it focuses on the possibility for rethinking the relationship between the professions and the wider society, through recent critical approaches to power relationships between service users and service providers. It also links these approaches to the wider questions about the nature of society and broad definitions of welfare.

My experience, as an author, of the global impact of the commodification of social welfare has been affected by my own biography. Moves between two countries and three universities during the writing of this book have left their mark: I think this is for the better. In acknowledging the critical support and assistance of colleagues the list is therefore longer than it might otherwise have been. My thinking on these issues has developed over several years in conversation and debate at Lancaster University (UK), Edith Cowan University (Western Australia) and Curtin University of Technology (Western Australia). The list of people who have given advice and provided information or support is long, but I would like to give particular recognition here to Steve Baldwin, Alastair Christie, Roger Clough, Roger Hadley, Patricia Harris, Sabina Leitmann, Peter MacDonald, Jeannine Millsteed, Marilyn Palmer, Dyann Ross, David Smith and Sue Wise. Pauline Carroll and Donna Runner-Ruda gave invalulable advice on the manuscript; Sue Burchell provided assistance with bibliographic searches. Any errors of course remain entirely my own responsibility.

Without the helpful patience of Jo Campling, consulting editor, and Frances Arnold at Macmillan this book would not have been completed. I am grateful for their forebearance.

Finally, I am indebted to all the service users, students, colleagues and teachers from whom I have learned so much about the issues addressed in this book. One person in particular stands out among all others, to whom this book is dedicated with respect and affection: Janet Finch – teacher, colleague, friend.

Western Australia   RICHARD HUGMAN

PART I

THE VALUES OF SOCIAL WELFARE

Introduction

This book examines the relationship between social values, the social policies which embody values, and the organisation and practice of caring professions whose work constitutes the main elements of social welfare services. The discussion is divided into three parts, identifying and emphasising three central themes. These themes are: the values which have been the foundation of social welfare as it has developed in Western countries through the twentieth century; the commodification of social welfare in the recent years of this period, which represents a major shift in values as well as in organisation and practice; and the implications of these recent changes for the future of caring professions such as nursing, the remedial therapies and social work in the social welfare arena.

Part I begins by examining the importance of values in the construction of social welfare institutions, including welfare state structures and the forms of professionalism which have emerged through the course of this century. This discussion engages with debates about the value dimensions of social policy. The place of professions such as nursing, the remedial therapies and social work in contemporary society has been defined in part by the role they are seen to play in the achievement of certain social objectives. However, values and the policy objectives which are related to them are highly contested (that is, they are open to dispute and disagreement). So, the key role of nursing, the remedial therapies and social work in debates about issues such as how health and well-being are to be achieved, and who is responsible for the various aspects of these, has been challenged as policies have shifted from social democratic to economic rationalist. Therefore, Chapter 1 examines the way in which the debate about the contemporary shape of social welfare, and the role of the caring professions within it, is concerned as much with values as with organisation and practice.

In Chapter 2 the meaning of key values for the caring professions is discussed in more detail. In particular, ideas about 'need',

3

'citizenship' and 'responsibility' are examined in turn. The concept of citizenship has been seen for much of the twentieth century as the basis for the determination of rights and responsibilities with regard to the meeting of need. These questions are at the heart of social welfare, because they are about the formal and informal relationships of obligation and responsibility between members of a society, including the state, the family and community. The more specific importance of professional values within the wider context is explored in Chapter 3. As professions offer skilled practices to assist others in the resolution of problems, there is a technical dimension (the means of providing for health and well-being) introduced into the discussion. Attempts to redefine the relationship between these means and the ends (objectives) of social welfare is shown to be part of the changes taking place in the overall values of social welfare. So, this chapter considers the implications of developments in the wider society as a whole for changes in professional values, organisation and practice. The argument emphasises that there are consequences in such value shifts for social welfare generally, as well as for the specific professions.

1

Values in Policy and Practice

Working in a World of Values

Values are inherent in both the methods used and the objectives of work sought by professionals. Not only do such occupations seek to operate in ways which are informed by value principles (often defined as codes of ethics) but the ends which they seek to achieve are value based. That is, the goals of professional work are expressions of those things which are socially valued. This is so whether the profession is concerned with health, education, law and personal welfare, or the apparently more concrete issues of architecture, accountancy, science and engineering. Yet to recognise this aspect of the professions should not obscure the extent to which their work, just like the realm of values on which it is based, is subject to debate, contention and even, at times, conflict. Rather it should alert us to the importance of value debates in any consideration of the practices and organisation of professions and their general standing in society.

This book is about the way in which the contested nature of the values underpinning health and welfare has had an impact on the practices of a range of professions. The focus will be predominantly on those occupations which have been described variously as 'semi-professions' (Etzioni, 1969; Hearn, 1982), 'mediated professions' (Johnson, 1972) or 'caring professions' (Hugman, 1991), although the broader field will be kept in view. Nursing, the remedial therapies and social work are selected as the key groups for discussion for several reasons. First, they share important aspects of their history and development, their contemporary organisation and

5

their standing both in relation to groups such as architecture, law and medicine and in the perceptions of society generally. Throughout the developed, industrialised world these occupations have had their practices shaped as much by 'outsiders' as by their own members. Second, they have also exercised much less control or influence over the social policies which have directed their work than have those occupations which are regarded as the 'classic' or 'established' professions (Etzioni, 1969; Johnson, 1972). For this reason, they have been more clearly subjected to the forces of change in the late twentieth century with which this book is concerned. (This is not to suggest that the more established professions have been immune to such forces – see, for example Halsey's 1992 analysis of the universities.) Third, that many of their important historical figures have been women and that gender remains a central aspect of their contemporary organisation and practice is a crucial element in their development (Walton, 1975; Hearn, 1982; Witz, 1992) and a point to which this analysis will return below.

The 'caring professions', defined thus, are those which serve not only the interests of their clientele, but also those of the state and of other professions. For this reason they can be understood as working 'between' these other groups (Philp, 1978). In such a position there is a need to interact with a range of practices and policies which reflect the values of outside groups. The state and other professions will usually be experienced as having greater power and authority, so that in situations of contention the values of nurses, remedial therapists or social workers may often be perceived as having lesser legitimacy. There is, then, a sense of contradiction, in that despite being held in social esteem because they embody positive social values (such as altruism, caring, dedication, other directedness and so on), when contention emerges the very core of these occupations may come to be questioned. This has occurred most particularly in the UK in the form of regular inquiries into social work, in which specific events are held to challenge the legitimacy of the profession as a whole (for example: Blom-Cooper, 1985; Department of Health and Social Security, 1988). Nor are nursing or the remedial therapies immune from similar fundamental questioning when individual members appear to confront the boundaries of acceptable action in the eyes of more powerful sections of society (Woods, 1987; Mackay, 1993).

Moreover, recent social changes in the developed countries

mean that the place of the professions generally is perhaps less secure than it has been for most of the twentieth century. Shaw's (1911) assertion that all professions are 'a conspiracy against the laity' has been seized with renewed vigour by politicians, journalists and other interested groups (such as service-user organisations) both as true and as unacceptable.

Across Australasia, Europe and North America the previously dominant position of (certain) professions in influencing if not determining health and welfare policy has been eroded rapidly (Cousins, 1987; Mishra, 1987). Partly this follows from the perceived needs of advanced industrial societies to reduce the extent to which the state is engaged directly in providing services in these areas. However, it is tied also to the emergence of a thorough-going neo-liberalism which has identified existing policies with 'undue restraint' and has sought to promote particular views of 'freedom', 'choice' and 'justice' (Johnson, 1990; Gray, 1992). This shifts the scope of the debate from the economic to the moral (to the point of engaging explicitly with social theology at times [Davies, 1993]). In other words, it begins to emphasise the extent to which recent welfare restructuring is driven as much by ideology as by economics (Jessop, 1994).

There are, therefore, two broad areas of 'value questions' with which we must be concerned in relation to the caring professions. These are the values of 'how' (the right means) and the values of 'what' (the right objectives). Discussions about these questions have tended to be seen as of narrowing focus or else of decreasing relevance in recent years. For example, Wessell (1992) suggests that in nursing 'ethics' often has become a matter only of decision-making in individual situations, while Shardlow (1989) noted that in social work 'value-talk' had for some time suffered an eclipse. Why should an apparent decline in the broad concern of professions with values have occurred? There are two possible developments within the caring professions which might explain this phenomenon. First, value statements have tended increasingly to be seen as too general to be realistic or of practical use (Timms, 1983). Second, the broad issues of social value have become defined as outside the sphere of competence of professionals (Cousins, 1987; Hugman, 1991).

The first of these answers comes from the 'radical' writings about nursing and social work (as well as the professions generally). Briefly summarised, this position is critical of codified ethical principles, which in the past have often been seen to be an essential characteristic of 'true' professionalism. Such codes, it is argued, decontextualise the problems and issues with which professionals deal. Being based on Kantian philosophy, ethical codes tend to stress individualist interpretations of the world, thus denying the social dimension to the needs of service users as well as of the professional identity and role (Simpkin, 1979, pp. 95–100). From such a critique it is argued that a more collective, necessarily *social* view should be taken of the relationship between professionals, clients and the state (Mullaly, 1993). (I will return to this point in Chapter 3.)

This critical perspective does not actually dispose of value concerns (Hugman and Smith, 1995). What it does is to reframe them from the realm of ethics to that of politics, or at least suggest that a political dimension is central to ethical issues (Purtilo, 1993). It is argued that either the origins of needs are social or that the available means of resolving needs lie within the social domain, or both. As the political sphere concerns the distribution and exercise of power and authority within society, the meeting of need must be grounded in power and authority over resources (including the technical skill and knowledge of professionals). Within this perspective individual(ist) ethics are subsumed within a broader analysis of social relations understood in terms of class, gender, race, age, sexuality, disability, poverty, culture and religion, and so on (Williams, 1994).

Increasing emphasis on technical competence forms the second explanation for the apparent decline in 'value talk' amongst caring professions (Issit and Woodward, 1992). Although there are other (epistemological) grounds on which the 'competence movement' can be criticised as it has taken shape in developed countries, one of its chief characteristics has been to increase the extent to which elements of work tasks are specified and routinised (Ashworth and Saxon, 1990). This process can be seen to separate out means from ends, rather than laying any stress on the relationship between them. That is, it is argued that the concern of professionals should be confined to the technical means of accomplishing their work, which is usually seen as highly complex and difficult to control or predict (Jamous and Peloille, 1970). At the same time it is asserted that the setting of objectives for such work belongs in another realm, with policy makers, politicians and managers. Thus the separation of means and ends creates a sense that choosing between different ends, beyond the level of the individual case, is not the proper concern of the professional practitioner. The practitioners' appropriate interest, seen from this perspective, should be in making sure they have developed the most effective and efficient techniques to achieve the broad goals which are set for them. To the extent that values are an expression of socially desired objectives, this will then exclude a concern with values from the professional domain.

The connection between this process and economic and ideological pressures on previously existing welfare state structures can be seen in two current trends. The first is the replacement of professionals with increased numbers of non-professionals, the creation of a more casualised professional labour force (short-term contracts, part-time working and so on) and other changes in the labour process (Jessop, 1994). This process has come to be called 'post-Fordism', referring to the demise of the labour processes of industrial capitalism of which the factory system of Henry Ford is taken as the epitome. That system presupposed full-time, specialised workers, each of whom had one job within the process of production, and in which such jobs were with one employer over a relatively long period of time. Large-scale hospitals and social welfare agencies are examples of 'Fordist' employment structures for the caring professions. In practice there are of course many examples of how the Fordist notion was more conceptual than real, such as the depression of the 1930s. The point is that it serves as a model for what is happening in the last decade of the twentieth century in various parts of the labour market, often using 'new technologies' as the means to create organisational change.

The second trend is in the tendency to seek to control and specify the work of professionals in ever more precise ways, through legislation, by changes in funding or remuneration arrangements, or through the promotion of a 'managerialist' ethos in which decisions about goals and judgements about techniques are separated. The conceptual terms which describe these shifts in the nature of professional work are deprofessionalisation (the down-grading of professional authority and autonomy) and deskilling (the removal of professional discretion in the choice of appropriate objectives, through limiting the professional overview of the whole care process) (Larson, 1980; Derber, 1983). For example, nurses may be controlled managerially through being excluded from decisions about wider aspects of hospital or service administration (Laschinger and Havens, 1996), and social workers may have the scope of their work determined by agency procedures (Parton, 1994).

Caring professions such as nursing, the remedial therapies and social work are subject to these changes in the labour process more than some others precisely because of their less-developed control over the 'uncertain' elements in their work (Cousins, 1987; Hugman, 1991). Consequently, their work is judged by more powerful social groups to be relatively easily specified (particularly in relation to its objectives) by non-members of the profession. However, even where a profession has widely recognised claims to skills and knowledge over tasks with uncertain outcomes similar controls may be developing, taking the form of a separation between the individual and the group. For example, medical practitioners may well increasingly come to be employed in the same manner as other professionals while medicine as an enterprise continues to enjoy a privileged position (Beck, 1992, p. 212; Dent, 1994). (I will return below to the corollary, that of 'flexible' employment as a developing trend amongst the established as well as the caring professions.) In such circumstances the concern with values will be seen to be concentrated on the technical 'means' of working at an individual level, while those relating to 'ends' will be seen as appropriately located at a social level (for example, in the relations between professional associations and state organisations). This reinforces the separation of means and ends discussed above.

That there have been strong movements towards graduate-level training in nursing (Castle, 1987) and social work (Sibeon, 1990) does not constitute a contradiction to these trends. What is happening in such developments is that the technical complexity of the work is reserved increasingly for *some sections of these professions*. This may increase rather than decrease the integration of professionalism with managerialism, by tightening both the definition of what counts as 'uncertain', that is unpredictable without the application of esoteric skills and knowledge, and the specification of exactly what a graduate professional should be able to do (Lorentzon, 1990). (It also provides a group within the profession for whom a move into management as a career step is also reserved.) As a consequence, the general routine aspects of professional work become separable from the more esoteric and uncertain elements and so can be allocated to paraprofessional or ancillary colleagues.

This process may appear on the surface to increase the professionalisation of fully qualified sections of nursing, the remedial therapies or social work. However, it does so in a context in which the managerialism and deprofessionalisation act as counteracting forces, limiting the extent to which control over the social objectives (values) of the work can be achieved by the professional practitioners. The consequence is a process in which 'technical autonomy' (the development of highly complex technical skills by advanced, or 'full' professionals) is enhanced at the expense of 'ideological autonomy' (the right of professionals to choose the goals towards which their skills are utilised) (Derber, 1983). This point will be developed in Part II of this book.

On the surface both these accounts of the demise of 'value talk' appear to rule out the possibility of an ethical discourse for caring professions which has any purpose beyond either an attempt to hold on to a semblance of traditional professionalism or else an individualistic interest in the appropriateness of techniques or procedures. However, contemporary accounts of 'values-talk' also share the conclusion that, rather than disappearing altogether, debates about the possibility of such a discourse have shifted from the realm of individual professional–client relations to the wider structural relations of the professions with other parts of society. In this sense ethics are to be seen as situated within a wider concern with values (Hugman and Smith, 1995). The former may still be focused on the rules for appropriate conduct at the individual level, but are embraced by the over-arching social values reflected in the pattern and structure of professional work (especially, for this discussion, in health and welfare). For this reason it is not only possible but necessary to consider the ways in which an ethical concern leads back to a concern with broader values. In other words, one may begin to ask if the exclusion of professions from the consideration of the objectives of their work is either wholly feasible or ultimately desirable.

Identification of these trends therefore points to the connection between values in professional work as statements of objective, the technical means by which these values are put into practice (including associated ethical principles), and the overall processes through which it might be said that these occupations are professionalising or de-professionalising. These processes take place in the context of a specific set of historical circumstances, structural and ideological, which are centred around the idea of 'welfare'. It is to this idea that the discussion now turns.

The Values in Question: Welfare

As a general principle, 'welfare' may be said to embody the notion that the well-being of all members of society is appropriately seen as a matter of public concern. For this reason, although the exact form will vary (Esping-Andersen, 1990), '[t]he contemporary debate in Western societies has almost invariably been about the *welfare state*' (Barry, 1990, p. 101, emphasis original). In other words, public concern has been focused predominantly around the structure and detailed purposes of welfare, exactly how it is organised and funded, rather than around the broad principle of welfare as such. The problem with welfare, Barry suggests (1990, pp. 50–4), is that it brings together questions of individual well-being with social and economic relations, neither of which sphere can be seen as free of subjective elements. Indeed, judgements concerning the good life are inherently subjective and the conclusions it is possible to reach will depend on the philosophical and political starting points (George and Wilding, 1976; Hewitt, 1992). Therefore it would seem to be impossible to take welfare out of the political arena, because it would depend then on universal agreement about social values, which, it is at least possible to agree, is not a likely event (Barry, 1990, p. 128; Taylor-Gooby, 1991, pp. 195–6).

Yet to imply that the focusing of concern around the structure and operation of the welfare state has precluded attention to matters of value and purpose would be, I think, quite simply wrong. Indeed, the debates since the late 1970s, as well as the pronouncements of governments around the developed world as to *why* certain technical or structural actions were necessary or desirable, have incorporated clear statements of value (compare, for example, Nicholls, 1992, and Young, 1992). Changes have not only been justified in terms of their effect on the economy, for example through the connections between reduced spending on welfare and levels of taxation, but also in their practical effect, such as claims that market mechanisms are to be seen as technically superior in service delivery. There have also been assertions that welfare-state structures are iniquitous on moral grounds (Nozick, 1974; Bauman, 1988). It is argued that welfare states involve a utilitarian coercion in which the rights of some are denied (through the mechanism of taxation) in order to meet the perceived needs of the majority (Gray, 1992). The charges against the welfare state are therefore based on values (ends) as well as techniques (means).

The work of the philosopher Rawls (1972) has offered one possible basis for shaping the debate, even if not resolving it. Rawls holds that the (re)distribution of resources is just if it is to the benefit of the least advantaged in a society. As a corollary, an inequality is to be seen as just if it is to the benefit of the least advantaged (irrespective of whether it also advantages others). Rawls also presupposed that in an ideal situation the rules for distribution and redistribution would be agreed without reference to the social position occupied by any one person. The defence of welfare might be constructed on such a proposition, because in a world of imperfect knowledge about one's own and others' situations a minimum level of benefit would be guaranteed for everyone in a society by universal welfare provision (Grace, 1994).

However, Le Grand (1982) has demonstrated that in the welfare state model of the UK inequity has not only persisted but at the same time has benefited the better-off to a greater extent than the worst-off (also see Castles, 1985, on comparable outcomes in Australia). The lowest level of inequity found was in the area of health, closely followed by secondary education. These forms of welfare, which are often quoted in discussion about equity, are those closest to the social democratic principles embodied in the welfare state (that is, they are seen as necessary for the continuation of life at a minimum standard). At the other end of the scale there are higher levels of inequity (where welfare benefits the better-off), such as those in mortgage subsidies and rail transport. These have recently become the subject of a reappraisal of welfare in the UK, considered from the perspective of 'access' (physically and socially to goods and services) rather than across-the-board subsidy for services (Cahill, 1994). Similarly, in Australia it has been argued that these forms of welfare should now be understood in terms of the advantage accruing to certain social groups or classes (Wearing and Berreen, 1994). Recognition of these factors advances the discussion about welfare beyond questions of the supply of particular services (although this remains part of the debate) to issues of their consumption. Such an analysis confirms the conclusion that, to the extent that the promotion of equity (or minimisation of inequity) is its purpose, welfare is in crisis and has been since the early 1980s (Hadley and Hatch, 1981; Mishra, 1984; Hewitt, 1992).

A different critique has been advanced by the 'New Right' in Australia, Canada, New Zealand, the UK and the USA with varying levels of impact. Hewitt (1992, pp. 38–45) argues that there is not one single entity which can be identified as the New Right, but that it should rather be seen as a set of positions which share certain core ideological elements. The most concrete of these is an opposition to a welfare state of more than the most minimal kind. In the realm of values there is an interplay between neo-liberal objections to the apparent limitations of 'freedom' through welfare-state structures, and neo-conservative objections to a 'dependency' on welfare which is seen to replace the 'natural' dependency relations of the family (Hewitt, 1992, p. 54; Sullivan, 1992, pp. 150–7).

There are a number of implications for the caring professions which derive from the practical consequences of these social values applied to health and welfare. Indeed, even if the position is adopted that such professions may be engaged legitimately in the debate about the objectives of social welfare, the broader context remains one in which many other groups also are involved in such debates. The chief characteristics of the dominant themes in the advanced industrial world (especially that which is English speaking) have been established by the New Right through its influence in government (Gamble, 1988; Hutton, 1995). Policy making and legislation have thus been constructed around ideas about 'the family' (and how that is defined), and the way in which health and welfare are seen either to buttress or undermine that institution (Parton, 1991; Weeks, 1995). Governments dominated by New-Right ideas have incorporated the use of policies which utilise deprofessionalisation and deskilling, and the deregulation of employment (including professional work) in the restructuring of social welfare. This connects the value position ascribed to 'the family' with the claimed agenda of reducing the scope of the state and the size of related government agencies. Even some social democratic administrations (such as Labour governments in New Zealand and Australia in the late 1980s and early 1990s) have shifted towards this position, at least in part responding more overtly to fiscal issues, yet with the same tangible implications for social welfare provision.

The ways in which these changes to the organisation of social welfare are brought together with the promotion of particular ideas about 'the family' can be represented as a set of smaller goals, each of which expresses aspects of the coalescence of neo-conservative and neo-liberal values:

- the reduction of the scope of social welfare (less government 'interference' in the lives of citizens);
- the reduction of the size of public (state) social welfare institutions (smaller government);
- more 'flexible' employment practices based on the use of 'contracting out' (reduced costs equalling greater efficiencies);
- more control over the objectives pursued by social welfare services (greater 'effectiveness').

These goals were then promoted as supporting 'the family' because they placed greater responsibility on to families, as well as (in theory) freeing families from what were claimed to be unwarranted intrusions by professionals in the name of health and welfare (Parton, 1991; Sheeran, 1993).

The way in which these goals have been operationalised is through the combination of restructuring with the introduction of the quasi-market processes. By increasing the use of contracts rather than direct employment as the basis of service provision, governments have been able both to control the costs of social welfare and at the same time control the objectives embodied in the work of the professionals and others delivering services. Indeed, one aspect of these developments has been the denial of the need for professional competence in some areas of work and the redefinition of competences in others. (I will return to these points in subsequent chapters.) An emphasis is placed on those services which can be seen either to 'support the family' or to 'promote social order' (in the form of limits to those actions which might be seen as disorderly, such as in child care, juvenile justice or mental health) (Parton, 1991; Bryson, 1992; Cheek and Rudge, 1994; Nellis, 1995; Rudman, 1996b). In comparison, services based on the provision of assistance to people who do not live in orthodox nuclear family relationships, or on helping (rather than punishing) offenders have received considerably less support under New-Right-dominated policies.

There is no major difference between the statutory practice which defines large sections of social work and community health services (especially in the historically state-based structures) and the non-statutory practice which pertains in other settings. In all settings the value choices of the means and ends of services are comparable. At the broadest level, the same loss of legitimacy for state-based social welfare available to meet the needs of certain sections of the community is shared by those working in the non-government sector. Indeed, it may even be that community development interventions are those which are most questioned, even by members of the caring professions, often because of the focus on a social level of need (with the accompanying attention to causes of need at that level). This is so in community nursing and allied health as well as in social work (Chalmers and Bramadat, 1996).

Two forms of social welfare which appear on the surface to contradict this analysis are services for older people and health education. The former has, throughout most of the Welfare-State period, been possibly the most popular aspect of social welfare, as older people are generally regarded as 'deserving' of assistance. However, in the last decade an alternate view has gained ground, in which it is argued that many older people are now prosperous enough to meet their own needs (for pensions, health and personal welfare) (Callahan, 1987). Moreover, the emphasis on the family can embrace this area of life, as younger kin also are regarded as in a position financially to support their elders. Again, the idea of 'the family' forms the basis for a redefinition of the role of the state in providing social welfare. (I will return below to the feminist critique of the implied concept of family within these policies.) For tax payers funding state systems, or payers of premiums to health insurance schemes, the activities of nursing, remedial therapy and social work become more important, as these consume a major portion of health and welfare funds, especially in providing care for those in later life.

Health education in respect of HIV/AIDS and drug misuse also continue to be funded by governments operating within the New-Right paradigm. These are both health issues where much has been made in the political sphere of the moral nature of problems faced by individuals (Bell and Williams, 1991). However, here too it is possible to see consistency with other contemporary ideological stances. Not only has there been a clear mandate only for health education measures based on notions of individual responsibility, with accompanying control of health education professionals through spending controls as well as direct instruction, but also the justification for such measures has often been couched in terms of social protection (McMurray, 1993, p. 215). Moral blaming of people who are HIV positive or who misuse drugs is combined with a sense that the main political concern is to protect *others* within society (Barbour, 1995; Martin, 1995).

In summary, therefore, the changes which have taken place in the realm of social welfare since the mid-1980s have been based on a significant shift in values. The consequences have included massive restructuring, an increased questioning of health and welfare professionals and, ultimately, a challenge to certain approaches to professionalism in this context.

These changes are entirely consistent with the philosophical distinction between the individual and the wider society which is shared by neo-conservatives and neo-liberals. Expressed briefly, the basis of moral thought (and hence values) in this perspective is the individual (cf. Nozick, 1974). Society is seen as the sum of individuals, each of whom remains sovereign in the sense that any one individual cannot morally be subsumed within the interests claimed for the collectivity against that individual's will. It is on this basis that taxation to pay for social welfare, the judgements of welfare professionals (unless in a policing role or privately paid for) and hence the welfare state as a whole are regarded as ethically as well as politically unacceptable. That which has been seen as 'need' within the era of welfarism becomes defined as 'want', 'choice' or 'preference', while 'rights' are accepted only within a narrower neo-liberal frame of reference (such as the right not to be attacked, or the right to engage in honest trade). In this context the value of social welfare is plausible only in so far as it contributes to a minimum level of state support for social order, or it can be subject to the mechanism of free market exchange. Even in the free market welfare is contested, as evidenced in debates about differential insurance payments by older people (Thurow, 1996).

Values and Social Divisions

A particular issue with which the caring professions have continued in recent years to engage in respect of 'value talk' is that of equal opportunities and anti-discrimination (Thompson, 1993). This discourse has been centred primarily around gender while – to extents which vary between the different professional groups – race and culture, sexuality, disability and age also have been of concern. The predominance of gender as an issue reflects both the history of these professions and their contemporary structures (Hearn, 1982; Hugman, 1991; Witz, 1992). Historically, nursing, the remedial therapies and social work were women's professions at all levels, although they were subject to external control by men through law, medicine and the church. Men have entered the caring professions in relatively small numbers, although the proportion of men to women in psychiatric nursing has always been relatively large, while in social work the number of men has increased markedly since the 1970s (Maggs, 1987; Hugman, 1991). However, at least since the end of the world war in 1945, men have disproportionately gained predominance in the senior positions in nursing and social work (Hearn, 1982; Witz, 1992; Ratcliffe, 1996). The remedial therapies remain women's professions at all levels, although the very small number of men have a greater chance than their female colleagues of promotion to senior positions (Rider and Brashear, 1988; Nicholls, 1995).

Issues of gender are manifest not only in the structures of the caring professions but also in their practices and the theories on which these are based (Castle, 1987; Chadwick, 1992; Kendrick, 1995a). It could be said, on first consideration, that there are some differences between the caring professions on this point. Gender issues have, arguably, been most overt in social work, where the tasks performed by the profession are more overtly focused on social relations as well as on the material needs faced by service users (for example, Dominelli and McLeod, 1989). 'The family' therefore forms a major object of professional concern for social workers. By definition, social workers are concerned with situations in which someone, either the individuals or groups in question, or else the state, considers that ordinary social relations or arrangements are not meeting needs. (As England expressed it, social work is provided not for people with problems but for people who have difficulty in dealing with their problems unaided [England, 1986, p. 13].) The equation between 'the social', domestic family relations and social need creates the situation in which the majority of social welfare service users are women and children (Finch, 1989; Doyal and Gough, 1991; Bryson, 1992). It is perhaps unsurprising, therefore, that the practices and theories of social work are influenced by forms of social science which are connected to a gender analysis of society.

Nurses and remedial therapists might be expected to be less influenced by this perspective. Given that, at least on the surface, their work is focused on physical well-being it could be claimed to be value free. However, here too we may see that in a majority of instances service users, as with social work, are likely to be women and children (McMurray, 1993). The largest users of health services are people in later life (defined as over 75 years), amongst whom the majority are women (Jones, 1996). Their family carers predominantly are women (Finch, 1989). Similarly, health services provided by nurses (including community nurses and health visitors), midwives and remedial therapists are used extensively by younger women in relation to childbirth and child-rearing (McMurray, 1993; Sandall, 1995). Even in occupational or physical therapy there may be implications of gender stereotyping that arise from the use of implicitly 'sex-role differentiated' activities (Bracegirdle, 1991; Babyar et al., 1996). As a consequence a gender analysis of need has increasingly influenced both the theories and the practices of nursing and allied health professions. This may be at the specific level, such as a concern with women's choices in childbirth, or at the general level of promoting the social and personal aspects of women's health (Harrison et al., 1995; Luker et al., 1995).

Other equal opportunity and anti-discrimination issues have not been so widely addressed, but nevertheless have also influenced the development of practice and theory in the caring professions. Questions of race and culture increasingly have been raised through the questioning of the assumptions of the caring professions derived from their origins in European culture (including the 'New World' societies of Australasia and North America) (Bryan et al., 1985; Dominelli, 1988; Eyles and Donovan, 1990; Pittman and Rogers, 1990; Babyar et al., 1996). Such assumptions are shown to be based often on ethnocentric concepts of the individual, the family and the community, and of health and illness. The result has been the imposition of the values of the white majority on people of minority ethnic or racial origin.

Opposition to discrimination on grounds of race and culture, and the promotion of equity in this respect, have come to be written into professional codes of ethics in Australia, Canada, New Zealand, the UK and the USA (see, for example: Australian Association of Social Workers, 1994, pp. 9–11; Jones, 1993; Loewenberg and Dolgoff, 1992, p. 146; Mullaly, 1993, p. 43; Curtin, 1994; Scully, 1995; Brockett, 1996). This may be connected to, or subsumed within, broader statements about 'promoting social justice' (Cortis and Rinomhota, 1996). However, in each of these countries the expression by professions of a particular perspective on this issue has generated contention. As Jones (1993) observes, to adopt a position regarding discrimination on grounds of race and culture (as on other grounds) is in effect to make a political statement. That is, it is to make claims about social structures and relations which have implications for the way in which *other people* act, as opposed to more 'traditional' codes of ethics which speak only of the actions of the individual professional person. From an individualist standpoint, such statements can be regarded as outside the prerogative of the caring professions. This critique of the anti-racist position adopted by such professions, and claims to be concerned with the promotion of equity in relation to race and culture, addresses a central issue in understanding the nature of professions in the contemporary advanced industrial world (Hopton, 1995; Hugman, 1996a). Professionalism, from this standpoint, necessitates the eschewing of the political. In other words, individualism argues that professionalism *should* be confined to claims over technical competence and not over ideological issues (as discussed above). It is, arguably, in relation to ideas and practices around race and culture that this criticism of the caring professions has most clearly been voiced.

Sexuality as a broad issue has been afforded less attention, in theory or practice, by caring professions than have either gender or race and culture. Where it is acknowledged it is often in negative terms (Jackson, 1995; Perkins, 1995; Bailey, 1996). Yet this issue has been of explicit concern, for example in relation to fostering or adoption by gay or lesbian couples (van Every, 1992). It is often implicit also in debates about responses to issues such as HIV/

AIDS, for example in the counselling of young people, health education work and nursing care for people who have terminal illnesses (Bell and Williams, 1991; Bunting, 1996). Caring professions can thus at times be accused of the 'promotion of marginal life-styles' (Cooper, 1993). Moreover, gay and lesbian professionals may be concerned that their sexuality may be used as the basis for discrimination against them if it becomes publicly identified (Jackson, 1995; White, 1995).

Disability and age may appear on the surface to be legitimate issues of concern to caring professions. These are aspects of life in which technical expertise may be claimed. For instance, the remedial therapies exist to help people alleviate or cope with various forms of physical disability, while nursing and social work in various ways have provided care for people with mental or physical disabilities, especially in old age (notwithstanding the fact that most such care is provided by family members) (Finch, 1989; Hugman, 1994a; Jones, 1996). However, caring professions are criticised also in relation to these issues. From the perspective of people with disabilities or who are aged, the caring professions have often focused on disability or ill-health to the exclusion of capacity and have concentrated on individual pathology as opposed to the structural causes of problems (social policies, physical access, the organisation of institutions and so on) (Oliver, 1990; Brandon, 1991a; Pilgrim, 1993; Sines, 1996a). This critique suggests that caring professions should be involved in the debates over policies and the organisation of practice to support the empowerment of disabled, ill and elderly people (Purtilo, 1993). Moreover, it is asserted that the professions have an obligation to place themselves (including their knowledge and skills) at the disposal of service users, and that unless they do so they will continue to represent the oppression of society against disability, illness and old age (cf. Brandon, 1991a; Jones, 1996, pp. 218–19; Sines, 1996b).

Against this, it may be argued that where professions become involved in structural changes in social responses to disability, illness or old age, they are exceeding their legitimate remit (Harbert, 1988). Here too the division between technical and ideological authority may be asserted by those who regard the nature of professionalism as centred on technical abilities to deal with individual problems. Furthermore, where the sanction for the professions' work (and the resources to meet salary and other costs) comes from the state, then this perspective argues that the involvement of professionals in such debates can only be as an ordinary citizen (that is, with no special right to be heard as an expert) or, where the professional is paid privately, to act on behalf of a 'client' (such as a disabled persons' group). The relation of disability or ill-health to the core knowledge or skills of a profession does not confer the right, from this standpoint, to engage with the ideological sphere in the definition of the objectives of social welfare for disabled or ill people.

The common link between the different issues of equal opportunity and anti-discrimination is the concern with the connections between social structures, the theories which explain the causes of (and hence possible remedies for) need, and the professional practices that follow from them. The debate around the concern of the caring professions for these issues turns on whether or not such a focus is to be seen as 'ideological'. It is on just such a basis that these professions have been challenged throughout the 1980s and the early 1990s. The individualism inherent in the dominant analysis of the needs with which such professions work combines with an individualism in the understanding of the professions themselves (with an emphasis on technical skills, individual competence and an orientation to single cases in practice). A structural analysis of discrimination and disadvantage is directly opposed to this dominant perspective. For this reason, it is when attention is given to equal opportunity and anti-discrimination issues, and to other structural explanations of need or disadvantage, that the caring professions (as, indeed, would any profession) have been seen to have exceeded their social remit by governments, policy makers and some service managers (Mullaly, 1993).

Attention to equal opportunity and anti-discrimination issues has also been criticised from within the caring professions, from a perspective which does not draw on the New Right (Webb, 1991a). Webb's argument is that the focus on anti-discriminatory values results in a moral prescription which he terms 'puritan' (p. 151). By this he means that the caring professionals who promote equal opportunity and anti-discrimination as a value base can be portrayed as 'morally legalistic', possessing 'moral certainty' and seeking the abolition of the object against which they are oriented. This is a different type of objection, which does not apparently deny the legitimate entry of professional ideas or actions into the realm of ideology. Webb's position denies the legitimacy of claims to a *specific* value position which he argues is being represented as the only one plausible for the caring professions. In contrast, Dominelli (1991) criticises Webb (1991a) on two important counts. First, she argues that the 'value neutral' critic inevitably will be caught in her or his own trap. The possibility of the pursuit of disinterest in academic or professional life has a long and at times quite disputational history, especially in the social sciences. In this context the gist is that an attempt to use academic sociology to critique the emergence of a strong value paradigm is not itself value free. Rather, it represents in itself another value stance; and, given its social origins (produced by people who have a specific social identity and experience, which provides a particular view of the world), it must do so. Secondly, Dominelli notes (1991, pp. 231–2) that the anti-discriminatory critique of 'orthodoxy' often has been based on empirical demonstration of the failure of the latter to fulfil the promise of its own values in practice. Indeed, orthodox values themselves may stand as an indictment of some practices within the caring professions on these grounds (Hugman, 1991, p. 223).

Historians of the caring professions also suggest that there is a strong thread of concern with issues of social structure, particularly in relation to discrimination and oppression, running from the mid-nineteenth through to the late-twentieth centuries (Woods, 1987; Sim, 1989; Forsythe, 1995). The ideas around which the professionalisation of nursing, the remedial therapies and social work was shaped very often came from a trenchant criticism, whether implicit or explicit, of the inequalities and oppressions of industrial society. This is not to say that radical opposition to these structures was always part of the early professional agenda. For some it was, while for others the objective was perhaps more to alleviate social ills or their consequences. However, whether radical or reformist, the ideas and values of the caring professions in their initial stages of development were constructed around issues of social division, inequality, disadvantage and discrimination. That all these professions primarily involved women, and continue to do so, was noted above as the reason why gender has been the most prominent social division in this respect. Nevertheless, because of this initial ethical orientation, the influence in the contemporary value frameworks of the caring professions of concerns about structural social inequalities should, after all, perhaps not be so surprising.

The Post-modern Critique

In recent years the caring professions have started to be analysed from the perspective of 'post-modernism' (Parton, 1994). For the purposes of this discussion, post-modernism is taken to be the position which argues that the modern period in Western thought (including philosophy, science, art, religion and so on), from the Enlightenment and Reformation to recent times, is now challenged by the breakdown of intellectual consensus (Lyon, 1994). This epoch, 'modernism', is defined as that in which all thought has become rationalist. The laws of natural science, and following this the 'laws' of society, can be known by ordered experiment and observation, from which it is possible to predict outcomes. Most of all, the accumulation of knowledge and technological skill have been assumed to represent a linear progress for human society. Indeed, modernism assumes that the history of this period is the story of 'progress' and that the rationalist scientific approach to knowledge produces 'truth'.

Post-modern theory argues that such a view of the world is flawed, because it fails to recognise that it is particular and hence partial. That is, modernism is the story of human development told from one perspective, when there are many other viewpoints which can and should be heard (Thrift, 1993). Modern rationalist thought is only one way of looking at the world. It is partial in that it is ethno-centric (it ignores non-Western views of the world and forms of knowledge) and it denies the plurality of perspectives even within Western society. Post-modernity (the social condition in which post-modernism suggests we now find ourselves) is defined by difference. Instead of a single explanatory world view, we should, therefore, be seeking to know and understand plural perspectives: there is no one 'truth', but rather a pluralism of truths.

At the very basis of the caring professions has been the use of modernist human sciences (social, behavioural and biological). This is so not only in Western societies, but also, through the impact of colonialism, in non-Western societies. Indeed, it may only be where Western thought impacts on non-Western culture that the idea of professionalism in relation to the practices that make up nursing or social work can develop (Azmi, 1997). Not all of the implications of modernism in human sciences are rejected by theorists of post-modernism (many of whom continue to trust their lives to modernist health care, for example, not to mention other uses of modernist technology such as aeroplanes or computers). However, the 'post-modern' critique of the ideas on which the practices of the caring professions are based poses problems of certainty and how to deal with plural perspectives on health and well-being. It suggests that a consensus on the definition of health and well-being may not be assumed; therefore, neither may agreement on the knowledge and skills used to address human need.

In summary, post-modernism challenges the certainties of both the structural analysis on which the bodies of knowledge and skill claimed by the caring professions are built and of the prescriptions for action suggested by this analysis (cf. Carter and Jackson, 1993). It does so because post-modern thought subjects all science, especially social science, to the same critique, questioning not only specific theories and methods, but more fundamentally the objective of a rational and predictive science of social life (Bauman, 1992; Lyon, 1994).

Although much post-modern writing focuses more on the ideas themselves than their consequences in policy or practice, some post-modern writing has recognised and addressed these implications (Rojek et al., 1988; McBeath and Webb, 1991; Howe, 1994; Parton, 1994). The implication for the caring professions of the emergence of the post-modernist critique is the further reinforcement of the contested nature of values in the issues with which these professions are concerned.

Attempts to codify ethics on rationalist principles, a common requirement of 'professions', will therefore be subject to internal contradictions. For example, statements of obligation to both client and the wider society ignore the possible conflicts of interest entailed (cf. Rhodes, 1986; Kendrick, 1992). This point is illustrated by reference to the ethical principle of 'confidentiality'. This principle has important connections to other concepts, such as 'humanity', 'dignity', 'respect', 'the person' and so on. The value of confidentiality is that it promotes the social status of the person as a human subject, whose dignity is threatened by not being able to determine who knows what about her or his life. Respect, in this sense, is the recognition by the professional of the service user's humanity, and the promotion of their dignity in the way information about that person is kept within the professional relationship. Without its location within this set of related concepts the idea of confidentiality would be very different, if it existed at all (Rojek et al., 1988, p. 129). Yet members of the caring professions may be required by law or by the procedures of their employing agencies to disclose such information about service users to a wide range of others (Scully, 1995; Shardlow, 1995). Moreover, the very notions of personhood and respect on which such a principle is based may be ethnocentric and so not shared by the service user (Azmi, 1997).

Rojek et al. (1988) are similarly critical of appeals to Marxism or feminism as the basis of truth because, they argue, the lack of precision of terms (such as 'collective practice' or 'patriarchy') is not accidental, nor is it remediable by greater exactness of thought. Rather, these are artefacts produced through language. The problems with these ideas, and the associated difficulties for professional values, stem from the specific circumstances of the present era, in which professionalism, along with the modernism in which it is grounded, is disintegrating. This may, and often does, lead to a fragmentation between various ways in which the world can be divided (including gender, race, culture, class, age, sexuality, disability, religion and so on) (Rojek et al., 1988, p. 173). As a consequence, the proposition of a value framework based on equal opportunity and anti-discriminatory principles either slips back into modernism (through appeals to an over-arching 'meta-theory') or else is doomed to failure.

Webb's critique of a value framework based unequivocally on equal opportunity and anti-discrimination could therefore be seen as post-modernist. Although more explicitly drawing on post-structuralist concepts of 'discourse' (referring to structured sets of ideas, language and their associated practices), Webb challenges the (modernist) certainties of the new value framework (Webb, 1991a, 1991b). He highlights the contested and shifting reality within which the caring professions operate. However, where Webb's argument falters is in the claim to find support in the work of Simmel and Weber, both of whom wrote in the classic modernist period of sociology and both of whom struggled to advance the idea of 'value freedom' in social science. There is a contradiction here, in that the openness to which Webb directs us is founded not on value *freedom*, but on value *pluralism*, at times even *relativism* (Lyon, 1994). The assertion of value freedom therefore is in itself an aspect of modernism which has failed, precisely because it represents a particular value position in itself.

Parton (1994) argues for a modest, but necessary appraisal of where caring professions, especially social work, find themselves at present. He argues that the idea of post-modernism is helpful, precisely because it deals with the shifts in social ideas and institutions. Yet he points to the way in which these are difficult to discern and are tentative (p. 10). The lack of certainty even in the move from modernism inclines Parton (among others) to write of the '(post) modern', expressing the uncertainty with parentheses. Not only might it be said that we know only where we are coming from, not where we are going to, but also that we do not yet know if we have departed: we are sure only that we, and the entire social world, is in motion.

Nevertheless, Parton's analysis identifies a number of shifts in knowledge, language and practice within which the caring professions are being re-formed. These are centred on their role between the state and citizens, in the relationships which have come to be termed 'the social' (Donzelot, 1988). This involves nurses, remedial therapists and social workers in the governing of citizens through the management of the (perhaps contradictory process) in which the autonomy of individuals and families is maintained, while at the same time the health and welfare of those who are weak or dependent is ensured. This can be most clearly seen in statutory work, but is not confined to those aspects as it can also be seen, for example, in health promotion and education and access to general, publicly funded services (Wessell, 1992).

In a period dominated by neo-conservatism and neo-liberalism the organisation of these professions increasingly is being distanced from the state. It is at this juncture that the post-Fordism of new employment patterns (defined above) and the post-modernism of the shifts in the wider social structures come together for the caring professions. Control over skills and knowledge, through which social power is exercised, changes form. It moves from the direct management of caring professionals through the medium of bureaucracy to an indirect pattern of control through quasi-privatised contracting arrangements. In such developments the processes of deprofessionalisation and of an emphasis on the governance functions of the caring professions are seen to connect. Quite simply, the state can use these changes to ensure that governance functions are met through those aspects of skill and knowledge for which it will contract. Social policing and social management are favoured over social development or social change.

However, as I have already argued, technique is no more value free than is the objective to which it is put. Both have meaning which is socially contextualised. Yet recognition of this does not of necessity rehabilitate the ideological nature of caring professions. What it does is to point to their contested nature and the way in which it is impossible to discuss matters of technique, or means, without also examining the objectives, or ends, to which they are put. Ideological as well as technical autonomy, the classic elements of professionalism (Greenwood, 1957), are thus placed firmly at the centre of questions about the future of the caring professions and the possibility of a new professionalism. Questions of values as well as of skills and knowledge therefore remain core concerns.

Social Welfare and Social Value

In the following chapters of this book the central argument is that the contemporary forms and the future directions of the caring professions are shaped by the social values that are expressed in social welfare. Although this may seem tautological, in so far as these professions are the vehicle for the provision of health and welfare services, there are two reasons why this relationship should not simply be assumed. The first is that the reference points concerning the nature of professionalism on which the caring professions may draw to promote their particular points of view are themselves subject to change from broader social forces. Deprofessionalisation and deskilling (see above) are trends which can be seen also in other professions. Second, the caring professions have been criticised not only by those who argue against extensive public welfare, but also by those who would wish to defend the idea of welfare as properly belonging in the social domain. So, the caring professions are a particular instance, on the one hand of professions engaged in the social arena, and on the other of a particular perspective on welfare (provided through professional knowledge and skill). Both elements express social value as this is attached to the means and the ends of social welfare. Throughout the following discussion, the balance between the individual and society is a recurrent theme. This is an old issue, but one which has a renewed urgency. From Rawls (1972) onwards there has been a resurgence of attention to this problem which has not been confined to the realms of philosophy, but also taken up in debates about political economy and the nature of society (Nozick, 1974; Barry, 1990; Grace, 1994; Hutton, 1995; Gray, 1996). From there it has begun to form the ground for ways in which the future of social welfare might be justified, if at all. So it is this question which forms the starting point for the following analysis of the relationship between social welfare and social values.

2

Values Revisited: Need, Responsibility and Citizenship

Caring Professions and 'Meeting Need'

Formal statements by health and welfare professions, in the guise of their associations or of academic commentators, frequently make reference to their purpose in 'meeting need' (Jolley, 1989; Ellis, 1992). Yet such statements cannot be taken at face value. Although plausible as a goal of social welfare, such statements have been repeatedly shown to be partial in that caring professions both meet need and at the same time impose constraints on the lives of their service users (Wilding, 1982). They are both caring and controlling. This contradiction has been explored particularly in the literature on social work, but also has been addressed in nursing and the remedial therapies (Abbott and Wallace, 1990; Hugman, 1991). The contradiction arises because it must be questioned 'whether the essence of nursing can be stated except in relation to the society in which it exists' (Ellis, 1992, p. 201). The same may be said of all the health and social welfare professions.

Placing social welfare professionals in the context of late-twentieth-century advanced industrial society, as we have seen in the previous chapter, raises issues of the goals to which their work is directed and the relationship of these to the means by which these goals are achieved. Whose needs? How are these defined? Who defines need? How do the social relationships between the different actors involved affect outcomes? What values are inherent in this process? These are all questions around which debates concerning the nature and purpose of the caring professions have centred and continue to do so.

Within such questions are to be found other, broader concerns with the structure of society and with social relations. If social welfare, and the institutions and professions through which it is provided, is to be understood in terms of the society in which it exists, then the nature of that society must also be grasped. For this reason, the connections between welfare and citizenship (membership of a society) are of particular importance in developing an analysis of the welfare state, including institutions and professions (Jayasuriya, 1996). Recognition of this point also indicates that the state too must be considered as an actor in legitimating the goals and means of social welfare.

Recent years have seen the collapse of the post-war Western consensus on social welfare. An aspect of these changes has been the thorough-going attack on the underlying values of welfare states. Philosophically the struggle over welfare has focused on questions of responsibility, liberty, obligations and rights; ultimately it is about the nature of society as a whole. As such the future of social welfare and the caring professions must be seen as a facet of the changing structures of Western society. So this chapter will examine each of these issues in turn and explore the ways in which they contribute to the potential for a justification of *social* welfare.

Need: Theoretical Approaches

In discussions of social welfare, two particular approaches have become synonymous with the concept of need. The first of these is the hierarchy of need defined by Maslow (1970). Five levels of need are defined in an ascending order of what Maslow termed 'prepotency', by which he meant the order in which it is necessary for them to be satisfied (pp. 38 ff.). These are:

(i)   physiological, such as food and shelter;
(ii)   safety, security in a psychological sense;
(iii) belongingness and love, in being part of a group such as a family;
(iv)   esteem, the recognition afforded by significant others; and

(v) self-actualisation, the achievement of things which expand or fulfil the spiritual, emotional or psychological aspects of personhood.

The basic principle of this hierarchy is elegantly simple, namely that each succeeding level can only be addressed when the preceding levels are satisfied. For example, it is difficult for a person to attend to psychological safety if he or she has chronic physiological needs. Need in this sense is the lack of something required in order to live as a human person.

Maslow's hierarchy has been used in professional practice to assess service users as well as in management of social welfare services to order the lives of professionals. In such contexts it has a clear heuristic utility. It is valuable also because it recognises the biological aspect of humanity, linking these with the psychological, emotional, social and spiritual. However, there have been many criticisms of this approach. Thompson (1987) argues that it fails to differentiate between circumstantial urges to act and the normative basis for choosing between actions. For example, human urges to do things which are harmful, such as the consumption of alcohol or tobacco, while not doing things which are beneficial, such as taking exercise, cannot be understood through Maslow's approach. The misuse of drugs would similarly challenge the assumptions behind the hierarchy of needs, as would those who put their safety at risk to achieve self-actualisation in dangerous sports (Doyal and Gough, 1991, p. 36).

These criticisms may be overstated. It is difficult to imagine a person going mountaineering or scuba-diving who is at the same time also homeless and starving. Likewise, the person misusing drugs may have begun to do so as a means of dealing with other basic needs before becoming addicted; the same explanation can be offered of the beer-drinking, cigarette-smoking couch-potato. What is perhaps more limiting in Maslow's approach is the extent to which, despite making connections with social and cultural factors, it remains focused at an individual level of analysis (and hence subsequently at that level in most instances where it is used in practice). Its appeal for health and social welfare professionals, and their managers, is that their work is organised predominantly around individual service users.

The other classic model of need in social welfare is that of

Bradshaw (1972). Unlike Maslow, who was principally concerned with a generalised theory of what need is, Bradshaw demonstrated that the way in which the definition of need is produced is related to the meaning of need which emerges. As a consequence, Bradshaw proposed a four-fold typology:

(i)   felt need (seen as personal perceptions);
(ii)   expressed need (explicit statements concerning a lack);
(iii)   normative need (judgements of need made by professionals or officials); and
(iv)   comparative need (comparisons between individuals or groups) (Smith, 1980, p. 17).

In particular, Bradshaw focused on the role of professionals in need definition. His underlying concern appears to have been to draw to the attention of caring professionals that their assessments would often be problematic because they failed to distinguish between different usages of the term need. In particular, the professionals' definitions might attempt to take in the service users' expressed assessment of their needs, but by not taking account of the way in which various factors distorted the exchange (such as agency policy, the service users' lack of understanding of what the professional could offer, and so on) the professional could misunderstand the felt need and so be imposing an unacceptable solution.

Unlike Maslow's hierarchy, Bradshaw's typology remains at the analytic level and is not able to be translated directly to the prescriptive. However, the typology serves two purposes. First, for practitioners it suggests that they might anticipate that there will be disagreement with their assessments where they impose solutions that do not relate to the perceived basic needs of service users. Second, it underlines the way in which the organisation of social welfare may itself be divorced from the perceptions of those who require services. The definition of need is not fixed, but is the product of social interaction in given circumstances. To locate agreement of 'basic needs' would require a shift in the relations between the state, professionals and service users.

Because it is dependent on the idea of basic needs, Hewitt suggests that it does not go far enough, in that this approach lacks a way to identify and satisfy them (1992, p. 177). Hewitt demonstrates that the problems of achieving the necessary consensus are neither simply technical or the consequence of professionalism *per se*. Rather, they stem from the ideological values inherent in the social relations on which welfare states have been built. In other words, because the structures of society provide the power for some groups, such as dominant groups within the state, to set the very terms through which needs will be defined, it is not possible to establish the consensus that is necessary for a just and democratic determination of needs to take place. This leads to perceptions of need that meet the interests of the state and its elite groups rather than allowing for everyone to participate. In such a context the definition of need remains highly relative, although Hewitt does conclude with some intimations of the potential to achieve a high level of social agreement on basic needs (1992, pp. 200–1).

The contemporary fascination with the relativist position has been challenged by Doyal and Gough (1991), who argue that the debate about need itself becomes pointless if we are unable to agree on certain basic suppositions. Using cross-cultural analysis and a combination of qualitative and quantitative factors, Doyal and Gough propose two key aspects of human life which, because they are fundamental, may be taken as the basic forms of need. These are physical health and autonomy (1991, pp. 49 ff.). Without the satisfaction of these requirements, they argue, it is not possible for human persons to engage in the primary activities of life, including production (food and shelter come into this category), reproduction and cultural transmission. They carefully avoid attaching specific definitions of what would count as appropriate relations of production or reproduction to this theory: it is at this level that cultural variation will play its part.

Nevertheless, Doyal and Gough are able to demonstrate the empirical application of this approach in cross-national comparison (1991, chapter 12). There are strong similarities in this exercise with objective models developed by Jordan (1987) and Taylor-Gooby (1991), and with Pieretti's (1994) concept of 'absolute poverty in a relative (that is, local) context'. Pieretti argues that absolute definitions of need (taking poverty as a particular example) may apply within a local context, whereas comparison with a different situation might suggest that no need existed (1994, p. 91). The person who is 'poor' in New York, London or Sydney might be well-off in a developing country, but this does not deny their poverty in the context of daily life.

Where these writers differ is in the extent to which Doyal and Gough apply their model outside western Europe. Indeed, this is crucial, given that both Jordan and Taylor-Gooby make much of concepts of social justice and fairness which are so heavily encultured, although Pieretti does allow for this without pursuing the point. In their wide cross-national comparison Doyal and Gough are able to show how the two elements of physical health and autonomy may have an effect independently of each other. That is, in a specific country physical health may be of a sufficient level for people to engage in normal social life, while political and social structures prevent their autonomy needs being met, or vice versa (or either, or neither). What Doyal and Gough share with these and other writers on this topic is the sense that there is an objective sense of need that is independent from the particular expressions of individuals, and the continuing importance of a limited role for the state in ensuring fairness and order. To avoid the previous imposition of arbitrary definitions of need, each of these writers, with some minor differences of emphasis, proposes participatory democracy as the means to achieve an appropriate balance.

Need: the Foundational Idea in Practice

As I have indicated above, the caring professions may be seen as having been established on the basis of their roles in meeting need. As histories of nursing and social work have shown, however, the way in which needs are defined and addressed, and who is involved, have always been highly contentious (Parry and Parry, 1979; Baly, 1987). The high point of liberal confidence in the task of the caring professions to define and meet need (Halmos, 1978) can be seen, therefore, as a short period in the development of these occupations. The history of nursing is one of a struggle to professionalise, in which the moment of 'full professionalism', seen as the autonomy to define and meet needs within a given scope, has never quite arrived (Jolley, 1989). For nursing, the remedial therapies and social work, 'full professionalism' defined in relation to autonomy over the arbitration of given needs, based on occupational control over the goals and techniques of practice, appears to have proved a chimera. Limited autonomy, for example in establishing the content of professional education and controlling entry through admission to qualifying courses, has been established. Yet even in this aspect of professionalisation the state and other more powerful professions have exerted constraints (Woods, 1987; Fry, 1992; Midgley and Jones, 1994).

In their discussion of social work, Rojek et al. (1988) write of 'traditional' social work, building on an assumption that the ideological and technical development of the occupation follows a line from the last century to the latter part of this. Other critical writers, such as Simpkin (1979) and Mullaly (1993), similarly identify 'orthodoxy' as a relatively unbroken line of descent. Alternatively it is possible to conceive of occupations' histories as more fragmented, with particular points at which shifts were made in response to outside influences. The partial displacement of 'scientific charity' or the 'settlement movement' in social work by analytic psychology in the 1920s is one example of such a shift (Parry and Parry, 1979). At the same time, complete displacements of previous ideas and practices have not occurred. For this reason, the ascription of 'tradition' or 'orthodoxy' should be seen as addressing the recent past rather than more distant times. Even 'radical' social work has a tradition going back over a century (Statham, 1978), although it may be ignored in contemporary accounts of social work conveyed to beginning students (Mullaly, 1993). Nursing, too, although it has claimed a scientific and technical basis, has an historical strand of action to promote health throughout society, especially where ill-health has its origins in social structures (such as poverty) (Salvage, 1985; Wessell, 1992).

The importance of these broad theoretical disputes running through the history of social work is that the concept of 'need' has a central place as a basis for debate (Smith, 1980). Reduced to their most basic terms, the divisions are between constructions of the individual person or society as the origin of need; individualist concepts also may be divided between those which do or do not use notions of moral causation of need. From such definitions follow the techniques and supporting theories used in response. If need is defined in social structural terms, then empowerment is more likely to be an objective than non-directive therapy. Where need is seen as the property of individuals' lives then counselling, therapy or casework will be seen as more appropriate; where moral culpability is attached then punishment may also follow.

Nursing and allied health professions have been affected by parallel debates about the meaning of need as the focus of their work. Although the medical model of health and illness has been predominant, the influence of ideas about the social context of health problems and solutions to them have always played a part (even if minor at times). In recent decades this approach has again been more to the fore, with, for example, the development of interest in advocacy and empowerment in nursing or occupational therapy practice (Witts, 1992), or of health education and occupational health as specialisms in which nursing or allied health professionals might appropriately be employed (Beattie, 1991; Borland et al., 1995).

However, such debates are not only central to the contentious business of occupational self-definition, but also constitute a major point at which outside forces exert pressure on the caring professions to direct their skills and knowledge in particular ways. That is, at a time when a strong form of individualism runs through policy in all advanced industrial countries, then the actions of governments towards social welfare have become couched increasingly in terms which validate individualist explanations of need and invalidate social or corporate explanations. This tendency finds expression in the emphasis on control and management functions, on individual behaviours in health education strategies and on forms of deregulation in occupational health that place the burden of responsibility increasingly on the individual worker (McMurray, 1993, pp. 36 ff.). The same process which asserts the rights of each citizen at the same time diminishes ideas of social or corporate (that is 'shared') responsibilities for the well-being of others, even when one owns the premises in which they work. Failures in health and social welfare, in such a world, are unambiguously the result of incompetence, incapacity or culpability, and responsibility for others is individualised on this basis. It is the individual employer who must take care of employees' health and well-being, in a system where the workers themselves are increasingly accountable. Explanations based on notions of social inequality or injustice are inadmissible. The implications for social welfare and the caring professions are that, in so far as their skills and knowledge are directed by social and not individual theories of need, they too will be seen as illegitimate. It is this process which explains the attacks by governments on such professions (Salvage, 1988; Midgley and Jones, 1994).

This returns the discussion to a point begun in Chapter 1, that the loss of legitimacy for the caring professions in advanced industrial countries is in part a consequence of the problems of legitimacy for the welfare state as a whole. The caring professions are variously seen as arbiters of need on behalf of the state (by service users), as going beyond their remit by often seeking to define need in the interests of marginal and disadvantaged groups (by the state), and as ascribing to themselves the exclusive capacity to define need (by both). The outcome has been for the certainties of the professional role in social welfare to be subject to the same challenge as all other aspects of the welfare state. The crisis of the welfare state is also the crisis of the caring professions, leading in particular to debates about the necessity or possibility of reformulating professional relationships with service users in terms of citizenship, rights and responsibilities (Hadley and Hatch, 1981; Croft and Beresford, 1989).

Citizenship

Social democratic concepts of citizenship, on which many models of the welfare state were based, derive their inspiration, at least in part, from the work of Marshall (1950). Citizenship in his terms is the set of social relations between people and the wider society of which they are a part, independent of their social-class relations (Barbalet, 1996). Marshall argued that citizenship, understood thus, forms the basis for engagement with the institutions of society, while these in turn promote the circumstances in which the exercise of citizenship is possible (Jayasuriya, 1996). Citizenship and social welfare in this sense can be seen as mutually integrative. An equality of status was linked in Marshall's concept to an equality of rights, forming the basis for the welfare state. It was precisely because this equality of rights was social rather than simply political or civil in nature that Marshall thought it gave a genuine strength to the position of all, as such social rights were seen as in opposition to the vagaries of the market. Moreover, they were distinct from the moral principles which underpin civil rights, being grounded in social and political institutions.

The theme of the separation between welfare and the market on the basis of citizenship was also developed by Titmuss (1958). Like Marshall, he was concerned to develop an understanding of the connections between private actions and public institutions which sustained the rights of all people to the means through which basic needs would be met. Like Marshall, Titmuss had no confidence in the market as a vehicle through which inequalities could be ameliorated. Both were also convinced that through the funding of welfare institutions by taxation all citizens would develop a shared sense of social ownership of the welfare state. The crisis of legitimacy in the welfare state can be seen, in the political sphere, as the breaking of a very weak consensus on this issue.

Several critics of Marshall and Titmuss have argued that the failure of their ideas was in many ways inevitable. These critiques divide into three main groups. The first is of those who see in the classic social administration theories the 'one nation' values of post-war Britain. Marshall and Titmuss, among others, represent the attempts of British social democrats and democratic socialists to use the prevailing culture of reconstruction to create the basis for social equality (Roche, 1992). Yet the perspectives of their time, for example the Keynesian promise of post-war economic growth (when it did start), in retrospect can be seen as having offered false hope (Barbalet, 1996, p. 59). Moreover, because of their antagonism towards the market they placed great reliance on the state as the agent of social citizenship rights. Subsequently this has come to be seen as the basis for the erosion of citizenship in practice, in the powers exercised by the state through its officials and professional staff, creating a de-moralising separation of citizen and state (Hadley and Hatch, 1981; Roche, 1992).

The second critique of the classic social administration perspective of citizenship is that it originated in and largely describes Britain, although its origins can be seen also in other parts of northern Europe (Roche, 1992). Other English-speaking nations, even those with historical connections to Britain, such as Australia, Canada or New Zealand, had developed their own civil, political and social structures, while clearly such ideas did not apply so easily in the United States (Esping-Andersen, 1990; Turner, 1990). Perhaps only in Scandinavia did the extent to which social citizenship was realised match that of post-war Britain (Esping-Andersen, 1990; Roche, 1992). The notion of the 'wage earner's welfare state' has been used to describe the reality of social welfare in Australia, based on the nexus between industrial and social 'wages' (in the form of pensions and child care, for example) (in Wearing, 1994, p. 180). In Australia, also, formal political citizenship is rather 'thin' in that it carries very few rights or obligations (Barbalet, 1996, p. 68). This is largely because such rights and obligations are based on 'residence' rather than formal citizenship. Barbalet observes that this is a progressive arrangement, separating civil and social rights from political citizenship. Yet it arises from similar industrial welfare patterns that now serve in New Right policies as a model for the retrenchment of social welfare across the advanced industrialised parts of the world (in restrictive rights, mandatory work or training, and so on) (Jessop, 1994, p. 24; Wearing, 1994, p. 181; Jones, 1996, p. 50).

The third critique of classic social administration is that it failed to recognise social divisions, other than those of social class which, it could be added, it treated in a relatively non-problematic way. Certainly the assumptions of economic growth were assumed to be able to create the circumstances for the spread of financial equality. Yet the ways in which questions of gender (Rose, 1981; Lister, 1991), race and ethnicity (Jayasuriya, 1996), disability or sexuality (Wearing, 1994) are silent in the discourse of classic social administration not only reflects the identity of the scholars whose work is under consideration but of the entire social and political discourse of the time in which they were writing.

Citizenship as the basis for social welfare, that in turn is oriented towards the promotion of greater equality, is therefore not only under threat from New Right critiques but also has become eroded from within through the social changes taking place since the 1960s. In particular, the emergence of social groups clustered around specific identifications has made explicit the divisions which were absent from earlier thinking about social welfare. Following Touraine (1981), these groups can be understood as 'new social movements', consisting of women's groups, black and ethnic minority groups, gay and lesbian groups, disabled people's movements, older people's groups, the environmental movement, and so on. For Touraine, the emergence of such groups is evidence that social-class relations are now only part of the picture, if they have any relevance, and that these other social divisions will become more important as the site of creativity in reshaping democracy (pp. 54–5).

Certainly, as noted above, these social groups in different ways have challenged the caring professions, who have responded through attempts to develop anti-discriminatory practice, for example. Where these have been effective (and that can be a contentious point in itself) then it may be that the response of caring professions has been directed towards the participatory (self-defined) citizenship of the service user. Yet Wearing (1994, pp. 193–4) cautions that new social movements in themselves do not guarantee democratisation. There is a risk, he asserts, that such movements may become exclusionary and fail to address the interdependence of social divisions (also see Thompson, 1993). The challenge is to avoid just adding another group to the list, but to deal with the problem of pluralism. By this is meant that a conscious effort has to be made to avoid a situation in which new groups of privilege or advantage develop, in seeking the common ground between new social movements as the basis for a revitalised social citizenship (for example, Pixley, 1993).

Citizenship and Practice: 'Special' Services

One of the primary ways in which thinking about citizenship, as the basis for social welfare in relation to new social movements, has impacted on caring professions has been in relation to the provision of 'special' services. That is, of constructing services around the self-defined needs of women, black and ethnic minority people, disabled people and so on. This is not to deny that the challenge to so-called mainstream services is unnecessary. Not to engage with this question can result in empty rhetoric which leaves specific minority groups ill-served (Rooney, 1987; Ahmad, 1990). What is being suggested here is that a means of achieving a pluralism is required that does not become totally relativistic or, by institutionalising separation of groups, reinforce divisions.

The concept of 'absolute need in a relative context' (Pieretti, 1994) or the basic objective needs defined by Doyal and Gough (1991) may provide vehicles for achieving this goal. In particular both these concepts include as a key element the question of the social constructed capacity for a person to play as full a part as they wish in their society. This notion provides a basis for considering 'special' services for specific groups. The principle is simply that these should first meet the basic (or absolute) need of autonomy or social engagement, without making special claims to citizenship over and against any other group. As Doyal and Gough show (1991, pp. 191–3), it may also be necessary for basic needs to be met through the satisfaction of 'intermediate' needs from time to time (clean water and sufficient nutritious food, a safe environment, significant primary relationships and economic security), some of which will be determined on a relative basis in context.

This approach can be illustrated with reference to services for elderly people in advanced industrial countries. Those people who are defined as 'old' by formal exclusion from the labour market (the exact age differs between countries) often experience significant levels of need defined in this objectivist way (Hugman, 1994a). That is, among older people in these countries there are greater than average levels of poverty, poor housing, low standards of nutrition, preventable ill-health and so on. The need for others to provide support in daily living is also greatest among this group (although the majority of older people do not require such assistance). This situation is buttressed by forms of social exclusion, of which compulsory retirement is the most obvious, but which also includes the organisation of social life around the interests of younger adults (Bytheway, 1995).

There are a number of special welfare services which are designed to address the needs of older citizens. All Western industrial countries have some form of age-related pension and some form of residential care provision for those who cannot live in other forms of accommodation. Age-related pensions are the most widely used form of social welfare, accessed by the majority. All other provisions are accessed only by minorities within the older population. For example, in the country with the highest level of social care usage (Denmark) the proportion of older people who receive such care (both domiciliary and residential) is 31 per cent (Hugman, 1994a, p. 125). Only four other countries (Finland, The Netherlands, Norway and Sweden) have levels of usage above 20 per cent. Of course, such figures are in part a consequence of what is available. There is also a cultural component: that most of these countries are Scandinavian reflects both the strong institutionalised welfare state in that part of Europe, as well as cultural acceptance of practical care from outside the family (Daatland, 1990; Siim, 1990).

There are two citizenship issues in care services for older people which will serve to illustrate the difficulties of balancing pluralism. The first is the situation of the older person from a black or ethnic minority community. Although such persons may have their physical health needs satisfied by social care services, their autonomy needs may remain unsatisfied because of cultural inappropriateness, language barriers and related communication difficulties and so on. One solution may be to create a special sub-group of care provision for older people by developing ethnically related services (see, for example: Torkington, 1983; Rooney, 1987; Ahmad, 1990). Or it may be that other additions may be made to mainstream services, for example through the provision of interpreters. The basis on which such difference or addition relates to citizenship is not that it is creating exclusion or elitism but that it is seeking to provide a basic standard for all potential service users and so is reformulating social citizenship around diversity and social division.

It is important also that such a justification for difference within a model of social citizenship does not simply reproduce the situation in which questions of social justice are asked only of those institutions which are constructed around the interests of dominant 'majority' groups (such as middle-aged, white, middle-class men). This leads to the point where a reformulated social citizenship requires the participation of service users in order that the terms of their engagement with social welfare institutions may be negotiated around their own understanding of their citizenship and how this relates to their needs. It requires open debate both *within* services, of *how* they are provided, and *about* services, of *what* should be provided. Services for elderly people provide an interesting example, because notions of empowerment, that address these dimensions, are often missing from professional practices or policy development. Without a move to develop an expectation that older people will be routinely involved in deciding how the care they receive should be provided, it seems unlikely that there would be a comparable shift in assumptions that older people should be a central part of the broader debate about social welfare as a whole. In this sense the minority of older people who require care services are subject to a sharply focused form of the ageism that affects *all* older people, namely that they will (or even should) withdraw from social life. Callahan (1987) argues that society should develop norms of excluding older people from social citizenship. To summarise, he adopts a utilitarian perspective in which limited health and welfare resources are to be targeted toward those for whom they will have greatest benefit (children, as future citizens, and younger adults as the current labour force). Attempts to ensure parity of citizenship for elderly people, expressed in rights to access fully the range of health and social welfare services in contemporary society, are seen as 'beyond our means'. Within this view, attempts to create participatory relationships between caring professions and service users is nonsensical, as elderly people who require care provision would receive it only on the basis of a residual citizenship right. Callahan's position, which he describes as 'generational *equity*' although it is clearly ageist because it proposes differential citizenship on grounds of age (Wisensale, 1988), is based on concepts of obligations and duties between generations, which raises issues of the relationship between rights and responsibilities in social welfare. So this chapter will turn to the questions of the balance in this relationship before examining the practice and policy implications of need and citizenship more widely for caring professions.

Rights and Responsibility (Equity and Fairness)

In their analysis of 'autonomy' as a basic human need Doyal and Gough (1991) note that along with the 'physical health' necessary for survival the opportunity to participate in social roles is also required. This leads them, among other things, to observe that while the state socialist regimes have largely succeeded in meeting the most basic physical survival needs of their citizens (although some, such as Cambodia and Ethiopia, may have failed on this count) all have to a greater or lesser extent been less successful in terms of autonomy. The evidence of the USSR indicates that as economic development advanced, the level to which physical health needs were met actually declined (Doyal and Gough, 1991, p. 284). It was this, accompanied by the long term failure to meet autonomy needs, which led to the 'collapse' of state socialism in the

USSR, rather than the hegemonic triumph of capitalism (p. 283). It is also this failure in other countries, such as China, which has limited the extent to which state socialism has been able to meet all basic needs.

The record of the major capitalist countries can equally be criticised (Doyal and Gough, 1991, p. 290). The USA, in particular, has a low level of achievement in relation to physical health needs. The highest achiever, Sweden, combines the approximation of need satisfaction in relation to both physical health and autonomy. At the same time, Sweden is the 'least' capitalist, in the sense that it has a highly managed economy in which social citizenship is accorded great value (Esping-Andersen, 1990).

Individualist Arguments for Responsibility.

The New Right agenda on state welfare has, at an ideological level, been driven by the claim that compulsory collective provision to meet need has caused personal moral responsibility to atrophy. This argument has been variously developed from the political science of Hayek (1960), the economics of Friedman (1962) and the moral philosophy of Nozick (1974). The common threads of these welfare-state critics is that by organising the alleviation of need through the state, based on compulsory contributions (in the form of taxes or national insurance schemes), the liberty of individuals to make their own decisions regarding the definition of need and its remedy is taken away. As a consequence, over time citizens assume a relationship of dependency to the state, in which all rights are possessed by the former and all responsibility ascribed to the latter. The majority of people become unable to comprehend welfare that is not provided by the state. The solidarities of family and neighbourhood break down, with a consequent increase in the numbers of people for whom taking responsibility for their own needs, or those of their family, has ceased to be an option in thought or in practice. Indeed, the presence of the welfare state may make it very difficult for people to exercise such responsibility.

This is the analysis of the contemporary social situation which was described in the previous chapter as a combination of neo-conservatism and neo-liberalism. It is neo-conservative in so far as it seeks to build values around previously existing social structures and social relations. An example of this is its vision of 'the family' which makes explicit reference to patterns of life in the earlier part of the century (Murray, 1984, 1990). It is neo-liberal because it propounds a very individualist moral liberalism. Such a position brings together Hayek's rejection of state welfare built on ideas of social justice – because for Hayek only individuals can be said to have intention and so be ethical – with Nozick's argument that the welfare state is morally unacceptable because it involves coercion (compulsory contributions) (Barry, 1990).

The practical implication of this analysis is that welfare should be 'privatised'. This has two senses. The first is that, as far as possible, welfare should be returned to the private domain of the household. A major intended consequence is that responsibility of individuals and families for welfare (that is, their own) will be promoted. The second sense is that in those situations where welfare needs must be met collectively, then this should be through private organisations, functioning on either a charitable or contractual basis. Much of the change in the organisation of social welfare in countries such as Australia, New Zealand and the UK in the 1980s and 1990s can be seen as an outcome of the implementation of these ideas in policy (Papadakis and Taylor-Gooby, 1987; Johnson, 1990; Beilharz et al., 1992; Hewitt, 1992; Sullivan, 1992; Wearing and Berreen, 1994).

Communitarian Arguments for Responsibility

The emergence of 'communitarianism' represents an attempt to rethink the basis for a collective approach to social welfare, in response to the impact of individualist policy. Unlike the neo-liberals, for the communitarians the ethical basis of social life lies in the conjunction of individual choice and responsibility with the *shared* moral life of family, neighbourhood, region, country and so on (Etzioni, 1995). There is some degree of similarity with neo-conservatism, in that the communitarian argument accepts the same sociological description of contemporary society. Changes in family structures (such as the increase in single-parent families), the growth of an 'underclass' (of people in chronic poverty), problems with crime and violence, the loss of legitimacy for bureaucratic state welfare institutions and of formal political institutions are all seen as problematic (Atkinson, 1995).

However, the analysis of the causes of these problems and potential policy solutions are not shared between communitarian thought and that of the New Right. The emphasis on 'community' within communitarian ideas places collective structures and relationships at the centre of the moral dimension of welfare and suggests that the means of defining and meeting need cannot be privatised.

Using the work of the German philosopher, Habermas, Hewitt (1992, pp. 114–16) points to the connections between our understanding of democracy, the failure in the legitimacy of the welfare state, and the move towards a reassertion of collective values in welfare. Unless there are connections between the everyday world as lived by members of a society and the policy decisions made about their welfare, then such welfare will lack public acceptance. It is for this reason that the New Right were able to obtain public support for policies which discredited large state bureaucratic services. However, the communitarian argument is that privatised services are as lacking in public credibility as are bureaucratic institutions. Where the former are seen as aloof and unresponsive, it is not inevitable that the latter have any greater public standing, particularly if they are seen as excluding the most disadvantaged sections of society.

Such an analysis connects Habermas' thought with that of Titmuss and Marshall (see above). Just as they saw the necessity of defining welfare in *social* terms, in both the origins of need and the integrative effect of shared responsibility, so too does the more recent concern with 'community' attempt to locate the grounds for collective welfare in the everyday experience of citizens. The most inclusive possible definition of citizenship (day-to-day membership of the same society) underlies this approach to community.

Of course, Habermas is not, as such, a communitarian. What is being suggested here is that his theory of communicative action (ideal democracy requires that all parties are free to engage in a rational discourse about welfare policy, unfettered by force) leads to the position that individuals must be located in a social context. The free person cannot be understood in isolation from society, which is why individualism has had such negative consequences (Etzioni, 1995). Cut loose from community, the individual becomes not morally autonomous but ethically dislocated. Where the only moral reference point is the self, as others can be understood only in relation to self, individualism leads to a moral 'free-market' in which ethical calculations must be seen in terms of cost, and benefit defined only in relation to the self. Such a process not only compounds the delegitimation of social welfare, but adds to it through the promotion of private, personal interests over and above those of the wider society. This in turn can be understood as a corrupted utilitarianism, that in its effect denies moral autonomy precisely because it displaces responsibility from the state to individuals without re-evaluating either the connections between rights and responsibilities or the nature and causes of need.

The practical implication of this analysis is that new forms of social welfare should be developed, which enable people to participate, balancing rights and responsibilities, on the basis of citizenship. Such arrangements would include a strengthened role for families, community associations, schools and other local services and voluntary groups (Hadley and Hatch, 1981; Atkinson, 1995). The notion of 'community' employed here predominantly equates with 'neighbourhood' (compare Baldwin, 1993) although it also allows for shared interests and sentiments.

Beyond Social Democracy?

Not all the recent critiques of New Right individualism have embraced completely the ideas of communitarianism as the alternative. Just as they share the communitarian concern with the effects of too great an emphasis on the individual as the locus of responsibility, so they also recognise the weaknesses of a collective approach that does not at the same time allow sufficiently for individuals. As Gray (1996, p. 58) notes, the social democratic vision of collective rights and responsibilities now belongs to history. The success of the individualist programmes in the 1980s has demonstrated the widespread 'demand for individual autonomy'. This reading of recent history is supported, at least in broad terms, by otherwise divergent writers, including Bauman (1988), Barry (1990), Doyal and Gough (1991), and Wearing (1994). At the same time these writers, and others (for example Taylor-Gooby, 1991), also point to the still widely held view that welfare clearly does have a clear *social* dimension, with implications for collective responsibilities and individual rights (as well as the converse).

Such a position leads to the conclusion that the Rawlsian understanding of social justice is tenable. The idea of shared responsibil-

ity gains credence from the assumption that individuals do not
'own' their natural abilities (Barry, 1990, p. 88). In consequence,
the balance of responsibilities and rights includes the responsibility
of each person to the welfare of others as well as their own welfare,
to the extent of their abilities. Following this, those who are least
advantaged may be said to have a right to welfare which does not
compromise the freedom of others (Bauman, 1988; Grace, 1994).
As Barry (1990, p. 89) notes, the preference people have for welfare (as shown in the work of Jordan, 1990, or Taylor-Gooby, 1991,
for example) does not necessarily imply preference for a particular
form of welfare. Specifics remain open to democratic debate and
decision. It is the assumption that only the state can deliver welfare
that has lost legitimacy, rather than social welfare as such (Hadley
and Hatch, 1981; Barry, 1990, p. 91).

In the era 'beyond social democracy' the question remains,
however, of what constitutes fairness in arrangements for social
welfare. Gray (1996) talks of 'complex fairness' related to 'local
justice', by which he means that agreement on the balance between
responsibilities and rights can only be arrived at through shared
social understandings to determine need, placed in the context of
everyday life. So the definition of fairness must be concrete, rather
than abstract, and local enough for social understandings to be
shared. Need, likewise, must be specific and related to the everyday
world. Gray arrives at this position through rejection of both the
neo-liberal negative view of freedom (from constraint) and social
democratic ideas about equality. Both are seen as incredible because both are indeterminate. Similarly Yeatman (1992), among
others, also seeks to replace notions of equality with 'equity'.
Variations in provision or outcome between different groups or
individuals might be seen as just if special provision and diverse
outcomes can be related to particular types and levels of need and
the social positioning of those in need. Yet irrespective of whether
the terms of fairness or equity are employed, the problem of being
able to create the political dialogue that leads to agreement in a
world where New Right individualism has dominated for over a
decade remains.

A further problem which any form of social welfare that incorpo-
rates a collective (social or community) dimension has to be able to
address is that of social divisions and the 'new social movements'.
We are returned to the point (see above) that by neglecting the

unfairness or inequity between groups in a pluralist approach to the contemporary problem of social welfare, such unfairness or inequity may be perpetuated. Issues of gender, race and ethnicity, disability, sexuality, age and so on all require explicit attention. A recognition of social divisions in considerations of local justice renders any ideas of fairness increasingly complex. Yet this is a factor which must be considered if injustices are not to be reproduced. As Bauman (1994, pp. 30 ff.) argues, if such care is not taken the particularities within communities may serve to create further divisions, internally as well as externally, that provide the seeds for future oppressions.

Values as Objectives

The related problems of establishing complex fairness and addressing social divisions constitute the contemporary crisis in the socio-political ethics of social welfare. To a large extent the related arguments owe much to Rawls (1972), whether or not this is explicit or implicit. Yet as Grace (1994, p. 87) notes, Rawls' theory of justice has a clear liberal character, being based on a procedural notion of justice and preferring the idea of 'right' to that of 'good' as the objective (also see Barry, 1990). Grace also shows that as a consequence of maintaining this 'thin' theory of the good, Rawls excludes some social elements which others might regard as fundamental. He points to 'politics' as such an element, and this has parallels with Doyal and Gough's (1991) view of autonomy as a basic need as well as the work of Finnis (1980) to which Grace refers. Grace's answer (1994, pp. 93–4) is to point to a different facet of the social democratic thread in social welfare, namely the extent to which it is a reflection of the broader social relations which constitute a society. In this, Grace implicitly develops that aspect of social administration represented in Robson's (1976) arguments for a welfare society which goes beyond the welfare state. That is, that unless a commitment to social welfare permeates society, state welfare structures will not be able successfully to meet need.

For Grace, questions of social justice are subordinated to those of moral life and social ethics. Without the latter, it is inevitable that a legalistic and procedural concern with rights and responsibilities will not give way to debates about fairness and equity. In focusing on social ethics, Grace proceeds to argue that opposition to extreme individualism is not to be found in a social justice liberalism (of the type developed by Rawls), but in the reassertion that society is not reducible to a market. Markets are to be seen as but one part of society. So, although it is reasonable to suggest that the property of one person should not be taken coercively (that is, taxed) just to give another a 'fair go', so it is also fair to suggest that where the survival of another is in question property rights are qualified, not absolute. Social welfare, as a social objective, is therefore a representation of social values. What are defined as the needs which should be addressed socially will come from the type of society which is sought by its members, and on which they may not necessarily agree. To questions of complex fairness and social divisions is added the problematic one of need definition, not as a technical but as a social and political issue.

What are the implications of such an analysis for the caring professions? The development of these professions seems cast about by the winds of change. In the post-war consensus, of Australia, Canada, New Zealand and the UK, the caring professions were moulded into the rapidly growing bureaucracies that were intended to deliver the social democratic promise. To a lesser extent they followed a similar path in the USA, where they have been largely based in organisations supported by social welfare policy if not in state agencies. Analyses of change and crisis largely have their point of reference in this era.

As the broader field of welfare policy has shifted under the force of the neo-liberal and neo-conservative New Right agenda, so too have the caring professions been required to adapt. The emphasis on individualism has affected their practices (with associated implications for the theories on which they draw) and also the forms of organisation in which they are employed. The former is a reflection of the debates about their purposes (the objectives of social welfare) while the latter is a consequence of the use of market principles as the vehicle to organise services. Not only has society become reduced to a market in terms of the principles on which the ethics of social welfare may be determined, but the means of delivering social welfare also are constructed in the market image (Bartlett and Le Grand, 1993). Caring professionals increasingly have become sub-divided between those who 'produce' services and those who 'purchase' (or, more properly, assess need and make arrangements for provision). Relations within as well as between specific professions and agencies have thus been structured on market principles.

In this sense it may be argued that the caring professions have been (re)modelled along the lines of manufacturing industry or business. The values which are represented by social welfare have taken on the public face of the market. The extent to which it is feasible for them to engage in the discourse suggested by Grace (1994) therefore is highly contentious, to say the least. Not only the organisational form but also the very nature of what it is to be a nurse, a remedial therapist or a social worker is open to question. What appears to be of particular significance in this development is that, although much of the history of each of these occupational groups has contained struggles to professionalise and grow, often in the face of opposition to specific goals, this is the first period for over a century in which they have been under sustained and concerted attack over their broad objectives. Moreover, this critical environment has persisted long enough to have had a profound impact on all aspects of these professions. So we are in a position, historically, to see what the effects of these changes have been.

In this chapter I have revisited and reviewed the core concepts of need, citizenship and responsibility that have driven debates about social welfare in policy and practice. In particular, it has been seen that although the legitimacy of previous ideas and institutions no longer stands, these three issues remain contentious. There *is* an alternative (perhaps several), although the creation of the grounds for the legitimation of new forms of social welfare is still 'in progress'. This is most especially because such legitimation cannot look simply to a neo-social-democratism as the counter to neo-liberalism. Such a conclusion presents theoretical as well as practical difficulties, because there was much of the social democratic era in social welfare that continues to be relevant and which should not be abandoned as an anachronism. The understanding of the connection between need, citizenship and responsibility as a *social* artefact is a prime example. This leads many of the proponents of non-market models of social welfare to argue that the (central) state should continue to play some role (although they differ widely on the extent of this – compare, for example, Hadley and Hatch [1981] with Doyal and Gough [1991]). While this is the case, however, very few would now argue that only the state should exercise the function of meeting need (compare Barry, 1990, p. 91). It is for this reason that hopes for a return to social democracy are widely seen as implausible. So, in the present, the defining characteristics of debates around social welfare and the roles of caring professions have come to be set by the neo-liberal market agenda. Understanding the implications of this for the caring professions is necessary therefore if their present state and future development are to be examined. It is that task to which this book is addressed.

In Part II of this book various facets of the market model of the caring professions will be examined, as the precursor to an exploration in Part III of non-market alternatives for future professional development. Before that discussion is embarked upon, however, I want to look in more detail at the value base of professionalism to which these occupations have laid claim and which provides the context against which market models were introduced. It is to this task that I turn in the next chapter.

3

The Role of Professional Values

Values and Professionalism

In the previous chapter the concepts of need, citizenship and responsibility were examined as the basis for defining the scope and purpose of social welfare. In this chapter the discussion focuses on the more detailed area of the caring professions which have come to be the primary source of social welfare in practice. In particular, this chapter examines that dimension of 'values talk', which is so often seen as a key feature of the professions, namely their occupational values or ethics. We are concerned here with questions of how professional values are constructed, what these are, and how they relate to the overall objectives of social welfare policy. Moreover, such questions lead to an examination of the role which caring professions play in the establishment of such objectives and so to questioning the nature of the caring professions themselves.

All professions to some extent make claims to a distinctive value base. Indeed, this can be seen as one of the defining features by which occupations make the claim to professionalism (Freidson, 1983; Jolley, 1989; Airaksinen, 1994). For Larson (1977) ethics constitutes the normative dimension of professionalism, matched by the cognitive (knowledge and skills) and the evaluative (autonomy and prestige). This implies that professionalism is a status, in which the role of ethics or values is to provide the normative relationship of the theoretical and technical aspects of work with claims to self-regulation and the high regard of the wider society. An ethical code, in this sense, forms the legitimation for the social independence of an occupation which makes claims to particular knowledge and skills. The occupation can be trusted with this level of independence, it is inferred, because it makes a public commitment to a certain moral framework, by which it may be evaluated and held to account for the way it uses the knowledge and skills. Formal ethics must be the basis of trust because in a theoretical and technical monopoly no other occupation can be as competent and no lay person can form a good enough judgement about the validity of any specific professional judgement or action. Only the members of the profession can be competent and so, as the basis of the trust required for the social sanctioning of their esoteric practices, they make a commitment to an 'objective' (that is, explicit and codified) set of ethics and values.

Critics of the professions, and professionalisation generally, have been severe in their judgement that, far from being a guarantee of trustworthiness, ethical codes merely serve to obscure the extent to which professionalism is often a means for occupational self-aggrandisement. Ethics, it is argued, form the ideological gloss on the social class and social status location of the professions. From this perspective, professions have been castigated as a 'conspiracy against the laity' (Shaw, 1911), criticised for having a 'trained incapacity' to take a broad view of social issues (Mills, 1956), attacked as 'disabling' (Illich, 1977), suspected of being 'privileged private governments' (Freidson, 1983) and questioned as potentially ethnocentric (Thomasma, 1994). Formal ethical statements are seen by the protagonists of professionalisation as, at best, representing statements of ideals that are rarely attained or even are unattainable. At worst they are decried as a smokescreen to divert public attention from partiality and self-serving actions.

Sociological analyses of occupational power structures have lent weight to these critiques. Johnson (1972), significantly highlighting social power as a dimension of professionalisation, showed that professionalism is not a type of occupational *form* but rather a type of occupational *control*. The most successful examples of professionalisation are those occupations which have gained the greatest degree of self-governance. This approach moved the debate about professions away from the formal and idealist concern with identifying traits or facets of professions into a more dynamic historical and realist frame of reference. An examination of social structures and relationships provides the basis for understanding how 'the professions' have been formed and how they are maintained, as well as their relationships with other occupations, the public and the state.

Following Johnson (1972), others have used this approach to examine the power exercised by certain professions and the impact this has on health and social welfare services (Wilding, 1982; Sibeon, 1990). A somewhat different development of this approach has been to identify the way in which professionalisation not only produced structures of social power, but the way in which that power reproduced aspects of the wider society, especially social divisions (Abbott and Wallace, 1990; Hugman, 1991; Witz, 1992). In particular, such an analysis reveals the extent to which professionalism as a concept obscured patriarchal and racist social relations. It was no historical 'accident', nor was it 'natural' that the so-called 'semi-professions' discussed by Etzioni and his colleagues (1969) were largely those areas of the caring services in which women predominated numerically. Evidence for the converse position, that men predominate numerically in the so-called 'full-professions' supports this conclusion (Hugman, 1991; Witz, 1992). It was not that the traits of unique knowledge and skills, formal association and code of ethics, with associated prestige, authority and autonomy, were necessarily lacking for nursing, the remedial therapies or social work. (Indeed, they can be shown to possess elements of each of these characteristics.) It was the way in which these were conceived and then attributed as the causes rather than the consequences of professionalisation. Not only were the forms of knowledge and patterns of skill in certain occupations valued over others in the earlier 'trait' approaches, but the types of prestige and authority were seen only as artefacts of occupational function, rather than related also to the identity of occupational members. In brief, men and 'men's work' were valued above women and 'women's work'. When gender differences were acknowledged explicitly by trait theory, it was to explain such differences in terms of 'how women are' (see, for example, Toren, 1972). The way in which power, authority, and autonomy are differentially allocated by social processes was not identified. It was the contribution of the analysis of professions as types of occupational control that provided the basis on which these issues could be identified as crucial to understanding professionalism.

As a value, therefore, professionalism is problematic. It contains a contradiction between notions of ethics, service and even altruism on the one side and exclusivity, monopoly and privilege on the other. All of these elements might exist, but they do so in particular social conditions; the contradictions reflect the wider society, in which apparently incompatible values appear to co-exist with regard to social welfare services and the needs which they exist to address.

When the members of occupations such as nursing, the remedial therapies and social work describe themselves as 'professional' they tend to be making reference to the former characteristics. The epithet 'caring professions' is seen as unproblematic because ethical standards, and principles of service and altruism, are regarded as positive objectives in themselves, as well as means to desirable ends (of good practice) (Jolley, 1989; Kendrick, 1995b). The idea that professionalism might also involve exclusivity or privilege is more contentious, addressed only by some members of these occupations, who make claims to other points of reference, such as 'skilled worker'. (I will return to these points and their implications below.)

Most recently a different aspect of the social processes affecting the caring professions has added a third dimension to the debate between professionalisation and its opponents. This is variously referred to as 'proletarianisation' (Derber, 1983) or 'deprofessionalisation' (Cousins, 1987). Although these terms imply that all vestiges of professionalism as it has been described above are being lost by the professions, this is not quite what the proponents of this debate are arguing. Rather they are describing a situation in which particular aspects of professionalism, those associated with autonomy over the goals or objectives of work, are being more tightly circumscribed. As part of this process, Derber (1983) argues, the technical (knowledge and skill) aspects of an occupation are emphasised while the right to establish the broad ends of the occupation are challenged and curtailed. Ideas about competence replace concerns with matching ends and means in the way professionalism is judged (see Chapter 1). Professionalism as a value is reduced as ideological autonomy is replaced by technical autonomy (Cousins, 1987), and with it the sense of doing what is 'right' is supplanted by a concern with doing what is 'correct' (compare Bauman, 1994).

Of course, it may be argued that the earlier concept of semi-professionalism was a construction around the partial success of occupations such as nursing, the remedial therapies and social work to achieve autonomy in the ideological realm. Subject to the mediation of the state and of other professions (primarily law and medicine), the caring professions have only been able to assert their ethical claims to the purposes of social welfare in limited ways. A clear example of such limitations can be seen in the struggles between nursing and midwifery on the one hand and medicine on the other, especially in the area of women's health and childbirth (Hearn, 1982; Woods, 1987; Robinson, 1989; Cheek and Rudge, 1994). Critical histories of nursing and midwifery reveal that the development of obstetrics and gynaecology can be seen as boundary disputes between those occupations and medicine, as much as it can be characterised by the scientific development of medicine in this field. In terms of social divisions it represents the exclusion of women by men in significant areas of women's health (Sargent, 1994, p. 146). Notions of ethics as the basis for occupational autonomy in nursing and midwifery are, therefore, highly problematic. Recent developments, for example in Australia and the UK, towards greater autonomy for midwives have been only partial in their impact on the balance of professional power between these groups and medicine. Parallel developments among remedial therapists have also generated some autonomy, but the use of the term 'allied health' in Australia in place of 'ancillary to medicine' disguises the degree to which medicine has sought to maintain its own hegemony over all areas of health work (Gardner and McCoppin, 1995).

Similarly, the autonomy of social work, for most of the twentieth century, has been curtailed not only by medicine but also by legal processes and the legal profession. Social workers employed in health settings are subject to the same boundary conflicts with medicine as are nursing and the remedial therapies. However, social work also plays a major role in the socio-legal realm, through responsibilities for children's welfare (especially child protection) and probation or correctional services (Parton, 1991; Davies, 1994). Indeed, social work may be said to face a multi-faceted set of constraints as, to an extent greater than other caring professions, it is located 'between' several areas of society which have been claimed by more established professional groups, including law, medicine, education and (at least in its early years) the church (Philp, 1978).

Under these circumstances the adherence by caring professions to formalised ethical standards can be seen as representing claims as much to independence from the established professions as to autonomy relative to the wider society. This is not to say that such autonomy is not sought, at least by some sub-groups of the caring professions; rather that limitations to their own development have been regarded for much of the twentieth century as more the consequence of boundary conflicts with other groups than the capacity to convince the general public that nurses, remedial therapists or social workers have clear ethical standards.

The emphasis on ethics may also at times have been used *against* the autonomous development of the caring professions. This point can be illustrated from nursing, in which the equation of a 'good nurse' and a 'good woman' has tended to buttress concepts of clinical subordination, a non-assertive stance industrially and at times occupational self-effacement (Oakley, 1984; Jolley, 1989; Bagguley, 1992; Fry, 1992; Koerner, 1995). Principled action, usually defined as altruism and service, have been used both by some nurses and by others to question the assertion of the capacity for greater professional autonomy and an associated social status for nursing. This takes the form of criticism for those nurses who attempt to define their skills and knowledge in autonomous terms, using notions of a 'lack of dedication'. Most especially any suggestion that nurses might be worth higher salaries produces the argument that it is important to keep salaries low enough so that people do not enter nursing for the 'wrong' (that is, financial) reasons. This has often seemed to nurses to be curious when the opposite argument, the 'need to attract the best' entrants with high salaries, is used in relation to medicine (Jolley, 1989). At the same time, there is general social support for nurses whose ethical standards are widely recognised: in more recent years the notion that nurses who assert their professional status, especially those who strike, are 'fallen' angels, is a political gambit by governments rather than a widespread attitude (Hibberd and Norris, 1991; Barry et al., 1992).

Ethical standards, despite being highly contested, are a core aspect of the types of professionalism that have been achieved by the caring professions. To the extent that traits have a limited meaning in describing forms of occupational control, ethics may even be said to be a more highly developed element than some others. So far this discussion has used the idea of ethics without

describing the sets of principles used in practice by these professions. In the next part of the chapter these ethics will be examined
as the basis for then analysing the way in which they are connected
to debates about the meaning of social welfare.

Professional Values – the Background

Nursing, the remedial therapies and social work are very much the
product of their time. Emerging as organised occupations during
the nineteenth century, within the context of industrialisation and
urbanisation, they can be seen as part of the 'modernist' epoch in
Western society (Lyon, 1994). As discussed in Chapter 1, modernism is associated with rationalism in thought, humanism in values
and a combination of empiricism and logical positivism in science.
These are the cultural and social foundations, at the ideological
level, of the broad enterprise of professionalisation. That the relationship of nursing, the remedial therapies and social work to this
enterprise has been full of conflict and difficulty does not detract
from the extent to which the elements of that process constitute the
caring professions as modernist in ways very similar to the more
established professions. Attempts to define demarcated areas of
knowledge and skill are reflections of the scientific dimensions of
modernism; the value bases of the caring professions, expressed as
formal ethical principles, are also part of their modernist origins.
More recent arguments about ethics may attempt to move beyond
these origins, for example through a focus on ethics based on the
action of 'caring' rather than rules (Fry, 1992; Thomasma, 1994),
yet the predominant basis of ethical thought in the caring professions has been a rational set of principles regarding the use of
systematic empirically based knowledge and skills (Hussey, 1996).
Moreover, both knowledge and skills are held to be empirically
verifiable and so ethics have become the objective rules for their
implementation.

  The ethical or moral philosophies which have been most highly
developed in Western society during this period, and which have
had the most impact in social welfare, are those derived from Kant
on the one hand and from the Utilitarians on the other (Simpkin,
1979; Barry, 1990). These philosophies in many ways are opposed,

and ethical debates within the caring professions have centred chiefly around the different implications of these two systems of thought. Kant's ethics were based on concepts of the individual person. Although he applied a 'maxim of generalisability' (what is claimed to be 'right' or 'good' must be applied to all persons) he held each person both to be an autonomous moral agent and to be an ethical 'end' in her or himself (for example, see Bowie, 1985). Not only does this mean that each person must take responsibility for their own choices and actions, it also means that it is inadmissible to use another person, contrary to that person's will, to achieve any end, no matter how good that purpose might appear. For Kant, ends can never justify means.

In contrast the Utilitarians determined that the good can be determined as the 'greatest possible good for the greatest number, achieved with the least pain'. Although containing some aspects of conservative and liberal thought, dominant in the period of the nineteenth century in which Mill and Bentham originated this school of thought, Utilitarianism differs from Kantianism in its implications for a collective view of ways in which what is good might be defined. Consequently, Utilitarianism can be said to allow for a social construction of the good towards which people might be directed in their actions. While it does not dispense with notions of individual rights and responsibilities, this philosophy subsumes them as secondary to the good of the greatest number. For the Utilitarians ends can justify means. Where Kantianism is absolute (*deontological*), Utilitarianism is relativist (*teleological*) in its assumptions.

Kantian principles have had a considerable influence on the construction of professional ethics in Western societies. They can be seen at the root of all *codes* of ethics, in their formulaic potential (they can be expressed as a series of distinct moral precepts) and in their idealist potential (they can be used to convey goals for action as abstract statements). They can thus be set down in the articles of a professional association, taught to beginning practitioners and then taken as measures of appropriate action in cases of dispute. Furthermore, as the work of the caring professions is directed towards specific people (as patients or clients), the individual focus of Kantian ethics may be experienced, even if not clearly articulated, as congruent with actual professional practices (Kendrick, 1995b). Finally, the congruence of means and ends in this perspective enables it to be applied to concrete practices. Kant's principles were particularly clearly formulated for caring professions by the work of Biestek (1961). In his 'seven principles of casework' Biestek sought to take the basic tenets of Kant's philosophy and to elaborate an ethical system that could apply to helping services, most especially those which involved a counselling or interpersonal dimension. These principles are:

1. unconditional acceptance of the client as a person;
2. a non-judgemental approach to clients;
3. the individualisation of the client;
4. the purposeful expression of emotion;
5. controlled emotional involvement;
6. confidentiality;
7. self-determination of the client.

These principles incorporate the human personhood of anyone in need of professional help and the responsibility of the caring professional to that humanity. They are both rationalist and humanist in their assumptions. Although sometimes misunderstood and/or misused, these principles have for several decades formed the basis of ethical codes in caring professions (Hugman and Smith, 1995). However, two main objections to Kantianism increasingly have been expressed in relation to these professions. Both concern the extent to which it is possible to make absolute statements about what should be done (categorical imperatives) without being able to consider the context in which action takes place.

The first objection to Kantianism is that, even when considering the actions of individual professionals in relation to individual service users, the context of the service must be grasped in order to make any ethical judgement (Fry, 1992; Loewenberg and Dolgoff, 1992; Kendrick, 1995b; Hussey, 1996). It is vital that the professional understands the limitations of choice within which they may be operating if they are to relate their actions to the 'good' of the person or people with whom they are working. These limitations may include imperfect knowledge about the situation, a lack of resources (within the service or in the wider community) or the lack of co-operation from others; they may also arise from a situation in which all choices involve a degree of apparent harm to some person or people. For example, the triage nurse faces such a dilemma as a constant part of her or his work, prioritising some patients over others. In a context of limited resources and potentially unlimited need such decisions can appear to involve highly relative criteria and so involve constant ethical compromise. In addition, Kendrick (1995b) cites 'whistle-blowing' and decisions not to provide care for which the nurse is not trained or equipped as examples where statements in formal codes may actually conflict in their implications (also see: McDowell, 1991, pp. 93–6; Sines, 1996b, p. 474). The alternative is to look for ethical principles that do not begin from 'categorical imperatives' (absolute statements of what ought to be done which are based on abstract categories of action). A social worker recommending the removal of a child from a family must deal with similar issues, in that the needs and interests of each party may be irreconcilable and a way has be found to reconcile competing interests or else give primacy to one or other point of view.

The second objection to Kantianism is that it fails to address the social construction of health and social welfare needs and of the individuals who experience them. This objection is most often associated with 'radical' perspectives on the caring professions (for example: Simpkin, 1979; Mullaly, 1993; Purkis, 1994; Koerner, 1995). These critics begin from the perspective that needs are artefacts of inequalities in social relations, as accidents of biography rather than personal moral culpabilities. The individualisation of the patient or client therefore leads to an inappropriate attention to problems at the individual level and diverts attention away from the collective level of responsibility, such as inadequate income support schemes in the face of endemic unemployment, poor housing stock and other social structural deficits. Such an analysis is based on a critical analysis of social class. In recent years this has been augmented by a recognition of other social divisions, most specifically around gender, race and culture, sexuality, age and disability. These factors too are judged to be the causal factors in health and social need, with implications for the societal level of analysis and so of intervention and thus ethical considerations. This perspective is frequently associated with social work and with community nursing, although radical nursing and therapy may also be found in hospital settings.

Both these critiques of Kantian (*deontological*) individualism rest on forms of Utilitarian thought. They are both relativist, the former with respect to the specific circumstances of any practice situation, the latter concerning the origins and causes of health and social welfare needs within social structures. Yet although they have the similarity of critiquing Kantianism they are different both in their logic and in their practical implications. The former can be seen perhaps as 'critical orthodoxy', in which the basic assumptions of the profession remain unchallenged while the contextual aspects of theory, practice and ethics are questioned. In the latter, more explicitly radical approach, a rejection of individualist assumptions about the nature and causes of need leads to a more thorough-going challenge to the basic professional ideas, practices and ethics. In effect, it becomes ethically anti-professional. The former is relativist (and hence Utilitarian) only in so far as it is obliged to be, as a 'realist' derivation of more idealist principles which, though unattainable, remain as a benchmark for judgement (Loewenberg and Dolgoff, 1992; Kendrick, 1995b). The latter is more completely Utilitarian, largely rejecting individualism and locating ideas, practices and ethics within an analysis of human life as a collective phenomenon (Simpkin, 1979; Mullaly, 1993).

This brief distinction of different positions has relevance to the way in which the ethical stances of groups within the caring professions connect with broader ethical debates about the nature of social welfare as a whole. In Chapter 1 the critique of publicly funded social welfare, paid for through compulsory taxation, was introduced as a neo-liberal attack on Utilitarianism. This raises some problems of consistency for orthodox professionalism, based on a type of (Kantian) liberal individualism and yet espoused by members of occupations that have depended throughout their development, at least in part, on employment in settings which either are publicly funded from taxation or else free at the point of service delivery through charitable or insurance mechanisms. Private practices in nursing, the remedial therapies and social work can and do thrive in many countries; however, the dominant mode has been employment in agencies which have formed part of the 'mediated' context to which Johnson (1972) referred.

This analysis, of the contradiction between formal ethics and the logic of practice situations, applies equally between countries where health and social welfare is based almost entirely in state-funded organisations (such as Sweden and the UK), those with more mixed modes of provision (Australia and Germany) and those with a predominantly private health and welfare structure. As Wessell (1992) argues, even in a hospital providing health care funded by private insurance there will be choices to be made in the provision of care. There is, therefore, no major difference between the government and non-government sectors in this respect. However, in another sense the nurse, remedial therapist or social worker will first have to make a significant choice about working in such a setting (where access may be based on ability to pay), or else seeking employment in the residual public sector (where access is free to all on the basis of citizenship). As other countries (Australia, Sweden or the UK) have moved towards models which in some way derive from the USA system, such ethical dilemmas remain. There is, as such, an in-built tension between the individual focus of much of the work, and hence an individual*ist* orientation in theories and values, while practice is embedded in situations structured, at least implicitly, on a Utilitarian logic. It is this tension to which both critical orthodox and radical arguments are directed.

(A similar tension can be observed in the more established profession of medicine in those countries where the dominant mode of practice has been some form of employment by state agencies, whether direct or indirect. For this profession also liberal individualist ethics represent a strong orthodoxy, while the realities of practice are the same as those identified above, in which relative choices constitute everyday life. That this is the case has not prevented medicine from using the potential for private fee-paying practice to exert strong political leverage; nor has it stopped the formulaic approach to ethical codes being seen as one of medicine's professional strengths.)

Under these circumstances the value tensions within the caring professions, between the professions and the state and between the professions and their clientele, can be understood as an aspect of the wider debates between individualist and collective views of social welfare and of society as a whole. The caring professions are bound up with an enterprise whose value foundations have been steadily challenged. The contradictions between individualism and collectivism may signal the weakness of the professionalisation for which nursing, the remedial therapies and social work have been, for the most part, struggling. Their future might be said to be tied too closely to the overall project of social welfare to escape the material and ideological changes which have been and continue to be wrought on it.

Social Welfare Values in the Caring Professions

Parton (1994), quoting Rose and Miller (1992), points to the apparent rapid end of a period in Western society in the late-twentieth century which can be defined as 'welfarism'. In this analysis Parton is focusing on the post-1945 period in which the welfare state became institutionalised through much of the Western world, providing the basis for the dominance of a particular vision of health and welfare professions as caring. The 'welfarist' ideology brought together the fiscal and organisational potential of the state to promote well-being for citizens. At the ideological level, therefore, it was interwoven with the developing concepts of citizenship discussed in the previous chapter. Forms of social insurance (the details of which differed quite widely between countries) were a means through which the welfare state was sustained economically and ideologically as a common social enterprise. Parton (1994) concludes that this welfarist period has been relatively brief, less than forty years, having largely been supplanted by the New Right and welfare pluralism. The emergent role for the caring professions is thus one of the management of social risk through the 'technologies' of assessment and surveillance (Parton, 1994, p. 25). This applies as much to nursing, in which the primary roles are seen as becoming those of managing illness and the dispersed control of deviance (Cheek and Rudge, 1994), as it does to the more obvious social control functions of social work in child protection or probation.

This major change in welfare values has only been partly reflected in the caring professions. Although some of their recent practices, such as the enthusiastic embracing of case management (Means and Smith, 1994), at one level are constructed around the more technical and instrumental approach to personal and social problems, at another level they are often combined with the same ethic as that which permeated the welfarist ideal. In other words, the overt commitments to notions of service, social justice, meeting need and respect for persons have not been abandoned. Nevertheless, it is when these values are confronted by the material realities of welfare pluralism and an increased limitation on resources relative to perceived need that a difficulty of fit between policy and practice may be experienced. This, for example, has been shown empirically to be a major reason why many nurses leave the profession (Mackay, 1989; Nolan et al., 1995). In the 'post-welfarist' environment, nurses face the question 'can respect for persons and social justice as values co-exist with social control and social management as tasks and a loss of legitimacy expressed in reduced funding?' Many are answering 'no'.

For many writers, of different theoretical (and political) persuasions, the answer also is either 'no' or 'only with great difficulty'. Jordan (1990), for example, sees social work as faced with a choice between the maintenance of its core values and their abandonment in favour of those of the neo-liberal state. Maintenance of core values, in this sense, leads to an oppositional stance regarding the instrumental technical approach to social issues which Jordan perceives to be developing. Similarly, Howe (1991), Clarke (1993) and Parton (1994) all refer, from different stand points, to the impact of the parallel movement ideologically and institutionally towards neo-liberal forms of social welfare on social work as a profession. The conclusion of each is that there is a clash of values, between 'respect for persons' and 'social justice' on one side and 'economy, efficiency and effectiveness' on the other. There is a tendency, encapsulated by the notion of an orientation towards the service user as a 'consumer', for standards of service to be prescribed in ways that ignore underlying complexities. Questions of the irreconcilability of the rights, needs and interests of all parties in many situations are reduced to a concern with the fulfillment of procedures. The problems of power relations involved in social-control activities also are obscured by the 'consumerist' approach (Hugman, 1994b). This can be seen, for example, in the apparent incongruity of consumerist principles applied to the investigation of suspected child abuse, as if this could go beyond principles of natural and formal justice shown toward the alleged perpetrator(s).

Nursing and remedial therapies, too, are challenged by this contradictory situation. Butterworth and Rushforth (1995) argue that there is a practical balance to be struck between the duties and responsibilities exercised by nurses, which may involve power over patients, and the rights and autonomy of those patients. They note that ideas about the latter are part of nursing values, while at the same time the contemporary situation requires nurses to give priority to their duties and responsibilities. Purkis (1994) similarly is concerned that by encouraging a decontextualised view of nursing skills, a 'taken-for-granted' understanding of nursing as 'what nurses do', leads to a subsuming of nursing values within those of the agency and so amplifies the deskilling process. While consumerism may appear to be congruent with the treatment of physical illness, by nurses or remedial therapists (for example, see Williamson, 1992), the social-control dimensions in some aspects of practice, such as mental health, are identical to those experienced by social workers (compare Beattie, 1991; Hugman, 1991).

Successive studies have argued that social power is an endemic aspect of relationships between the caring professions, service users and the state (Hugman, 1991). 'Solutions' to this 'problem' have tended to divide between those who believe that full professionalism is a sufficient safeguard to the rights and autonomy of service users, and those who propose consumerism as an antidote to the potential for professional power to be misused. Yet neither side of this simple dichotomy is adequate if power is endemic and consumerism is tied to the neo-liberal goals of reduced state expenditure and increased social control/management. What is required is what Husband (1995) has termed the 'morally active practitioner' and Sellman (1996) has defined as the person with moral sophistication and fluency. By these terms they mean the professional who is able to weigh means and ends, to identify value choices and to base their practice on the conscious exercise of such choice. However, in an era of increased attention to technique and prescribed standards over independent thought and autonomous responsibility, is such a person a dying breed? Indeed, did such a person exist in the welfarist caring professions? Arguments for professional values in social welfare depend, in part, on whether such a person would be historically possible or whether this image is itself part of the welfarist ideology.

Delegitimising Professionalism – the Values of Proletarianisation

The radical critiques of professionalism have, at their centre, a shared value orientation, which is based on a socio-structural understanding of need. In other words, this perspective argues that the causes of need lie in the structural arrangements of society. Although variants of social democracy and Marxism underpin the different contributors to this perspective, they can be seen as sharing an analysis based on conflict theory, namely that society is composed of groups whose interests are in conflict – and the resulting structures and relationships can only be understood in terms of the underlying conflict (Mullaly, 1993).

There is a long history of the influence of the radical perspective in social work (Statham, 1978) and in nursing (Maggs, 1987). It has a lesser influence among occupational therapists (Irvine and Graham, 1994). However, not only do all three groups share conflict theory as a basis for their understanding of the needs which their work addresses, but they also have in common ideas about the implications this approach has for their respective occupations. The first is a value orientation towards the relationship between means (practices) and ends (goals), the second concerns the type of occupational formation which is sought.

The value orientation of radical nursing, occupational therapy or social work seeks congruence with the structural understanding of need. For example, the notion of 'respect for persons' is seen to require contextualisation, without which it can have no meaning (Mullaly, 1993, p. 34). In practice, this may lead to a relativist stance concerning the degree to which respect may be afforded to persons of different social background. Those in need may be afforded greater respect, in so far as their needs will be seen to have priority over the rights of others (for example, to enjoy low levels of direct taxation) (Simpkin, 1979). There are implications also for forms of practice that are seen to be appropriate, favouring collective practices and, as far as possible, using individual interventions only where these might serve the purposes of helping people to change their material circumstances.

As indicated above, such an orientation is Utilitarian in its ethical construction and so takes a very different approach to the idea of 'respect for persons' than does the more orthodox *deontological* perspective. Radical theory, accepting that an abstract and absolute perspective is inherently contradictory, takes sides and chooses to favour those who appear to be disadvantaged by contemporary social structures. It also takes sides with people who are subject to structural discrimination, including women, Black people and other ethnic minorities, gays and lesbians, disabled people and older people. The greatest good of the greatest number may not be seen only in crude numerical terms, but also in relation to social advantage. As an occupational orientation it clearly is in overt conflict with the neo-liberal and neo-conservative forces which have come to dominate social welfare policy (Johnson, 1990), especially in so far as these policies tend to favour the advantaged (Wearing and Berreen, 1994).

At the same time, the 'radical perspective', as described by a number of writers, is not unremittingly relativist. Mullaly's (1993) starting point is in the humanitarian and egalitarian principles of social work; his criticism is that orthodox practice cannot implement these principles, rather than an attack on the principles themselves. (Similar points are made by Hugman [1991] and Fook [1993].) In the same way, radical nurses and occupational therapists are seeking to promote health and well-being; their difference with orthodox professionalism is the route they take, guided by their analysis of the causes of illness and disease. Even the detailed practices may have close similarities. What emerges is a compromise or blend between ideas that have their origin in *deontological* thought and a recognition of the relativist context of inequalities in social structures and social relations. It is for these reasons that it is possible to talk of radical and orthodox branches of the *same* occupations or professions.

The consequence of the radical view on occupational formation is the other area in which a distinction may be drawn with orthodox professionalism. Indeed, the issue is often whether the notion of professionalism has relevance at all, or if it is to be seen as part of the problem. This leads to critiques both of the overt processes of professionalism and of the enthusiasm with which these have been sought by nurses, remedial therapists and social workers.

One form of this critique can be seen as explicit anti-professionalism. This approach argues that not only are the facets of classic professionalism practically unattainable for the caring professions, but that they are theoretically undesirable as well. This analysis draws on the understanding of professionalism as a separation of groups on the basis of skill and knowledge, in which social inequalities are augmented and those who are structurally disadvantaged are further oppressed through the power accorded to professionals. The solution is to seek a different occupational model, one which stresses the reality for nurses, remedial therapists and social workers of being employed and managed within agencies. The model is that of the skilled worker (Simpkin, 1979; Koerner, 1995; Parkin, 1995). As a consequence, it is argued that the process of proletarianisation should not be rejected, but is to be grasped as the contemporary reality. Only by seeing themselves as employed skilled workers will members of these occupations be able to make appropriate judgements about their work. Following from the self-identity as employed workers, trade unionism is promoted over and against professional association as the appropriate form of collective relationship and action.

The other form of the critique of professionalisation can be seen as a radical or critical professionalism. In this approach the social status of classic professionalism is rejected, while it is recognised that there are distinct forms of knowledge and skill which are developed through training and can be made available for service users. To different degrees, Barber (1991), Hugman (1991), Fook (1993) and Mullaly (1993) represent examples of this approach in social work. It exists also in health and nursing (Maggs, 1987; McMurray, 1993; Twinn, 1996). This perspective tends to see the possibility of a combination or a collaboration between relevant trade unions and professional associations, both of which are regarded as requiring major reform to divest themselves of elitism and discrimination while maintaining the values of the respective occupations towards humanitarian and egalitarian service (Thorpe and Petruchenia, 1992).

As the 1980s progressed, and the impact of the New Right on social welfare policies and institutions increased, so the arguments for radical or critical professionalism have tended to replace anti-professionalism as the dominant critique of tradition and orthodoxy. There are two factors which have created the circumstances for this development. The first is the way in which the New Right also has attacked the professions; the second is in the development of anti-discriminatory and anti-oppressive practice as a vehicle for changing both the caring professions and social welfare more generally.

The New Right and Deprofessionalisation

Part of the New Right agenda in reshaping social welfare has been to use the professionals through whom health and welfare services are provided to implement the practical and institutional changes necessary (Johnson, 1990). For this reason policies have tended to focus on technical components in the role of professionals, while the institutional shift to a managerial culture has sought to separate the determining of means from ends in social welfare (Cousins, 1987). The former are seen as the province of professionals, while the latter are reserved for (senior) managers and policy makers. Proletarianisation or deprofessionalisation, with its accompanying deskilling and limitations of autonomy that was envisaged by Haug (1973), Larson (1980) and Derber (1983), developed steadily in Canada, the UK and the USA. In Australia and New Zealand, Labour administrations also created the conditions in which the same processes could operate (Beilharz et al., 1992). (It should be noted that in other countries left-of-centre administrations also had implemented policies that produced the conditions which enabled a more thorough-going reappraisal of the welfare state to take place; see Hewitt [1992] and Sullivan [1992].) At the ideological level, the criticisms of professionalism which had shaped the internal critiques by nurses, remedial therapists and social workers were utilised also within New Right social policy. Managerialism and consumerism, based on private-market models, were proposed as the solution to the separation of bureaucracies and professionals from service users, because they were seen as the vehicles through which economy, efficiency and effectiveness could be promoted (Cochrane, 1993).

Anti-oppressive and Anti-discriminatory Professionalism

As attacks on professionalism became clear as attacks also on both the caring professions and the health and welfare services they provided, the internal critiques of professionalisation have tended to focus less on embracing proletarianisation and more on reformulating professionalism around a service-user focus. Ideas about creating links with service-user groups and attention to the barriers between professionals and service users (particularly in relation to anti-discriminatory and anti-oppressive practices) have become the centre-point of radicalism (see, for example, Langan and Lee, 1989). However, although such developments appear to start from the same point as consumerism, they move in a different direction, stressing the active involvement of service users in the definition of needs and services, and promoting the possibility of partnership between service users and service providers (Brandon, 1991a; Hugman, 1991; Sines, 1996b). I will return to this issue in more detail in Chapter 6.

The impact of anti-oppressive and anti-discriminatory ideas and practices on the contemporary values of the caring professions can be seen as a direct development from their histories. Although there have been points of significant change during the twentieth century, these should not be seen as fractures. The values of what is recognisably nursing or social work throughout this period have always included a concern with the structural inequalities of society as the origin of much of the need with which these professions are required to work (Wessell, 1992; Forsythe, 1995; Gottleib, 1995). This is not to deny that these professions have also, at the same time, combined the exclusionary aspects of professionalisation with the disciplinary intent of the state. That is, they have at times sought to professionalise by claiming sole expertise in areas of social life useful to the state in the control of certain social classes (in particular the poorest and most disadvantaged). The history of each profession contains contradictions. What is to be seen, however, is that there is also a rich tradition in the caring professions of feminist and anti-racist action (Statham, 1978). The attempts in the 1960s and 1970s (the period in which contemporary orthodoxy was established) to separate the personal and the political (compare Halmos, 1978) may be seen as a denial of this professional heritage.

The appeals to proletarianisation and arguments against professionalisation, therefore, are to be seen as of their time. They highlighted the tendency within professionalisation for occupational knowledge and skills to be reified over and against service users. Yet the extent to which the alternative would lead to the use of deprofessionalisation to attack the existing basis of social welfare was not anticipated; nor could it have been. The origins of the proletarianisation strand of radicalism lie in a period that might be characterised as the 'high point of modernity' for the caring professions (Parton, 1994, p. 22). At this same historical point, the crises of the welfare state discussed in Chapter 1 were emerging. From these changes it was possible, even necessary, for the caring professions to rediscover the values of anti-oppression and anti-discrimination, and to tie them to a consideration of new forms of professionalism. This more self-critical professionalism could be seen as a potential bulwark against ideas and values more hostile to social welfare. Not only did it make a structural analysis of social issues and problems its central concern, but it sought to rethink professional 'autonomy' in the context of the needs and interests of service users. In particular, widespread moves from bureaucracy to market models of organisation in health and welfare have made such a reassessment plausible, introducing ideas about empowerment and consumerism.

Bauman and the Holocaust: Bureaucracy or Business?

Bauman (1994) argues that there has been a choice in the dominant form of social organisation arising from modernism, which has defined all social life in the twentieth century. This choice is between bureaucracy and business, not only as structures, but also as associated value systems. Bauman's distinction is reached through an examination of the relationship between social thought, ethical values and human action which was rendered problematic by the holocaust in Europe in the 1930s and 1940s (Bauman, 1989). The 'problem' is one which has shaped Western social science in the latter part of the century, and which events in Cambodia, Bosnia-Herzegovina and Rwanda re-emphasise, namely how a society can become caught up in genocide in a very short space of time.

Bauman's answer is to be found in the connections he makes between a sociological analysis of bureaucracy and business as forms of social organisation and the value systems inherent within them. The ethical principles of bureaucracy are contextualised in the operation of impersonal rules, codified as procedural rationality (Bauman, 1994, p. 6). The individual employee does not need to be concerned with the objectives of the organisation; what is required are, first, an understanding of the procedures and, then, the technical ability to accomplish tasks. Indeed, the particular employee may be removed from the ultimate consequences of the work undertaken. This situation produces two ethical sentiments: loyalty to the organisation and loyalty to fellow members (p. 7). An action is right if it is technically correct, follows a legitimate command and is not disloyal. To be 'only obeying orders' becomes a virtue. It if for this reason that 'whistle-blowing', although motivated by a concern with standards of service and a commitment to service users, can come to be seen as 'unethical' (McDowell, 1991).

In the alternative organisational form of modern society, business, the procedural rationality of bureaucracy is replaced by instrumental rationality (Bauman, 1994, p. 10). The 'ends' of business are to be found in the maximisation of benefits from using available resources. Thus 'honesty' tends to be the paramount moral principle, while the virtues include efficiency and effectiveness, measured through profitability. The example Bauman gives is of the relatively recent concern with environmental issues or ethical investments, which have become accepted only when they have been shown to 'make good business sense' (p. 11). An action is right when it makes an honest profit, and so profit becomes a virtue.

For Bauman, ethical persons must be seen as autonomous in their capacity for thought and action. Therefore, neither form of modern social organisation creates the social conditions in which a truly ethical person can act. Both bureaucracy and business require individuals to subordinate their moral autonomy to the requirements of an organisational logic. So neither can satisfy the requirement for an ethical basis to society, and the prospect of the search for ethical values in the late stages of modernity can only be seen as a period of uncertainty. Bauman's solution is to argue that what is required are ethically active citizens, able to balance rights, risks and responsibilities in exercising choice. Such persons would seek to determine right from wrong, even if this was at odds with the prevailing orthodoxy. Social justice might be chosen against bureaucratic procedure or business efficiency, recognising that debate about what constitutes social justice is itself a part of moral activity (compare Grace, 1994). The ethical person is the one who seeks to take ethical responsibility in morally autonomous action (Bauman, 1994, p. 14).

The issues here for the caring professions are to be found in the implications of Bauman's analysis for their organisation and the connections this has with both professionalism and values (including ethics). In an era in which the perceived attacks on social welfare are based around a breaking-up of large government bureaucracies, it seems difficult to construct their defence if Bauman's criticism is taken seriously. Impersonal chains of command, the dominance of procedures and the sense of organisational loyalty are all part of the consumerist critique of public services and the professions which staff them (see above). Yet the same criticisms suggest that the replacement of bureaucracy by business organisation in social welfare leaps from the procedural frying pan to the instrumental fire. If, as was discussed in Chapter 2, the legitimacy of social welfare is based, at least in part, on shared social values regarding need and responsibility, then instrumentality is no better a guide than procedure for determining what is right or good. Moreover, the ethical person described by Bauman has a marked similarity to the image of the professional in sociology, whether functionalist or critical (Freidson, 1983); it is the morally active (Husband, 1995) or the morally fluent (Sellman, 1996) professional discussed above. The ethical professional fits the business ethic with no greater ease than that of the bureaucracy. Such a construction of professionalism suggests that organisations which permit, even demand, the application of skill and knowledge in a conscious balance of risk and responsibility would be the required outcome. Such a model of organisation is not what social policy makers inspired by the free market have offered in the place of bureaucracy.

Towards a New Model for Professional Values

Professional values in social welfare are caught up in the same lack of certainty that permeates Western society, whether this is seen as late-modern or post-modern (Lyon, 1994). In every aspect, including both the understanding of professionalism and the nature of social welfare, nursing, the remedial therapies and social work find themselves in a situation where the former moral language of professionalism in large bureaucracies no longer makes sense, but the values of the market place clash with ideas of service and anti-discriminatory practice. There is a search for a new approach to professional values that goes beyond teaching ethical principles and codes in qualifying training courses. This requires education for the exercise of responsibility, for fluency and sophistication in dealing with the values of caring work (Fry, 1992; Sellman, 1996).

Of particular note in this respect is the extent to which recent commentaries on values in nursing and the remedial therapies have questioned the previous formulaic use of a deontological (Kantian) perspective (Elander et al., 1993; Kendrick, 1995b). Education for professional practice is seen to require a recognition of the complexity of the situations faced by practitioners in the context of actually doing the work (Thomasma, 1994; Bucknall and Thomas, 1995). Professionalism in this sense can be seen as 'ideas in conversation with context' (James, 1995, p. 161). Values are the language of this conversation and fluency requires that such language is capable of grasping the complexities faced in practice. It is for this reason that decontextualised formal ethical codes are no longer seen as sufficient.

At the same time the stark dichotomy between deontological and teleological approaches that characterised the earlier radical critiques of the caring professions is now avoided (Tschudin, 1994; Hugman and Smith, 1995). In particular, the boundaries between abstract individualism and collectivism are no longer so clearly defined. For example, the attention to anti-discriminatory values draws on liberal views of the individual, including ideas about the rights of individual service users to have service responses to their identity as they perceive it, while at the same time allowing for the ideas of a shared or common understanding of social need (based on a particular facet of identity, such as gender, culture, sexuality and so on). Such an approach presupposes that a liberal right of individuals to define themselves in relation to collective entities (or not) is maintained (Ten, 1993; Gray, 1996), even though the caring professions are engaged in the definition of need, and appropriate responses to need, based on a *social* (shared, collective) approach to the identity claimed by service users (Wise, 1988, 1995; Langan and Lee, 1989). Some commentators have argued that there is a cognitive and emotional level to nursing, remedial therapy or social work which requires that the professional and service user share the objective facets of social identity. That is, they would consider it necessary for women service users to be helped by women professionals, for Black service users to be helped by Black professionals, that a professional must have experienced disability to help a disabled person or that gay and lesbian service users should be helped by gay or lesbian professionals. In contrast, others have argued that it is both possible and necessary for all caring professionals to learn about the life situation and world view of others as core professional knowledge and the ability to mould their practice around such knowledge as a core professional skill (Dominelli and McLeod, 1989; Chinnery, 1990).

The ambiguities of this situation can be seen in the way in which the orthodox liberal value of respect for persons (Butrym, 1976) can be applied in situations where professionals are responding to the need of people who are other, in terms of gender, race and culture, sexuality, age or disability. Browne (1995) describes nursing practice in a First Nations community in Canada, in which the meaning of respect for persons was not only easily grasped by people from different cultural backgrounds, but in which they practices that demonstrated the professionals' respect for persons towards patients was clearly understood as good nursing by all involved. It included listening to what patients were saying about their problems, making responses which were seen as relevant, explaining procedures and not exposing the patient to a lack of dignity. Comparable comments can be made about occupational therapy (Hume, 1991) and social work (Dominelli, 1988).

The central point, however, is that this is not simply a reflection of a multicultural perspective, seen as knowing about other cultures as a series of facts (Cortis and Rinomhota, 1996; Culley, 1996). Rather, it requires a commitment to establishing relations between professionals and service users in which respect for persons is linked to a rejection of discrimination and informs all aspects of a cross-cultural exchange. Similarly, applying such a value in ways which combine individual and collective dimensions would relate to an exchange between an able-bodied and a disabled person, between a woman and a man, a homosexual person and a heterosexual person, or people of different ages in grasping the social construction of disability, gender, sexuality or age and applying that understanding to practice (Chinnery, 1990; Perkins, 1995). It is in this way that anti-oppression and anti-discrimination can be seen as values (goals of practice) as well as a means to the end of providing services. As such, they point to the prospect of overcoming the division between individualist and collectivist approaches to values and to the possibility of a discursive ethics in the caring professions.

In Part I of this book I have examined the context of social welfare in the late twentieth century and the relationship of social welfare to social values, with particular attention to the implications for the caring professions. The crisis of legitimacy in social welfare (see Chapters 1 and 2) contains within it a crisis for the role of professions in defining the goals of their own practices. This is a crisis for the legitimacy of professionalism itself, in that it denies moral (as opposed to technical) autonomy by denying the right of the caring professions to engage in the establishment of the goals of social welfare or of the values which underpin those goals or the means of achieving them. What is happening to the caring professions is thus part of the broader processes of change in the definition of need, citizenship or responsibility in policy or in practice. In Part II I will look in more detail at the impact of the specific historical changes which have affected social welfare, especially ideas about market mechanisms and consumerism, and the challenges these developments create for the morally autonomous professional in nursing, the remedial therapies and social work. Finally, in Part III of the book I return to this theme in a discussion of alternative possibilities.

PART II
THE COMMODIFICATION OF SOCIAL WELFARE

Introduction

In Part II different facets of the impact of the processes described above as deprofessionalisation and deskilling are examined. Chapter 4 looks at welfare as a 'product' and the way in which such a perspective has been used to claim the legitimacy for increased managerial controls, changes in organisational arrangements and the reshaping of the welfare state. The idea of health and welfare as 'industry', emphasising the way in which something is created rather than just consumed in the process, may at first sight appear to be positive. Yet this is a contradictory development. It is indeed possible to see it as positive from the perspective of those who work in these services: they do contribute to the social and economic wealth of society through their labour, in the health and well-being which are created by their work. However, with this reinterpretation of professional services into productive labour has also come a recasting of the professional role, from one of relative authority to that of the skilled operative, the ends of whose work can (or must) be directed by others. The question remains, however, as to whether the others are those who directly use the services, or those who control the agencies of the state through which professional practices are licensed, organised and financed.

This discussion leads, in Chapter 5, to a consideration of professionals as producers. The central questions are how this will affect the caring professions and what will be the impact on core values claimed by such occupations. Following from this discussion, in Chapter 6 the focus shifts logically to service users as consumers. However, this is not just the other side of the same coin, as the critiques from service users of the values expressed through professionalised social welfare are more diverse than the neo-conservative and neo-liberal arguments. Moreover, there are dimensions in the range of service-user views which provide the basis for a more radical reconsideration of social welfare and the role within that of the caring professions. The service-user perspective creates the potential not just to salvage pieces from the wreckage of the welfare state, or to indulge in a simplistic approach to the post-modern problem in a 'pick-and-mix' assemblage, but to go beyond that and to develop patterns of social welfare that reflect *social* values. It is on this point that the ground for the discussion in Part III of the future role of the caring professions in social welfare is established.

4

Producing Social Welfare

Welfare as Service or Product?

Ideas about the 'production' of welfare emerged in the UK from the work of the Personal Social Services Research Unit at Kent University (PSSRU) in the late 1970s and early 1980s (Davies and Knapp, 1988). Derived, at least in part, from equivalent developments in the USA, this approach sought to explain the relationship between the characteristics of welfare services, the needs of welfare recipients, the costs of welfare provision and the outcomes of welfare systems (pp. 2–3). Beginning with the assumption that social resources for welfare are not limitless, this approach sought to understand whether the ways in which services are provided are the most efficient or effective that might be feasible. The primary object of this research was the sector of care for those older people who require welfare support, but the approach became applied also to mental health, to child care and to general hospital services (Knapp, 1988).

Efficiency as a concept in this context can be described, in summary form, as the best use of available resources (Davies and Challis, 1986, p. 20). It was analysed by the PSSRU as a measure of whether society obtained the greatest success in achieving the objectives of welfare programmes (effectiveness) at the least possible cost (economy). The 'best' service therefore is not that which is the cheapest, but the one which delivers the optimum outcome for the amount of resource utilised (also see Bartlett and Le Grand, 1993, pp. 14–15). Such an approach clearly owes much to formal orthodox economics and to the models employed in business and commerce.

However, as PSSRU researchers themselves acknowledged, decisions about intended outcomes and the amount of resources in the field of health and welfare are primarily social and political in nature (Knapp, 1988, p. 150). Thus the balance between outcomes and resources is based not only on technical judgement but also reflects social values. As a consequence, efficiency cannot be seen as a neutral concept, but is inherently charged with values concerning the answers to questions of 'who', 'how', 'what', 'where' and 'when' of social welfare services (including health). For example, if the intended outcomes of a service system include the promotion of choice, then whether choice has been created will form an important measure of success. This will be so even if such a system costs more than one in which the same response to other needs (such as relief of poverty, or restoration of health) has been met without any choice being available. The judgement about such an outcome being the most efficient will, therefore, only be possible if an economic value can be placed on the difference between the two systems, and if the costs associated with other means for promoting choice can be known. In other words, whether the cost of choice is worth it remains a political (and therefore social value) judgement.

Notwithstanding such conclusions, and the explicit caveats contained in the PSSRU findings that the contracting-out of social welfare services would have limited efficiency gains (Knapp, 1988, p. 168), the government of the UK throughout the 1980s and into the early 1990s eagerly pursued policies towards various forms of privatisation or semi-privatisation. These measures have tended to become blurred with 'community care' because the policies have sought to combine welfare *in* the community (that is, as far as possible, not in institutions) with welfare *by* the community (that is, as far as possible, by a mix of voluntary, private and informal provision alongside a reduced public sector) within a restructured welfare state (Hadley and Clough, 1996).

The UK is not alone in this process. Not only do these policies mirror the system prevailing in the USA, but also many other countries which previously had large-scale public social welfare systems moved in the same direction at the same time, or have quickly followed. Australia, Canada and New Zealand, along with countries of the European Union and other parts of Europe and Scandinavia have all in some degree moved towards mixed economies of welfare in this period. This is so, despite the strong support for extensive public welfare systems in Scandinavia, for instance (see, for example, Daatland, 1992). The advanced industrial world, it seems, has been caught up in a policy current in which various forms of privatisation (including partial and quasi-privatisation) have become a global trend.

That social welfare in the period of the late 1970s to the early 1990s should have been characterised in this way across so many different systems can be seen as related to three underlying factors that are shared by many countries (as discussed in the preceding part of this book). The first of these is a loss of legitimacy for some aspects of publicly funded social welfare because of perceptions about social (in)justice. Such criticisms have even been shared across the political spectrum, with conservative analysis reaching some limited accord with social democratic criticisms, in that the *intended* beneficiaries of welfare policies may be seen to be not those who actually gain the most from it. This curious agreement is evident in a comparison of Le Grand's (1982) argument that the middle classes, not the most poor, are the primary beneficiaries of the welfare state, with similar claims made by Jenkins (the first Thatcherite minister of health) in 1980 (Webb and Wistow, 1987, p. 93).

Second, the sustainability of large-scale public welfare has been questioned increasingly because of the demographic shifts which are taking place in advanced industrial society. This is the argument about the impact of ageing populations on the levels of welfare state provision which it will be possible to maintain as the balance between age groups shifts. As that proportion of society which can be classed as economically active moves from the majority to the minority, it is argued, the burden of social welfare cannot continue to be met from transfer payments. The solution which has become the norm is to create mechanisms whereby private individuals are increasingly responsible for the costs of services through payment *at the point of use* (directly or through personal private insurance cover) rather than through taxation and rights based on citizenship. This is usually referred to as the 'user pays' approach.

Third, evidence about the impact of the welfare state is also held by some critics to have shown that large-scale public (state) institutions are simply inefficient in delivering their services. That is, the same resource would achieve more services or better services (or the same services could be provided at lower cost) if these were provided through different organisations (Bartlett and Le Grand, 1993, pp. 15–19). Such criticisms include a lack of flexibility and responsiveness, a lack of choice (of type or source of services) and a form of equity that leads to the predominant usage of public welfare by those not in greatest need.

Taken together these three criticisms have been used as the basis for widespread attacks on state welfare and as points of reference for devising alternatives. Indeed, they are closely linked. For example, it would be more difficult to question the legitimacy of the welfare state if the state institutions were regarded as highly efficient; perceptions of the rising costs of providing public welfare to an ageing population would have a different impact if state services were seen as legitimate; and so on. However, there are subtle differences between these three points in relation to the logical conclusions which might be drawn concerning the alternatives that could or should be developed. In particular, although the first and second criticisms of welfare state provision point to (degrees of) privatisation, the third could only do so if the view was taken both that bureaucracy is inherently inefficient and, at the same time, public services can only be forms of bureaucracy.

According to Papadakis and Taylor-Gooby (1987, pp. 22–3) there is a more fundamental issue which has fuelled the other criticisms of the welfare state, which they term 'accumulation crisis'. Problems with the legitimacy of public welfare, with the paternalism of bureaucratic professions or with failures in redistribution might each have been subject to different analysis if it were not for the growing dominance of the view that advanced societies cannot broadly afford the levels of social welfare which had developed since 1945. Moreover, the analysis which underpinned this view was shared by critics from left and right perspectives. Not only were New Right theorists arguing that social welfare was inimical to wealth creation, but, at the same time, the Marxist (or neo-Marxist) contribution was to question whether social welfare represented productive activity or consumption. As the New Right gained ascendancy across the advanced industrial parts of the world the conclusion has been, almost uniformly, that expenditure on welfare can only be justified if it is seen to fit the criteria of market-place industry and commerce: efficiency, effectiveness and economy. Where it can be literally subject to the market place there has been a push for privatisation; where it cannot there has been a range of experiments with the introduction of principles approximating to the free-market (quasi-markets) along with an emphasis on the contribution of families, friends, neighbours and so on (Howe et al., 1990; Edgar, 1995; Hadley and Clough, 1996).

A mixed economy of welfare, which at the same time introduces a quasi-market system into public services, appears therefore to be the best possible compromise between these different critiques. The mixed economy breaks with the previous era of state welfare dominance, it is seen as encouraging choice, whereby direct payment gives greater choice, and it (re)forms public services in the mould of private enterprise through the creation of competition. It is in this latter aspect that the notion of production has gained credence in a sphere which was understood previously in terms of service. Along with this notion has also come the sense that welfare can (and should) be seen as an industry or a business, reinforcing the claim that tests of efficiency are not only appropriate but perhaps long overdue. In the remainder of this chapter the implications for the values of welfare which arise from this commodification, the recasting of social welfare from services performed on behalf of society to something produced for consumption, will be discussed.

The Values of Production

It seems reasonable to ask why the contrast between ideas of service and of production should matter. If it can be shown that the objectives chosen through accepted democratic processes are being achieved in a way which balances outcomes with costs, why should the commodification of welfare be problematic? Even if the process of commodification results in different quantities of services than previously, why should the principles of supply and demand be any less acceptable than those of professional judgement? These questions can be seen as important if it is recognised that behind them lies a concern with broader issues. Can social needs be determined separately from professional judgement? Does social welfare make a productive contribution to society or, by being a form of consumption (moreover, one for which the end users do not have to pay), is it somehow simply one way among many of spending social wealth?

Of course it must immediately be recognised that none of the preceding discussion ignores the fact that the providers of health and welfare are 'doing something'. The concern with the notion of production does not depend on such a basic criticism. What is being debated is the extent to which the activity of health and welfare service workers should be seen as contributing to the product of society as defined in economic terms, or whether *in these terms* it should be seen as consumption. For the economist the measurement of product (for example, in Gross National Product) is possible only when a monetary value can be attached to an artefact or activity. The 'value' of social welfare in these terms, therefore, begins with the 'cost' of social welfare.

Yet for economic theory, as much as for other approaches to such issues, the question of value cannot be reduced to costs seen only as the actual resource used. This would more accurately be seen as 'price'. A more complex definition of cost would also involve consideration of the alternative uses to which the resources could have been put: 'opportunity cost'. It is in this respect that the 'accumulation crisis' mentioned by Papadakis and Taylor-Gooby (1987) can be seen as the thread running through the late-twentieth-century critiques of large-scale public social welfare. Problems with legitimacy, founded on shifts in dominant social ideologies, are problems of the disposal of social wealth and the calculation of opportunity costs involved in the provision of health, education, housing, income support and personal social welfare through state funding against manufacturing and commercial investment.

Earlier proponents of the (social) welfare state were less concerned with such formal economic theory. As was shown in the preceding part of this book, their understanding of the value of social welfare was *moral*. Within that framework the notion of a good was focused on the desired outcomes for a particular form of society. The good which was sought was both a particular form of service and a certain consequence for the way in which society operated. Goods as artefacts or activities were conflated with the 'good' life. What was produced was not only the tangible outcome (health, education and so on) but also the 'good society'.

This conflicts markedly with neo-liberal economics, in which the moral and price dimensions of the meaning of value are quite separate. A good in this sense can be seen as either a product or as a moral condition, but it is not seen as the business of economics to link the two. Such a linkage is regarded as the sole concern of private individuals, subject to the minimum necessary constraint of law. In such an approach the value of social welfare services is best determined through their direct purchase by users. Only in this way, it is argued, can the relationship between value and price be most efficiently determined. Any connection between moral and economic value is, therefore, not the proper concern of the state (other than to ensure the maintenance of order through minimum constraint).

It is as this latter approach to the issue of the value of social welfare has come to predominate that the ideological construction of social welfare as productive, or the field of social welfare as an industry, has developed. Among the earlier proponents of a production approach to welfare, such as PSSRU (see above), the objective was not so much to criticise the type of services, those who provide them, or even their location in state agencies, but to construct a rationale for them which took seriously and accepted the basic premises of the formal economic perspective. Indeed, Challis and Missiakoulis (1988) identify strengthening the professional role of social workers, through the creation of an empirically verifiable test of effectiveness and associated service practices (case management), as an intended outcome of much of that unit's work. In other words, by showing how the productivity of social work could be evaluated in terms of economic efficiency, it was hoped that both their role and the quality of the services for which they are responsible (in this instance access to residential and home care for elderly people) would be enhanced.

Similarly, it may be argued that those who work in health and welfare have gradually accepted terminology such as 'production' and 'industry' to describe their work precisely because these terms are now seen as positive in comparison to the negative image of 'consumption'. It is as if a claim is being made that such services have a value, because they *produce* something (health and welfare). Walsh (1994) notes that what is distinctive about such services, indeed of many public services including health and welfare, is that they are produced at the point of consumption. Thus the productive aspect of the activity may be obscured. This will especially be the case if the activity itself is not accepted as legitimate by an observer (including government). It is against this difference of perception that professionals and other defendants of the welfare state are struggling by emphasising that aspect which can be seen as production.

The values of production, however, do not sit easily with previously dominant views of the nature of professionalism. The meaning of 'service', as with 'good', can differ according to the basic assumptions from which they are understood. Such problems are not resolved simply by replacing the idea of service with the idea of production. Where service *is* what is produced, then the definition of a service as legitimate remains crucial. Moreover, defining and legitimising a service cannot be confined to the particular circumstances of its production. In other words, it has to be widely accepted socially as well as by those involved in the interaction between individual service users and professionals. (This point will be developed in greater detail in the next chapter.)

As the welfare state has been dramatically reconstructed through the late 1980s and early 1990s it has become increasingly clear that this position has not been sufficient to provide the defendants of public (state) social welfare with a strong position. Put simply, the debates are still centred around the scale of resources to be allocated to social welfare provision, and the forms of organisation desired to deliver such services. Knowing what are the most efficient means of achieving given ends does not resolve choices about what those ends should be; this remains a (moral) value judgement. The notion of production and its associated measures of efficiency and economy may be necessary for survival within an economic rationalist framework, but they are not sufficient to resolve questions of welfare objectives.

It is for these reasons that the promotion of privatisation, quasi-markets and the welfare mix should not be seen as ends in themselves but rather as means to an end (Bartlett and Le Grand, 1993; Evers, 1993; Ernst, 1994). The ends which these means of reconstructing state involvement in provision are designed to achieve are: a shift away from a direct towards an indirect role for the state in service provision; a combination of a greater reliance on direct payment by the actual users of services (at the point of use, as noted above), and targeting state funds to particular types of service (and hence service user). This strategy is based on two related elements. First, it permits an emphasis to be placed on user pays. Second, it enables those services which cannot be funded through direct charges to be limited, increasingly through targeting services to those who are judged to be most in need. A degree of legitimacy is restored because that which can be is subject to market forces, while the supply of that which cannot is carefully limited by 'responsible' government.

The legitimacy claimed for user pays in social welfare, as in any other sphere, is that of consumerism. The power of the purchaser is the driving force of the market, so understood. However, the meaning of consumerism for health and welfare is far from straightforward (Hugman, 1994b). This concept will be examined further in Chapter 6, but to make connections here with that discussion it is necessary to note two things. First, because of the political and social importance of maintaining a fairly broad safety net, however targeted, the extent of consumerism developed in practice will be limited by its context. The state and the professionals it employs must continue to play a major role in determining the nature and scope of services. Second, there are some services which it is difficult to conceive as the responsibility of any social entity other than the state, such as those related to criminal justice. This is so no matter how indirect their actual provision might be.

Such qualifications to the idea of consumerism point to a basic question behind the restructuring of social welfare through the economic rationalist agenda. This is the question of what actually is being produced by welfare services? It is to this issue that the discussion will now turn.

What is the Work of Welfare?

In the previous chapter the question of the contemporary role of the caring professions was briefly discussed. It was noted that an important aspect of the recent development of nursing, social work and the remedial therapies (as well of most allied health occupations) has been the increasing emphasis on the related tasks of social control and social management. In particular, the ideas of Cheek and Rudge (1994) and of Parton (1994), that the period of welfarism is now ending and the main task expected by the state of caring professions is the management and control of risk groups in society, was related to the deprofessionalisation of these occupations. In place of the earlier trend towards classic professionalism, it is argued, a move towards a trade-off between technical and ideological autonomy has emerged.

The prevailing professional norms in nursing, the remedial therapies and social work can be seen as that of caring (Salvage, 1985; Knowlden, 1991; Ellis, 1992; Boyce, 1997). However, what this means in more concrete terms varies between the different professions and also within them. For example, Knowlden (1991) characterises this as a combination of 'being caring', in the sense of a commitment and concern for the well-being of the patient, with 'doing caring', in accomplishing the everyday performance of tasks such as checking intra-venous tubes, operating a balloon pump and so on (pp. 204–5). In contrast, Ellis (1992) appears to differentiate between the nurse who is able to care through showing concern and the nurse who simply performs the same tasks as if mechanically (p. 204). In practice, Ellis acknowledges, this may be more difficult in highly technical contexts such as intensive care but, even in that situation, caring is about the way in which the necessary tasks are performed. Caring may involve both 'activity' and 'attitude' (p. 206). There are strong parallels here with the analysis of caring in the lives of people who provide assistance to relatives in the community (Ungerson, 1990). That both spheres can still be understood in terms of the predominance of women is not coincidental (Salvage, 1985; Ungerson, 1990; Ward, 1991). The work of nursing, as of 'women's work' more generally, is characterised by this combination of practical accomplishment and social–emotional expression. Without both aspects what happens is not 'real' nursing or not 'good' nursing. This applies even where the context demands that the nurse is involved in social control or coercion, such as in some aspects of psychiatric nursing, or community health in situations of child abuse.

In social work the concept of care has long been regarded as only part of the picture. For example, Satyamurti (1979) identified a contradiction between caring and controlling which she argued had been part of social work for most of its history (from the nineteenth century onwards). This view is reflected by other writers from different perspectives, such as Rojek et al. (1988) and Davies (1994). Here too, however, there was the sense that in so far as the objective of the tasks undertaken by social workers could be construed as for the welfare of the service user, then a sufficient degree of caring could be said to be accomplished. Even though such a view may be influenced by the specific form taken by the institutional welfare state in the UK (Payne, 1991, p. 7), it is also possible to apply this analysis in the USA, in Australia, in New Zealand and in Canada, to situations in which social workers exercise power over their service users (Barber, 1991).

Caring professions have struggled with the tensions between caring as work and caring as commitment (doing and being, action and attitude), alongside the requirements to exercise both aspects through control and even coercion. Constructing health and welfare work as production denies one side of this contradiction. The focus on the quantifiable aspects of social welfare, and hence those which are accountable in an economic sense, precludes any sense of attitude or commitment as part of the service provided. Caring comes to be seen solely in terms of the tasks performed.

The impact of this shift in the meaning of professional caring work is illustrated by reference to the development of care management in the UK (Department of Health, 1991). The move from *case* management to *care* management, although based on an argument that the word *case* is demeaning to service users, also reflected a shift in the central ideas and practices. Case management, as originally perceived in the UK, was intended to provide a structured service in which the focus would be on the individual service user's needs. What was to be managed (that is, 'the case') was to be the access to appropriate care services (Challis and Davies, 1986; Onyett, 1992). However, the outcome has been the management of services (that is, 'care') in order to target resources to those deemed to be most in need (Hadley and Clough, 1996; 'Sammy's Dad', 1996). In the early stages of the wholesale implementation of this system in community care in the UK there was debate about the recording of 'unmet need', but this was quickly abandoned on the grounds that service users might be able to use legal redress in situations where services were not provided (Hadley and Clough, 1996).

An American critic, Schorr (1992), noted that the community care system being introduced in the UK was based on the evidence of experiments which not only were local rather than national, but which were specially funded as trial projects. As has already been noted above, the research unit on whose work much of these developments were founded themselves had pointed to the cost implications. What is being argued here is that such an outcome is not accidental. The implementation of this system universally within the UK took place in the context of parallel developments in the structuring of acute health services and many other types of state services, in privatised or quasi-market forms. As a consequence of this industrialising of services, the two different but complimentary aspects of caring have been separated. The work of health and welfare is now the production of concrete, if highly complex, tasks and not of meaning or of moral value. This bifurcation must therefore be seen as part of the broader neo-liberal agenda in the public sphere.

That the tasks which have now come to constitute the limit of the official definition of care are highly complex has been accommodated within such developments. All advanced industrial societies may be regarded as undergoing significant changes in the nature of professional work. Processes of deprofessionalisation, or proletarianisation, of professional labour, however, do not necessarily imply a total loss of the autonomy suggested by the idea of professionalism (Larson, 1980; Derber, 1983; Hugman, 1991). Whether in acute health services, community care, child care, juvenile justice and so on, occupations such as nursing, the remedial therapies and social work can be seen as having continued to develop practices which are technically complex and at that level require a large measure of autonomy (Davies, 1994; Weir, 1995; Boyce, 1997). The meaning of 'deprofessionalisation' in this context concerns the way in which autonomy is confined to specific practices with individual cases. Moreover, the separation of action and attitude is accompanied by the denial of that part of professionalism which links means and ends. The goals of practice are established for professionals by managers. There may even be a move to control objectives so tightly that, in effect, techniques also are circumscribed. In this way the characterisation of health and welfare work as 'production' may not succeed as a strategy for protecting technical autonomy but may act as a device for further managerial control. The substitution of technical for moral rationality may lead to the denial of moral freedom or responsibility (Bauman, 1989). (I will discuss this issue further in the following chapter.)

Such a conclusion would be supported by an examination of the way in which certain forms of practice have increasingly become marginalised in the early 1990s (Butcher, 1992). As the notion of community was co-opted as the location for privatised forms of care, moving away from the more collective ideas about community that were expressed in community development or community action, radical practice in many places became focused on advocacy and rights (Brandon, 1991b). Community development and community action are now usually located in the non-government sector, even if provided with government funding. However, this also is under attack as governments reduce or withdraw such funding on the basis that issues of access, equity and participation with which such work is concerned is the business of private citizens and not of the state (Wearing, 1994). In its place can be seen the growth of community management (Taylor-Gooby and Lawson, 1993), and the struggle over advocacy and related practices which may be reduced to arguments on behalf of specific individuals in relation to the rationing of resources (Brandon, 1991b; Onyett, 1992).

So, does this mean that Cheek and Rudge (1994) and Parton (1994), examining nursing and social work respectively, are correct that the end of the welfarist era is to be seen as the reduction of care to social management and social control? Certainly this is the assumption contained within neo-liberal and neo-conservative policies. Their vision of the caring professions is of skilled social technicians capable of managing the process of targeting resources to disabled or elderly people who require assistance, of controlling disorderly families (including the protection of children at risk) and delinquent youth, and of providing the end services such as hospitals and clinics, residential homes, counselling and so on.

To this extent the constituent parts of professional work, including assessment/diagnosis, intervention/treatment, monitoring and review, and so on, which in broad terms are common to acute and long-term services (Onyett, 1992; Weir, 1995), are the means to the ends of health and welfare. The outcome sought, in other words the product, is a restoration of health, or well-being, to a level where the person can as far as possible engage in normal social life. Yet although a great deal of agreement can be reached within the professions, between professions and governments, or between professions or governments and service users, that this is the case, there remains considerable disagreement about both *how* these services are to be provided and *why* they are required in the first place. Indeed, the latter question is at the heart of the struggles between caring professions and New Right governments.

The industrialisation of welfare, with its emphasis on the technical rather than the moral dimensions, obscures the fact that *all* approaches to health and welfare are based on social values. The processes of industrialisation, privatisation, creation of quasi-markets and targeting services, are based on an analysis of needs as individual in nature, often in cause as well as effect. Even where needs are not seen to be caused through the exercise of individual responsibility, they are, nevertheless, not to be seen as a matter of collective responsibility. As Barry (1990, p. 90) notes, neo-liberalism is predicated on the belief that because no one person intended this situation to exist, no one is responsible except either the person to whom the misfortune of need falls or the person who freely chooses to respond to another's need.

Social welfare in the late twentieth century and the professions which deliver it (as discussed in Part I) have come to rely to a large extent on theories and rationales that are based on a different perspective, namely that although individual need is unintended it can be foreseen (Barry, 1990, p. 91). Even in their most orthodox forms, the ethical basis of the caring professions derives from the view that there is a social (collective) responsibility for the distress that is the responsibility of no one individual. In this view, social welfare is a matter not of benevolence but of social justice. The struggles between the caring professions and New Right governments can, therefore, be seen as being based on a variance between social philosophies which are fundamental to differences about definitions of social welfare as production or consumption.

The strategy of emphasising the productive aspect of service provision and other professional work can, on this basis, be seen as inherently flawed. The argument that welfare is contributory to society and not simply a form of consumption to be rationed by political whim is only a weak defence of welfare services and the professions which work within them. The underlying issue is not whether such professions are productive (or even whether or not they work hard, or are paid at the right level), it is about the meaning and purpose of the services they produce. Adoption of the industrial view of social welfare appears to have been an important step in the process of its delegitimisation and the basis for privatised and quasi-market models to be introduced.

That welfare services are produced at the point of consumption has also given weight to the often quite enthusiastic use of consumerist ideas by both the proponents and opponents of the welfare state. The major difference in this respect, as with all others, is between a view of social welfare as a right of citizenship on one side, and as a good on the other, subject to market principles (and the minimum possible intervention of the state). For the former the meaning of consumerism is accountability to the end user of services; for the latter it is to be found in being subject to the abstract relations of the market (Johnson, 1990, pp. 179–82). In practice it may often be confused (Strong and Robinson, 1990, p. 182). An acceptance of an industrial production vision of social welfare fails to challenge an individualistic view of judgements about the quality of services. The opinion of each service user is separated from those of all others in decisions about specific service use, except through market research processes in which the agenda is controlled by managers on behalf of the state (Beresford, 1988; Hoyes and Means, 1993, pp. 109–10).

The implications of the industrialised model for the social relations of professional work in agencies (with particular reference to managerialism) and with service users (with particular reference to consumerism) will be elaborated in Chapters 5 and 6 respectively. It will be seen that it is, in reality, a quasi-industrial model in so far as caring professions are subject to the same patterns of change in labour relations as the workforce in manufacturing, commerce or other commercial services (Jessop, 1994). An understanding of social welfare as production has occurred at a time when all other forms of production also are facing major restructuring arising from the globalisation of economies and increasing 'economic rationalism' of national governments (Stilwell, 1994; Dalton et al., 1996). So before proceeding to examine these two more detailed aspects of social welfare relations, the remainder of this chapter will look at the consequences of the broader reconstruction of social welfare in terms of whose interests are met and whose values are reproduced.

Who Benefits from (the Production of) Welfare?

In the social democratic formulation of the welfare state it was intended that both individuals in need and society as a whole would benefit. For the individual the benefit was to be in the alleviation of need; for society as a whole the benefit was to be in the impact of welfare on the meaning of citizenship. In other words, not only could any one person be assured that circumstances would not lead to poverty, ill-health or other lack of welfare below a common standard, but at the same time all members of society could share the sense of common purpose in the knowledge that they too could access the welfare state if needed. For Hobhouse (1922) the formal structuring of welfare by the state would lead to a more equitable society in which personal freedom would be balanced by opportunity for each member of society to exercise that freedom free of the most basic want. The basis for this view of social justice was reciprocity, between rights and obligations, and between members of the society.

One of the major social democratic theorists of the welfare state, Titmuss (1958), identified three sectors of welfare. In addition to the public welfare system, the formal welfare state represented by hospitals, schools, income-maintenance schemes and so on, Titmuss argued that there are two other sectors. The first of these is occupational welfare, including employment-based health and pension schemes; the second is fiscal welfare, comprised of taxation benefits and indirect governmental support for non-government welfare. In making this distinction Titmuss was concerned to argue against those who challenged the post-war development of an institutionalised welfare state. In some senses this might have been seen as surprising, as Titmuss (1970) later showed greater regard for altruism than reciprocity as the basis for social welfare. However, this analysis aimed to demonstrate that although only some sections of society benefited in an immediate tangible way, other sections of society were also gaining from the invisible forms of welfare (largely funded through tax relief to individuals or companies). Moreover, this invisible welfare created more socially valued outcomes, for example an occupational pension instead of supplementary state pension.

By the late 1970s, the impact of the two invisible sectors of welfare, combined with the universal nature of many direct provisions, could be shown to be creating large levels of inequality (Le Grand, 1982). Put simply, the middle classes were gaining the most from the welfare state, which was failing to meet the needs of those who could be judged by objective standards to be most in need. This was not only because of the working of the indirect welfare systems (occupational and fiscal), although they did make a significant difference, but also because access to the formal direct welfare state was easier for those in middle and higher income groups. Examples of the proportionate gains, taken as a ratio between the top 20 per cent and the bottom 20 per cent, include: for health care 1.4 : 1; for higher secondary education 1.8 : 1; for public buses 3.7 : 1; for university education 5.4 : 1; for housing 6.8 : 1; and for rail transport 9.8 : 1 (Le Grand, 1982, pp. 126–8). Clearly these figures combine direct and indirect forms of social welfare, but even in the largest direct forms of provision (health and schools) the richest fifth did better than the poorest fifth of the British population. Comparable findings in Australia were expressed in the term 'the workers' welfare state' (Castles, 1985). Those in work and earning, and their dependents, did better from the welfare state than those who were unemployed and in the poorest circumstances. Indeed, Australian welfare policy, in contrast to that in the UK, has always been focused more on the support of occupational welfare than direct provision (Papadakis, 1994).

Papadakis and Taylor-Gooby (1987) conclude that the continuing presence of occupational and fiscal welfare, alongside private forms of direct welfare, in even the most highly developed welfare states suggests that the 'welfare mix' is long-standing. What has been the issue in the last twenty years is the balance between the different sectors and the role of the state (pp. 30 ff.). Quoting Le Grand and Robinson (1984), Papadakis and Taylor-Gooby note that privatisation, and quasi-privatised arrangements, may still involve a strong state role in subsidy or regulation, as well as in the direct provision of some services. There may also be the possibility of shared responsibility for service provision. They argue, therefore, that privatisation is not the same as 'rolling back the state', although it may be used as a rhetorical device to add legitimacy to changing institutional arrangements. Instead of restricting the intervention of the state in welfare, its activity is redirected (p. 33). The important question is to determine who shall be the producer of a given service.

It is in this context that the reformulation of welfare as a form of production legitimates the withdrawal of the state from direct provision, to the more indirect roles of subsidy and regulation, while at the same time encouraging private providers to enter the scene in larger numbers than previously. This is so whether or not the providers are not-for-profit non-government agencies or profit-making companies. The beneficiaries of this move can be seen as these agencies and companies, who are able to enter the (quasi-)

market, as well as the government which is able to divest itself of direct institutional control. The claims for such changes also include the direct users of services who, it is argued, benefit from choice (created by competition), which lead to greater responsiveness and improved quality, and so to more efficient services (Department of Health, 1989).

As alluded to above and in previous chapters, possibly the greatest single perceived pressure on welfare spending in advanced industrial societies is in the rapid increase in the numbers of older people as the direct users of services (de Jouvenal, 1988). The argument, that all advanced industrial nations will face a demographic crisis in the early years of the next century, is based on a calculation of the balance between those in the labour market and those who are not. This dependency ratio, as it is termed, will shift towards a dominance of society by those who have left the labour force and are in receipt of retirement pensions. These are also the people who are the largest user group of health and welfare services (Callahan, 1987). It is this perceived crisis that provides much of the impetus for current policy changes in the level and institutional arrangements of social welfare. Although most older people are relatively healthy and independent (Hugman, 1994a), care provided to these age groups comprises a large proportion of all social welfare, and indeed of some countries total GNP (World Bank, 1994). For example, in the USA 16 per cent of GNP is spent on health services, of which half is for people in receipt of retirement pensions (Thurow, 1996). As service users or recipients, older people can now be seen as primary beneficiaries of social welfare.

Several criticisms can be made of the assumptions behind the crisis concept (Estes, 1986; de Jouvenal, 1988; Johnson and Falkingham, 1992; Hugman, 1994a). Although not always explicitly articulated, these assumptions are embedded in the concept of demographic crisis, the social welfare policies which are based on it (or justified by it) and the powerful advocacy for their global adoption by organisations such as the World Bank (1994).

Retirement Equals Economic Dependence

In the advanced industrial countries retirement, or old age, pensions have been a normal part of the social welfare system for many decades. Although this has not prevented many older people from experiencing poverty (Walker, 1986), this form of social welfare has provided basic support to large sections of the older population. As many as 80 per cent of older people in some parts of Europe rely on state pensions for a minimum income (Bianchi, 1991; Robolis, 1993). However, as there has been a rapid introduction of occupational pension schemes in many countries, the level of direct involvement of the state has declined, to be replaced with regulation and subsidy (through tax exemptions on superannuation contributions in the UK, for example) (Walker, 1994). Most advanced industrial countries have made significant moves towards occupational pensions as the main source of income for retirement, *among the current cohort of workers.* So, although present need for state pensions is regarded as high, the continuing state responsibility for direct income support can be expected to taper off into the next decade.

The argument that people on retirement pensions in the future will constitute an economic burden can be seen, to this extent, as an extrapolation of the current situation. Moreover, such a perception of retirees is, to say the least, an extremely partial interpretation. The current cohort of pensioners have an expectation that their taxes or contributions (as in the UK scheme) constituted a form of social insurance. Even though such schemes were, for the most part, unfunded (the money was used in transfer payments to existing pensioners and not invested), there is a strong public belief that such pensions are one of the most fundamental rights (Taylor-Gooby, 1991). Yet even while this belief persists, older people living on occupational pensions already form a growing part of the tax-paying population, and as indirect (purchase based) taxation replaces direct (income based) taxes this might be expected to continue (Johnson and Falkingham, 1992). Retirement increasingly may not mean economic dependence.

Retirement Patterns are Fixed

The predictions of demographic crisis assume current patterns of retirement. However, the age at which people retire, gender differences in retirement and the impact of wider developments in labour markets can all be expected to continue to change in the coming decades. In the early 1990s the predominant ages for retirement were 60 years for women and 65 years for men (Drury, 1992). In only a short time this has reduced and is anticipated to continue to reduce to the year 2000 (Graycar and Jamrozik, 1993). One of the reasons for this appears to have been the connection between tax and pension policies, which have encouraged people to retire earlier, especially in countries such as Australia and the USA (Jones, 1996, p. 128). However, in many instances this may also be a euphemism for late-career long-term unemployment, as the proportion of men aged between 55 and 64 can account for as much as 50 per cent of people unemployed for over one year (ibid.). Given the policies that many governments are developing, for example through changes in occupational pension rules, including the use of state subsidies, there appears to be a good deal of flexibility in the way in which responses to the volume of retired people within a population can be managed.

A problem which may have to be faced is whether the large cohort of people now in middle age (the 'baby boomers') will reach the 'third age' with expectations of a lifestyle oriented towards leisure, to be funded by their occupational welfare entitlements, and backed up by direct state support if they live into late old age. It is the last part of this scenario to which attention could now be paid, without compromising other aspects of current welfare provision. Tax and pension policies are socially structured and can, with appropriate planning, be developed in response to such issues. Although there is evidence that in all advanced industrial countries some steps are being taken, this will require a high level of government intervention, and it is *that* which may be politically unpalatable for neo-liberal governments.

(Un)employment Patterns are Fixed

This factor follows from, and is interlinked with, the previous one in so far as both are based on current practices in labour-market participation. Projections tend to assume that the current pattern will at least continue, with a sharp decline in labour-market participation over the age of 55 (for example, Australian Bureau of Statistics, 1994, quoted in Jones, 1996, p. 128). Yet as we have already noted, a large part of the withdrawal from the labour market by men aged over 55 is disguised unemployment. At least part of this has been the consequence of restructuring (or downsizing) in industry, business and government in *contemporary* circumstances. Added to this, the proportion of women entering and staying in the labour force has grown in recent decades. Assumptions that they too will leave again at age 55 or soon after can only be based on present experience. The commitment of the present mid-life cohort of women to careers, however, shows some differences and these could equally well be assumed to be a factor in future changes (Graycar and Jamrozik, 1993).

It is feasible to argue that as the balance of age groups shift, the dependency ratio will also be affected by changed opportunities for younger people to stay in the workforce. The reference to old age as the problem separates this cohort from the rest of society; seeing the issue as one of the whole society suggests that by considering means to promote and support labour-market participation at younger ages, and to later ages, than at present may in itself be sufficient to reduce or remove the sense of demographic threat.

Health and Social Care Demands Must Increase

Portrayal of the ageing society as the cause of major shifts in social welfare values relies on an assumption of dependency in old age. This is a presumption of decrepitude and decay as characteristic of that part of the life-course. This assumption draws on fact, in that the incidence of ill-health and disability rises with age and is pronounced among people over 80 years of age (Callahan, 1987; Victor, 1991). However, most older people (defined as retired from the labour market) are neither ill nor disabled to the extent to which they might require either acute or long-term care (Hugman, 1994a). Moreover, the demand for health and social care is affected greatly by the social construction of old age and of the professions which provide services to older people. In particular, the finding that a vast proportion of health care is provided in the last year or two of most people's lives suggests that health costs are associated with the stages of dying (or the ill-health which leads to death). In the USA this issue is now acute, as up to 4 per cent of GNP is devoted to health and related care for people in the last year of life (Thurow, 1996).

Why has this happened? In part, it may be claimed, the pattern of health and social care usage is a reflection of a number of factors, including family sizes and relationships, the changed role of women in Western society (especially labour market participation) and so on. That families, especially women members of families, do not form a waiting army of informal carers is now widely recognised as a social and demographic reality (Finch, 1989; Bryson, 1992). However, patterns of health and social care usage are also greatly influenced by attitudes to *professional* care, particularly medical intervention. There are demand and supply factors in this situation. While there is evidence that most older people, as well as families, would prefer the intimate work of care to be performed by professionals (Allen et al., 1992; Daatland, 1990, 1992), there are also concerns about litigation if relatives consider that 'not everything was done'. This leads to a situation where medical and health care in Western societies now operates as if death can or should always be avoided. Therefore the growth of medical and health care costs, with the consequent implications for social care provision, must be seen as a result not simply of demographics but of socio-political choices. As such, health and welfare costs for older people cannot be assumed to be rising simply because people live longer (Fries, 1993). This phenomenon must be seen as an issue of the medicalisation of ageing, and death in particular, and not of old age as such.

Enterprise Values in Welfare Production

So, if old age does not necessarily produce economic dependence, and if retirement and (un)employment patterns might be expected to change, and the increase in demand for health and welfare services also is not determined, are older people really the primary cause of the wholesale reconstruction of social welfare seen in advanced industrial societies in the last couple of decades? The answer, it appears, is not that society cannot afford public welfare, but that a certain type of society does not fit with the levels of taxation and direct state intervention in service provision which this requires.

Claims to economic benefits from the large-scale reduction of direct state welfare (Young, 1992) point to another way of conceptualising the interests served by defining welfare services as production. It was noted above that one of the driving forces in reconstructing the welfare state is the argument that advanced capitalism can no longer afford the type and size of welfare institutions which had developed in the preceding decades. By tying the ethical principles embodied in privatisation and quasi-markets to the reshaping of the welfare budget (Hadley and Clough, 1996), governments can obscure or deflect the political responsibility which should accompany such decisions. The level of state spending on direct provision or subsidy thus also becomes a technical rather than a political (and hence moral) issue. In this sense the prime beneficiary is the state itself, which is able to resolve the accumulation crisis alongside the legitimation crisis. The link between welfare as production and privatisation can be seen, in this way, as an important aspect of the policies which have been implemented in many countries.

However, the extent to which privatisation policies have actually achieved these ends must be questioned. These policies, as applied to social welfare, are part of wider strategies adopted by many governments to create free markets in previously state-dominated sectors, including the sale of government-owned primary and commercial businesses, and to deregulate the private sector (Ernst, 1994). Stilwell argues that in six key respects such policies have not been successful at the national level, as follows:

- Financial deregulation created an economic milieu conducive to speculation [and consumption] rather than productive investment.
- ... The balance of payments current account deficit got larger and subsequent fluctuations in [currency values] seem to have no consistent effect on nation's [*sic*] overseas indebtedness.
- [Reduction of the government deficit] in the late 1980s also failed to eliminate the ... current account deficit, despite claims by the proponents of the 'twin deficits thesis' that reining in one deficit would also resolve the other.
- Tariff cuts have caused major job losses [in manufacturing industry] while doing nothing to promote new industrial development.
- Wage restraint has redistributed income from labour to capital but without any corresponding redirection of profits to [investment].
- Restrictive monetary policies caused high interest rates which added to the balance of payments problem by sucking in more capital from overseas. ...

(Stilwell, 1994, pp. 230–1)

Although written about Australia, this critique also applies in slightly different ways to New Zealand and the UK. Of course it may be observed that most of these implications do not apply directly to social welfare services. However, this would not be an accurate conclusion. Examples of a tangible impact would include the entry of international private health-care firms to newly expanded markets or of the provision of higher education across national boundaries (Halsey, 1992; Walsh, 1994). At the same time, however, the pressure on welfare spending is seen to increase rather than decrease because of the pressure on national economies implied by these effects of 'economic rationalism'.

Privatisation and the commodification of social welfare therefore can be seen as part of the development of a globalised economy. The future of social welfare in ageing societies is only partly addressed by current policies to reduce taxation. If that was the case governments could be expected to be transferring the benefits of taxation to subsidies on occupational and private welfare (such as superannuation) and maintaining levels of taxation while gradually shifting from direct to indirect sources. That rapid reductions in taxation are funded by sharp reductions in social welfare spending, relative to *present* demand, suggests that reducing current account deficits, and creating a climate in which the workforce is more flexible, in other words making the present economy more amenable for global capitalism, are the priorities of governments in advanced industrial countries. On such terms welfare can only be afforded if it can be commodified, constructed as a form of production and subject to the logic of the 'free' (global) market.

The values that are embedded and expressed in the emerging forms of social welfare are, therefore, those of global capital (Wearing, 1994). They are the values of enterprise written into the welfare domain (Heelas and Morris, 1992). The means of achieving this remodelling of health and welfare have been based on the idea of social welfare as production, although this was not the intention of those who coined this term. It has required new forms of organisation for service provision and it has been bound up with new ways of constructing the relationship between service users, service providers and the state. So, in the following chapters the impact of these changes on professionalism and consumerism in social welfare will be considered.

5

Professionals as Producers

The Rise of Professionalism

Professionalism is one of the defining features of modern society (Perkin, 1989). Explanations of this phenomenon have emerged from sociology and social history, locating professionalism clearly in the context of industrial capitalism as a form of the social organisation of particular types of work (Johnson, 1972; Wilding, 1982; Friedson, 1983, 1986; Abbott and Wallace, 1990). That is to say, the form of occupations which are called 'professional' historically have accompanied the development of industrial capitalism. Perkin (1989, pp. 120–1) notes that in the period of rapid social change in the early to middle nineteenth century, in which the boundaries between the aristocratic and middle classes were in flux, a division emerged between the professions and business. Both areas of activity were arenas in which the values of work and of respectability were able to be reconciled, but they produced in turn quite different, even divergent, values. The outcome by the twentieth century was a mutual distrust, each of the other. The dichotomy which came to be well established separated 'culture' from 'industry' and 'intellect' from 'technique'. For Perkin (1989, pp. 122–3) it therefore seems to have followed that the professionals of this period came to regard the values of free market capitalism as inhumane, even inhuman.

Particularly influential in the analysis of the process of professionalisation has been the Weberian concept of 'closure' (Parkin, 1979). The principle of closure is that of exclusion. From this perspective, the professions are seen to be occupations which have succeeded in staking claims to social territory in the form of knowledge and skills. Such claims are buttressed by the assertion of values discussed in Chapter 3 above. To take the example of medicine, by defining it as an occupation which should be restricted to those who have recognised knowledge and skills, not only is medicine defined as an activity, but also the boundaries of its membership are set. The process of defining who can be accepted as a medical practitioner at the same time designates who cannot be accepted.

This approach may be understood as a 'process' perspective on professions (Sibeon, 1990). It has already been noted in Part I that the professions developed in a particular social and historical context. In that discussion it was seen that attempts to define professions by reference to characteristics or traits has largely given way to analysis that takes account of the historical process. This process analysis focuses on the class and status location of the professions, arguing that the criteria used to define traits are, in fact, claims made by the occupations in question to support a particular social identity (Hughes, 1958; Friedson, 1970; Elliot, 1972; Johnson, 1972; Wilding, 1982; Cousins, 1987; Hugman, 1991; Witz, 1992). That is, assertions concerning knowledge and skills, and the formulation of associations with codes of ethics, can be seen as devices to support occupational self-government and other forms of autonomy (see above, Chapter 3). They are not simply the reasons for the growth of professionalism but, to a great extent, are defined by that process itself. In other words, the traits are not the *causes* but the *consequences* of professionalisation. This is not to say that the knowledge and skills in question are fraudulent, but rather that their organisation in the specific way that they are at present is the outcome of social processes; nor is it the end of the story. The boundaries of closure continue to be the site of debate and struggle over who can be admitted, who is kept out, and even whether the lines can be redrawn. The exclusion by doctors of nurses and midwives from diagnosis and prescription, and their gradual readmission to these areas of activity, is an example of the historically dynamic nature of such boundaries (Hearn, 1982; Woods, 1987; Weir, 1995).

For Johnson (1972) the important issue is occupational control. His three types of professions are three types of professional power. The first, *collegiate* professionalism, is the self-government by an occupation, in which the terms of its work (both objectives and means) are controlled by the members of the profession. The

second, *patronage* professionalism, is where the terms of the occupation's work are negotiated between members of the professions
and their clientele. Power is shared between the professionals,
through possession of skill and knowledge, and patrons through
payment. The third type, *mediated* professions, involves a three-
way relationship between professions (knowledge and skills), the
state (law, organisation and resources) and the clientele (citizens).
Not only does the state mediate between the professions and citizens, but also the professions mediate between citizens and the
state (Wilding, 1982; Hugman, 1991). Historically, these types do
not exist in pure form. For example, medical practitioners may
operate within all three types of professionalism in different contexts, although the collegiate form is that to which strongest claims
are made. Similarly, it may be possible for elements of all three to
be incorporated in the practices of nurses, remedial therapists or
social workers, although elements of the mediative type have dominated, especially in the latter part of the twentieth century.

Larson (1977, 1980) takes the issue of power further in her
argument that professionalism can be understood as a claim to
occupational autonomy. That is, the extent to which an occupation
can be said to have professionalised is an indication of the extent to
which it has successfully defined areas of (social) life in which it can
exercise discretion over its objectives and the means by which these
objectives are pursued. Professionalism is a claim to autonomy
over the ends and means of work. For the medical practitioner it is
the right to diagnose and prescribe, and to exercise authority in
defining health issues. Similarly, for the teacher it is the right to set
a curriculum, to select teaching methods and to manage the class-
room, and for the social worker the right to assess a social situation
and to intervene on the basis of that assessment.

Closure can thus be seen as a means by which occupations maintain sufficient autonomy over the ends and means of their work.
Jamous and Peloille (1970) argue that the major component in this
process has been in relation to knowledge. Where the knowledge
claimed by an occupation can be codified and communicated in a
set of rules, which they call 'technical knowledge', then professionalism will be weak. Where there is a high level of indeterminacy,
knowledge is not easily codified or communicated, then professionalism will be strong. As Laffin (1988) observes, a high level of
indeterminacy does not protect a profession from outside forces,

but it does provide a basis for exerting some control over the impact of external change and the nature of any responses.

Where several occupations work in the same context, the process of closure may produce challenges between them for control of specific actions. This is most clearly illustrated by the relationship between medicine and other health professions, especially nursing. The doctor's right to diagnose and prescribe extends to the direction of nurses in their work. It is based on claims to a high level of indeterminacy in medical knowledge and a high level of technicality in nursing knowledge. Arguments by nurses that their role should encompass the definition of health problems and ways to respond (diagnosis and prescription) are, therefore, challenges to the closure of medicine. In this nursing is asserting a claim to indeterminacy of knowledge and therefore autonomy in practice. There are similar struggles between medicine and other professions, such as psychology, the remedial therapies and social work. Outcomes vary between countries, reflected in the terminology 'occupations ancillary to medicine' in the UK (which normally excludes psychology and social work) and 'allied health' in Australia (where psychology and social work may be included) (Boyce, 1997).

This process can be seen as 'usurpation', in which the territory of another group is claimed and attempts made to occupy it (Parkin, 1979). The outcome of usurpation may take one of three forms. First, it may result in attempts to strengthen closure, as in doctors' struggles to exclude nurses and midwives from independent practice in childbirth (see above), or to discredit nurses gaining university-degree-level qualifications (Ross-Kerr and Paul, 1995). Second, it may lead to a partial admittance of elements within the challenging group, as in the acceptance of a small number of nurses as clinical practitioners. A form of closure can be seen in the assumption that such nurses are taking on the role of *junior* doctors (Lamberston, 1995). The same analysis applies to attempts by remedial therapists to gain more independence from doctors in assessment and treatment work (Helewa et al., 1987; Mattingly and Fleming, 1994). Third, usurpation may lead to the emergence of a new professional grouping located between the professions out of which it has developed, such as the nurse practitioner or the health visitor (in the UK) (Dingwall et al., 1988).

A similar process can also be identified in the way an occupation might leave behind parts of the work it has previously undertaken in order to professionalise further. This has been explained as 'ditching the dirty work' (Howe, 1986), as such a process usually involves delegating the less expert or glamorous activities to ancillaries or para-professionals (Davies, 1994). The underlying logic is that of separating the indeterminate and the technical aspects of work, with only those activities that contain relatively high elements of indeterminacy being claimed as central to the identity of the profession (Early, 1987; Mattingly and Fleming, 1994). This process highlights a contradiction, in that the tasks to be abandoned may often be those on which the occupation was founded, such as the physical care of sick bodies in nursing (Johnson, 1978; Baly, 1987; Salvage, 1988). I will return to this point below.

Professionalism can therefore be understood as a dynamic set of aspirations and goals for occupations in achieving control over their work in terms of both objectives and techniques. In this sense professionalisation is the process by which such control is achieved. However, as Laffin notes (1988, p. 29), this process can be precarious because it is vulnerable to changes in technological progress and in public opinion. The importance of the latter can be seen in situations where a profession is seen to contradict the conventional wisdom of a society (p. 28). Examples of this include the public image of social work, where its judgements can often be portrayed as defending the indefensible and failing to act for those who are widely perceived as deserving (Aldridge, 1994), and nursing, where some stereotypes focus on inappropriate behaviour (the 'battle-axe' and 'naughty nurse' images) (Bridges, 1991; Holloway, 1992).

The Critique of Professionalism

In Part I of this book the critiques of professionalism were explained as pointing to exclusion not only between occupations but also of the rest of society. In particular, it was noted that the sense of conspiracy against the laity creates problems for professions in maintaining their legitimacy. At the same time it is important to recognise that the laity is not a unitary group. It is divided by social class, gender, race, ethnicity, age, disability and sexuality (as also are the professions). Moreover, different external groups stand in different relations of social power to the health and welfare professions. For example, the experience and objective status of exclusion is not the same for a single mother with a disabled child, living on state benefits, as for a married couple who have a child with an acute serious illness, who have a high income derived from work in managerial or professional jobs. Being part of a racial or ethnic minority would further compound such situations (Bryan et al., 1985; Williams, 1989). Indeed, the criticism of the inequalities in public welfare (Le Grand, 1982) are often based on evidence of the disadvantage experienced by people as a consequence of their socio-economic circumstances. In so far as the practices of caring professions do not recognise and respond to these disadvantages, then they serve to compound social divisions (Beresford and Croft, 1986; Dominelli, 1988; Hugman, 1991; Witz, 1992).

Such critiques do not argue that knowledge and skills are imaginary. Rather, what is being suggested is that the boundaries set around forms of knowledge and skill are arbitrary. As such they form the borders of territory which are used as the basis for control not only of the profession but also of the lives of those who require the services of the health and welfare professions. This is of particular importance when it is recognised that these boundaries implicitly but powerfully incorporate social divisions, such as class, gender or ethnicity (Hugman, 1991; Williams, 1994). Knowledge and skills may be constructed around an understanding of the world that fails to recognise difference because it contains implicit bias. An example of this may be seen in the way health and welfare professions may in certain circumstances respond to families that do not conform to the perceived normal pattern for a society (Abbott and Wallace, 1990). From a perspective that sees the purpose of the caring professions as that of social control and management of the population then this may not be problematic, but in terms of the professions' own self-images, of service and care, it presents a very serious challenge. It is only relatively recently that such an understanding has begun to have an impact on the way in which caring professions see themselves (Cheek and Rudge, 1994; Henderson, 1994), although because of the inclusion of social analysis in its theoretical base this may be said to have applied to social work over a longer period (Simpkin, 1979; Rojek et al., 1988). Whether it has had any effect on mainstream social work practice is more debatable (Mullaly, 1993).

Furthermore, the process of closure seeks to exclude not only other occupations and service users but also managers and policy makers (Laffin, 1988; Walsh, 1994). Larson (1977) had argued that most professions in the latter part of the twentieth century are, to some extent, organisationally based rather than individually independent in their employment. This follows an observation by Mills (1956) that bureaucratisation was as evident in the large law firms or medical practices as in government agencies or commercial enterprises. Especially in the USA, the hospital doctor, the engineer and the corporate lawyer can be seen as subject to bureaucratic constraint as much as nurses, remedial therapists, school teachers or social workers. In some countries, such as Australia or the UK, this may also be the case, in so far as senior hospital doctors are formally contracted rather than employed. However, junior doctors are employees in all these countries, and increasingly their senior colleagues also are subject to being managed by non-medical general mangers (Strong and Robinson, 1990; Pollitt, 1993).

Under these circumstances the challenge to the legitimacy of professionals' rights to determine their own actions, and so to the basis of professionalism itself in occupational autonomy, is greatest from the state as represented by managers and policy makers. The reasons for this can be seen in two interconnected aspects, in the nature of the work undertaken by these professions (and so the forms of knowledge and skill involved) and in the orientation of these occupations to the state itself.

Laffin (1988) points to two types of competence claimed by the professions, which are derived from the relationship between indeterminacy and technicality which was discussed above. The first of these is cognitive competence, which is the possession of and capacity to apply knowledge that is socially accepted as relevant to an issue or problem. This is competence, as discussed above and as it could be expected to be more widely understood among nonprofessionals. The second form of competence is normative, relating to the capacity to identify and pursue the *right* course of action (Laffin, 1988, p. 29). It is in this arena that the question of indeterminacy becomes more problematic. Judgements about the right course of action are value laden in so far as they are socially contextualised. Where what is right can be established as a material issue, and the division between cognitive and normative dimensions broken down, then the claims of professionals may be strong. Engineers and most doctors (such as physicians and surgeons) have enjoyed this position for some time. However, it does depend on the success of an occupation in eliding the cognitive and normative elements of their work, as illustrated by some claims made by medicine in debates about euthanasia (Hassan, 1996).

Where a profession primarily addresses the problems of the social world the normative form of competence will be weak because it is subject to counter-claims by many powerful outside interests, of which the most significant is the state. Nurses, remedial therapists, school teachers and social workers would all fit this latter description in some parts of their work. The attention by some branches of professions concerned with the *psyche* (psychiatry, psychology) to sustain a positivistic natural science orientation can be understood in this way, as attaching to the material mode of normative competence. In this sense right derives from technically correct and can only be judged by the professional.

Between the service user on one side and the nexus of powerful others (the state, managers and policy makers) on the other is a contradiction. This can be seen whenever professions ground their claims to the normative basis of their actions in what is right for the service user. Although, as an ethical proposition, addressing the rights of service users may be seen as incontestable, the question of *who* should determine those rights is likely to be highly contested. In contemporary democracy, to deny people's rights in an overt manner is unlikely to be a successful strategy. However, the paternalism of traditional collegiate professionalism has in effect done precisely this covertly through claims to know what is best for the service user (Croft and Beresford, 1989; Witz, 1992; Mattingly and Fleming, 1994). The critique of the professions in this respect has been utilised by the New Right administrations in many countries in the 1980s and early 1990s as part of their strategy systematically to confine the arena of determining rights to that of government (Levitas, 1986; Marquand, 1992; Jessop, 1994). In the guise of creating small government, and reducing the power of professionals and bureaucrats, the central state has in fact been strengthened. This has happened because the reality of change has for the most part meant modifying the nature of government agencies and shifting the balance of power from professions and officials to the state through new forms of employment such as contracting out (Bartlett and Le Grand, 1993; Pollitt, 1993; Walsh, 1994). It has not meant an overall reduction of state responsibility or activity. In this process the legitimate role of other institutional actors, such as professional associations and community groups (even though this latter could be said to represent service users corporately), has been systematically reduced.

In this context, for professions to challenge the state, which is simultaneously conflated with the government, is seen as exceeding their social remit. There emerges a struggle between the professions and government as to which understands and best represents the interests of service users. In this process the state employs two devices. The first of these is to use earlier critiques of professionalism as 'conspiracy against the laity' (notwithstanding the irony that such a critique emerged from left-of-centre thought) to challenge the legitimacy of their normative competence. This has been done by overtly including the control of professionals in policies as necessary for the control of costs, and so of taxes. In this way a direct link is made between state and citizen which constructs the professionals as 'other'. This plays on the idea that professionals act in their own interests and not in the interests of service users or other citizens. The second device is to strengthen direct controls over professionals through management and the centralisation of the policy process (Laffin, 1988, 1989; Strong and Robinson, 1990; Bartlett and Le Grand, 1993; Pollitt, 1993; Hadley and Clough, 1996).

The Fall of Professionalism?

Changes in the social form of the professions as managed employees has been variously termed de-professionalisation (Haug, 1973) or proletarianisation (Larson, 1980; Derber, 1983; Cousins, 1987). Drawing both on Mills' (1956) analysis of employed professionals and on Braverman's (1974) understanding of deskilling, it is argued that the classic professions may be subject by social forces to a shift in the direction of the occupational forms demonstrated by the so-called 'semi-professions' rather than the latter taking on the classic form.

By deskilling Braverman (1974) was referring to the fragmentation of the work process such that the span of control over the whole was reserved for a managerial role. This, he argued, was the effect of the industrial revolution on the artisan, through the concentration and routinisation of work in factories. A parallel process can increasingly be observed in the situation of professional workers in the late twentieth century (Haug, 1973; Larson, 1980; Derber, 1983). However, the case that this represents an inexorable and inevitable dynamic is open to question (Cousins, 1987, pp. 39 ff.; Hugman, 1991, pp. 62–3). Braverman made several assumptions about the monolithic nature of the control of the work process that can be challenged empirically. Most importantly, to secure the co-operation of the workforce management must allow some autonomy, so that the creative potential of that workforce can be utilised. Also, the impossibility of supervising every aspect of the work process in health and social welfare provides opportunities for control to be subverted, if only in small ways (Pithouse, 1987; Cousins, 1987).

As a consequence of this situation, attempts to limit the power of professionals employed in health and social welfare have resulted in the development of a struggle over control of the work process. This has taken the form of structured decision making and limits to the resources available with which a service can be provided. Examples vary between professions and between contexts (Hadley and Clough, 1996). In the UK the increasing use of contracts, with very tight specifications that limit areas of discretion (indeterminacy), are evident in general medical practice as well as some branches of nursing and social work. The standardisation of practices using specifications set by managers, such as in community care assessments in the UK, is another example.

In those situations where contracts form the basis of the relationship between the professionals and the state, two elements can be seen to be incorporated in the changing nature of professional work. The first is that the use of contracts or the establishment of quasi-autonomous units form a means of managing professionals by restricting their discretion. More accurately, the process turns professionals into managers (Hoggett, 1994, p. 43), by making them responsible for finding ways of implementing externally set policies through a combination of their own skills and knowledge and the resources available (also set from outside the immediate situation of practice). The second, contingent, element is a blurring of the divisions between professional and ancillary roles. As the junior professional roles become more tightly specifiable by professionals-as-managers, the distinction between junior professionals and ancillaries ceases to have the same significance as it has done historically (Johnson, 1978; Richards, 1995). Indeed, the ancillaries may become the junior branches of the professions in question. Senior professionals in this sense can be seen as those who take on management roles as well as, or even instead of, the more complex and indeterminate forms of practice.

To some extent such a development can be seen as the logical outcome for the semi-professions. As has been noted above, they have largely emerged in organisational contexts and grew through colonisation of those hierarchies (Laffin, 1988; Hoggett, 1994). However, what has become more clear in the detail of recent changes is that the particular type of deprofessionalisation or proletarianisation which this represents is one which accompanies managerialism. A trade-off can thus be seen in the way the supposed decentralism of the contract culture enhances technical autonomy against the diminution of ideological (or normative) autonomy (Derber, 1983; Cousins, 1987). Where the professional is permitted to undertake autonomous action it is circumscribed by the demands of managing (a budget or an 'independent' unit); more junior roles can be controlled by the use of detailed assessment schedules, time-sheets and other regulatory mechanisms which have been utilised for many years in manual work. Approaches to the assessment of performance thus stress the instrumental and ignore the ideological (Balogh et al., 1989; Balogh, 1992).

One response to this position can be seen within the strands of the caring professions which have been regarded as radical. This response is to argue not only that such proletarianisation was inevitable but also that it should be seized as the basis for the formation of opposition to the reduction of the scale of public welfare (Simpkin, 1979). By allying health and welfare work to the trade union movement, it was suggested, it would be possible for caring professionals to make the necessary links with the rest of the population who form the vast majority of service users. The struggle for classic professionalism was criticised not only as reinforcing the division between professionals and service users but also as impossible to achieve and therefore illusory as a means of ensuring occupational autonomy (Salvage, 1988).

Although the history of the subsequent decade is that of attacks by New Right administrations on trade unions also, and a significant reduction in their power (Jessop, 1994), this strategy continues to inform some radical criticism of orthodox professionalism (Parkin, 1995). From the vantage point of the 1990s this can be seen in part as a rejection of the compromise necessitated by the position of professional-as-manager. It places the responsibility for rationing of resources and decisions about social control with managers as the representatives of the state at the local level. This is a value position which emphasises the connections between nurses, remedial therapists and social workers and their service users as fellow citizens of a strong and centralised state. It harbours no illusions about the power of caring professions to effect changes in social welfare policy through their practices. Moreover, it establishes the values associated with the defence of social welfare as *oppositional* to the agenda of the state under New Right government.

Yet the success of New Right governments in reconstructing the welfare state through the reduction of the direct role of the state in funding and provision raises questions about the extent to which proletarianisation as a strategy can enable caring professions to be effective in their opposition. Although this is an approach which has not substantially been tried, rather than tried and found wanting, the impact on organised labour of the 'disorganisation' of capital (Lash and Urry, 1987) suggests that it is unlikely to be the strong defence sought by Salvage (1988) among others. The reshaping of late advanced industrial society through various interconnected 'post' forces (post-Fordism, post-industrialism and post-modernity) (Lyon, 1994) indicates that other strategies will need to be adopted. These will have to focus on the defence of the continued development of the welfare state rather than of a particular historical form. In so far as class relations may no longer be the only major social cleavage to be taken into account, but cross-cut by gender, race, ethnicity, disability, age and sexuality, then proletarianisation may no longer be adequate as the basis for an oppositional perspective. As the lives of service users are affected by a diversity in the combination of these divisions it could be seen as self-defeating for caring professions to align themselves with only one way of understanding inequalities of power in social structures.

Professionals and Production: the Implications

It is in this context that the construction of social welfare as a commodity and the role of professionals as producers can be seen to have implications for professionalisation. The industrial images evoked by these terms demonstrate the current dominance of the materialist strand in Western culture (Perkin, 1989: see above). They also suggest that a parallel can be drawn between the managers and operatives of social welfare and industry respectively. Indeed, the current enthusiasm for referring to social welfare as an industry is premised on the relative value of the former and the latter in a neo-liberal context.

Community care developments in the UK, and the similarities these have with changes in the USA, Australia, Canada and New Zealand, provide the clear evidence that just such a shift has taken place. Two specific issues can be identified. The first of these is the increased use of regulatory controls over practice, such as assessment schedules. The use of such schedules is intended to limit the area of discretion of the individual practitioner. The rationale is that it enhances equity between service users (for example, Department of Health, 1991). By providing a structure within which the information to be included in an assessment is specified in advance by someone other than the person meeting the service user, it attempts to ensure that the discretion of the individual worker does not enter the decisions that are subsequently made (Sibeon, 1990). Similarly, in the fields of counselling, child protection or of juvenile justice the areas of discretion are limited by the use of highly specified procedures and policies (McCallum, 1990; Parton, 1991; Smith, 1995).

Because these changes reduce the indeterminate aspects of the work they could be seen as the final stages of proletarianisation. It is in this way that the increased technical dimensions of the work blur the boundaries with ancillaries. Derber's (1983) suggestion, that a trade-off between ideological and technical autonomy would form the basis of continuing professionalisation under such circumstances, seems implausible, given that the closure principle suggests it is the *technical* activity which aspiring professions delegate to ancillaries (Early, 1987, p. 6). In so far as it is associated with the demise of ideological autonomy and emphasis on the technical aspects of work, the industrial production metaphor in social welfare could be seen as the end of professionalism. Criticism of the community care reforms in the UK and of the reduction of the state role in community services in Australia, Canada and New Zealand, is partly directed towards the increase in regulation of professional practitioners accompanying the apparent de-regulation of social welfare (for example, Hadley and Clough, 1996). It is in this respect that case (or care) management in the UK has come to be seen as a Trojan horse for the attack on public welfare provision.

However, two caveats must be mentioned here. First, the historical context in the UK means that, for the most part, direct work with service users in the areas that are now embraced by community care have *always* been undertaken primarily by ancillaries rather than by qualified professionals (Howe, 1986; Richards, 1995). In Australasia and North America the historical legacy is similar (Mauksch, 1966; Castle, 1987). In such contexts the traditional role of the qualified professionals has been to supervise ancillaries. This includes hospital nurses and remedial therapists as well as community-based practitioners (Dingwall et al., 1988; Mattingly and Fleming, 1994; Richards, 1995). In this respect the separation in practice and management of ancillary and professional is a return to the past as much as a new situation, as with so much else in the present era. It was only in the more high-status areas of work, such as child health and welfare, that community nurses and social workers had gained greater autonomy *in the direct work with service users*. Procedural constraints in these previously more autonomous areas of direct practice consequently take a less overt approach. Nevertheless their logic is the same, to restrict individual discretion by spelling out good practice in a highly technical manner.

The second caveat is that there is actually a material difference between the production of social welfare and the production of consumer goods. Here Walsh's (1994) observation that services, including health and welfare, are produced at the point of consumption connects with the issue of deprofessionalisation. Although schedules and procedures restrict the area of discretion for the practitioner, they do not do so absolutely; nor can they, unless the practitioner is to be directly observed by a manager in the completion of the task. Completing an assessment form or following procedures involves the use of discretion. It requires communication between practitioner and service user(s), the interpretation of information and the application of that information within the relevant policies. While the mechanical type of interaction which may be produced is experienced as an affront to notions of good professional rapport with service users (Hadley and Clough, 1996, p. 145), the necessity for judgements to be made and skills employed in undertaking even this type of work can provide opportunities to exercise discretion, albeit limited.

Both these qualifications on the absolute nature of deprofessionalisation demonstrate the contradictory nature of these occupations that has been endemic from their early days. The struggle between professionalism and bureaucracy was highlighted by Wasserman (1972) in the USA in the observation that social workers in public agencies could not purchase an order of groceries for a service user without managerial permission. The more recent imposition of detailed assessment schedules and highly prescriptive procedures is of a different level but not of type in the relationship which may develop between practitioner and manager. What is perhaps evident in the contemporary situation is the changing nature of the bureaucracy and the underlying concepts. While social welfare as service contained collectivist sentiments, social welfare as production is highly individualistic. The production-of-welfare era can, in this way, be seen as the unfinished business in the struggle between professionalism and bureaucracy translated into the neo-liberal frame of reference. The sense for practitioners therefore may be that after the developments of the previous four decades the position might have been one of a gain in professionalisation. The reality is that of having moved sideways (to a different form of semi-professionalism) rather than forwards (to greater professional autonomy), but this is experienced as moving backwards. The contemporary situation is perceived by members of these professions as less than it was expected they would have achieved by the 1990s.

The Rise of Managerialism

A further defining value since the 1970s has been that of managerialism. Pollitt (1993, pp. 6–10) argues that managerialism is as much a value as a description of a mode of organisation precisely because it draws on ideological referents and beliefs. Good management is good, better management is better, without the requirement of saying what is to be managed or why. It is possible to introduce a discussion of managerialism in social welfare without specifying the objectives of the services which are managed (which Pollitt defines as 'social need, professional standards, deprivation, community or equity', 1993, p. 11). As a consequence the introduction of managerialism from manufacturing and commerce to social welfare has been experienced as the invasion of an alien belief system. This belief system is one in which the discourse of work objectives (discussed as ideological autonomy above) is separated from the technical performance of complex work. Managerialism is, therefore, the necessary antithesis of proletarianisation. Because of this connection it thus must also be seen as inimical to professional autonomy and to be accompanied by deprofessionalisation (as this has already been described above and in previous chapters) (Laffin, 1989).

Earlier critiques of social welfare services and professions in large organisations, as has been shown, were based on the perceived contradiction between professionalism and bureaucracy. It was argued that work control which is derived from bureaucratic structures allows no one person to possess discretion, and so all persons are subject to the regulations. A benefit of managerialism, it has been claimed, is that it individualises work control (Pollitt, 1993). As opposed to the rigidity of bureaucratic organisations, in which no one may take final responsibility for decisions or actions, managerialism brings with it the benefits of the business culture in which individual independence and the possibility of risk-taking are valued (Bamford, 1990; compare Bauman, 1994).

Bamford argues that the rise of managerialism in social welfare has been partly fuelled by shifts in the public image of caring professions (1990, pp. 111–13). This analysis is based on the peculiarities of the British child welfare system, which has been subject to repeated public inquiries into failures to protect vulnerable children. Although primarily focused on social workers, this view encompasses health visitors and other community nurses, as well as, on occasion, paediatricians (also see Campbell, 1988). Yet this situation does not pertain in quite the same way in North America and Australasia, where a comparable development of social welfare managerialism has taken place. For this reason Bamford appears to be more accurate when he connects the control of child protection with control over resources and costs (1990, pp. 117–22). It is the concern with costs and general legitimacy that has international comparability in this sense. Therefore it seems more plausible to argue that managerialism serves the purpose of effecting greater control over the whole of social welfare, in both the ideological and technical spheres.

The control which has been sought is not that between levels of staff in organisations, but of social welfare services by policy makers and politicians (Laffin, 1989; Strong and Robinson, 1990; Pollitt, 1993). Managerialism within these services, and of the caring professions, thus is part of the wider agenda of social management by government (Jones and May, 1992, pp. 387–9). The rise of managerialism has been a partner to increased concern at the macro-economic level to reduce welfare expenditure and the consequent reduction in the level of provision. Nowhere can this type of work control be equated with *growth* in public social welfare.

A further aspect of managerialism which requires critical attention is that by emphasising the separation of practice from work control it further opens the social cleavages which were already endemic in the caring professions (Abbott and Wallace, 1990). Put simply, it exaggerates, even though it does not create, the extent to which hierarchies embody the control of women's work by men, of Black and ethnic minority workers by White management and of disabled people by a system geared to those without such disabilities (Grimwood and Popplestone, 1993; Williams, 1994). In this situation it therefore should not be surprising that so little progress has been made towards the resolution of these divisions and inequalities (Ahmad, 1990; Williams, 1994). Increases in the numbers of disadvantaged groups in the social welfare workforce tend to be in practitioner roles and to be subject to the same pressures facing skilled and professional workers elsewhere, of increased casualisation, temporary contracts and part-time employment (Whitaker, 1992, p. 187; Hutton, 1995, pp. 105–10). Managerialism avoids addressing such issues by regarding them as ideological. Attempts by caring professionals either as individuals or through organisations such as trades unions or professional associations can thus be opposed as illegitimate (compare Harbert, 1988).

Moreover, the managerialist revolution contains the implication that, along with everything else, work itself is reconstructed as a commodity (Hutton, 1995, p. 99). This turns the notion of a free market on its head, or at least exposes the deficiencies of viewing the labour market by the same principles as that of the market in consumer goods and services. That is, while it may be the case that power belongs to the purchaser, the identity of the purchaser belongs to employers (as it always has). The terms of exchange in the labour market are established by employers as suppliers of work rather than workers as suppliers of labour. In a situation of high unemployment this is heightened because the demand is for work not for workers. Under such circumstances employers may only change their actions if forced by the market for their product. As no such shortage exists in social welfare (indeed there is an excess of demand in these terms) the pressure for change can appear to be weak. Those changes which have been made can be seen as located in areas which are less easily controlled, because less visible politically, or else as a response to political pressure from outside the services themselves (Williams, 1994). This does not mean that no change originates within services, but that, when it does, it is subject to strong resistance and a sense that other matters have a higher priority. This is underpinned by the ideology that such matters are essentially political and therefore of no legitimate concern for professional practitioners.

Managerial Control: the Example of 'Whistleblowing'

An example of how managerialist social welfare organisations can react to challenges to this culture can be seen in the treatment of those who make public any perceived deficiencies or failures in service provision. These acts, usually termed 'whistleblowing', are often constructed by employers as industrial deviance (Hunt, 1995; Kendrick, 1995b; Jan and De Maria, 1997). Hunt (1995, p. xv) connects the threat to professional autonomy and the attempts by social welfare services to gag employees through specific clauses in employment contracts. Through the early part of the 1990s a series of health-service professional staff in the UK were sacked as a consequence of their making public statements critical of standards of service or discrimination. A common feature was that the individuals involved had attempted to use the normal channels (that is, organisational hierarchies) to express concerns about the risk to service users of insufficient standards or deception in research findings before making their concerns public, but were not responded to positively (also see De Maria, 1996). This has happened also in the non-government sector as well as in state agencies (Hunt, 1995, p. xviii). For Hunt (p. xxi) such developments follow directly from the move to a market approach to social welfare and the introduction of managerialist principles into this sector, based on private market business models.

However, it is also the case that in this respect business ethics ought not to be so far removed from professional ethics. Bauman (1994, p. 11) notes that honesty is claimed as a prime value in business, and it is this value to which whistleblowers in caring professions are oriented. Yet honesty in this sense often is reduced to compliance with the terms of a contract, and business may sometimes find its morals equated with instrumental rationality. That is, what is good is what makes good business sense and uses resources rationally. Under this ideology the number of nurses on duty in a hospital can be seen as a technical matter for managers and not an ethical issue for professionals (McDowell, 1991; Kendrick, 1995).

Some legal protection for social welfare professionals (and others) has been introduced in the USA (Purtilo, 1993; McHale, 1995). This has not always proved easy to operate and stands in some contradiction to the minimal regulation of American employment, in which an employer does not have to show just cause for dismissal. Under the federal employment protection legislation, however, the issue becomes one of public interest and the plaintiff (the dismissed person) has to show that disclosure of information fulfils this criterion. Even this type of protection is not as clearly available in Australia, New Zealand or the UK, where the principle of confidentiality may be used to separate professionals from their own ethical obligations to service users by prioritising obligations to employing organisations and their managers (McDowell, 1991, pp. 88–9; Hunt, 1995, pp. xxii–xxviii). Confidentiality to service users is thus seen as relevant only to information about specific individuals.

The logic behind the use of the principle of confidentiality in this way is that of the separation of normative competence and ideological autonomy (the perceived capacity and right to choose work goals) from technical competence and technical autonomy (the perceived capacity and right to choose work methods). Within the deregulated commodified social welfare organisation it is the latter which is seen as the prerogative of the professional. The processes of deprofessionalisation and proletarianisation would thus seem to be complete.

New Cleavages and Closures

Can management therefore be understood as a new class? This was the conclusion reached by Burnham (1945). His central argument was that the increased technical complexity and sheer scale of modern society meant that effective power was passing from those who owned the means of production in a formal legal sense to those who controlled them. In short, he heralded the triumph of Weberian pessimism over Marxist optimism. Since then a series of critics have demonstrated that by failing to understand the more subtle relationship between ownership and control Burnham overstated his case. Mills (1956), for example, pointed to the way in which the increasingly sharp divisions within professional as well as manufacturing work were creating a class of professionals who were separated from ownership *and hence* control over their own work. Braverman (1974) followed this lead, and it is from this critique that the proletarianisation thesis originated (see discussion above). For those professions employed by the state, the control of the means of production (the offices held in those agencies) lies with managers, but the ownership clearly rests with the state itself. For this reason it may be argued that Burnham not only misunderstood the Marxism he sought to criticise but also the Weberian concept of bureaucracy on which he drew. Indeed, for Weber the bureaucrat could never be said to 'own' the office held, no matter how great the degree of control over the work process.

For these reasons, the proletarianisation thesis, although used by radical critics of the claims of professionalism in nursing and social work (Simpkin, 1979; Salvage, 1985; Parkin, 1995), could also be seen to be most accurately applied to the more recent moves to create a deregulated quasi-market in health and social services. There are two aspects to this development which can be understood as forming a new cleavage, or social division, within social welfare services. The first of these is the introduction of general management, not only in practice but also as an ideology

(Bamford, 1990; Strong and Robinson, 1990; Cox, 1991; Pollitt, 1993; Hadley and Clough, 1996). General management as a principle is based on the assertion that management is a distinct, skilled activity in itself, for which appropriate training is required, and which can be applied to any activity in which the manager need not have any practical experience or detailed knowledge. An example of this is the claim by Griffiths (1988) that managing community care is much like managing a firm of supermarkets.

What Bamford (1990, p. 115) recognised in this development were the growing divisions between the different levels within caring professions. Not only are these reflected in organisational hierarchies, but also a clearer separation has opened between practice and management. Attempts to merge practice and management, based on a professional model, have been limited and often short-lived (Ralph, 1989, p. 75). There has even been the undignified spectacle of those professionals who have 'made it' to the higher echelons of management rushing to distance themselves from the professions from which they rose. An early example of this tendency is Harbert (1988), although Bamford (1990) shows that the counter-tendency is possible (see also Cochrane, 1994).

The second, related, aspect of managerialism has been the introduction of managers who have no experience in the actual provision of health or social services. Hospitals, residential services and community services can all in this way be seen as equivalent to supermarkets. What is perhaps more challenging to the professional ideology is that clinical practice and other direct work with service users is subsumed under the control of general managers along with buildings and other infrastructural aspects of the work. The recent history of nursing is that of the separation of these two aspects from the earlier role of matron (Dingwall et al., 1988). However, the process did not stop there, but continued so that the clinical area has become subsumed under the growing field of general management (Cox, 1991).

The importance of the status of general managers in relation to professionals, or of those who have left their profession to become managers, is that they are frequently perceived by the professionals as the agents of government in the implementation of damaging attacks on social welfare (Cox, 1991, p. 99; Pollitt, 1993, p. 67). The orientation of caring professions towards the needs of service users, and of managers towards the wishes of government, emphasises the division and begins to indicate quite distinctive class orientation. Managers may not have ownership, but their interests are increasingly allied to those who do. In this context it should perhaps come as no surprise that whistleblowers will be treated as subversive or traitorous and not simply as exercising independent professional conscience. A code of ethics, so much a part of the professionalising strategy, may thus often be compromised and challenged by the managerialist ethos, and vice versa. Loyalty is claimed by the manager over and above the profession, and professionals may experience this not just as a conflict but as an attack on their professionalism. This also is a point at which the struggle between ideological and technical definitions of autonomy can be seen. The professional who chooses general management can also therefore be seen as joining the attack (Cox, 1991, p. 102).

In addition, the further sharp separation of management and professional practice introduced with general management has had the effect of highlighting continued work segregation. Although a form of dual labour market may still be seen between the professions and ancillaries, there is also a strong division between practice and management. Black women and men, and white women, continue to be less likely to be represented in the ranks of general management than are white men and in comparison to be highly represented in practice and clerical work (Hugman, 1991; Grimwood and Popplestone, 1993; Williams, 1994). What is emerging is a multiple rather than dual labour market, in which the divisions are more complex and multi-dimensional.

Professionals as Managers

Commodification of social welfare, combined with the neo-liberal moves to restructure state involvement, have led to the creation of the quasi-market approach which was discussed in the previous chapter. For professionals this has created new demands on their work through the development of new roles. Specifically, the emphasis on social welfare as a product, together with the determination of governments to control costs through controlling professionals' actions, has led to the distinction between the roles of purchaser and provider (Bartlett and Le Grand, 1993; Propper,

1993; Hadley and Clough, 1996). These two roles can be summarised in the following way:

- *purchaser* – the role of specifying a service to be delivered, of allocating resources to ensure delivery, of establishing contracts with the provider (supplier), of monitoring the standards of service – the purchaser role will also normally include the assessment of need with the service user, as in case management and brokerage;
- *provider* – the role of working with the service user to meet the identified need (such as in clinical practice or other direct interventions).

The purchaser/provider split, as it has come to be known in the UK, and is being introduced to Australia and New Zealand, contains several elements that reflect its origins in the restructuring of social welfare (Degeling and Thomas, 1995). These include work (and hence cost) control, emphasis on a technical definition of the work (especially on the provider side) and, through role and task specialisation, the tendency for the overview of work to be available only to general management.

The principle of the purchaser/provider split is that of the market place, in which the power of the purchaser is intended to provide the basis for the most efficient and effective service to be obtained for the service user. This principle is based on two assumptions. The first is that single agencies which assess need and provide services are inherently inefficient because they do not permit choice between service alternatives. The second is that through competition between providers, working to contract, the quality of services can be improved while costs are kept as low as possible. Efficiency is thus tied to economy, and so should promote effectiveness.

However, in the USA there is growing evidence that these quasi-markets are not able to operate in the manner intended (Propper, 1993). The need to maintain consistency for service users may lead to 'sweetheart' deals that tie a purchaser to a provider and so minimise the power implied by being able to go elsewhere. Moreover, the demands of forming and monitoring contracts, with service standard specifications, creates a new set of responsibilities which in turn promote greater central costs and may lead to the growth of new bureaucracy (Dageling and Thomas, 1995; Hadley and Clough, 1996). In particular, as the managers of contracts are usually separated from the staff who assess and work with service users, and both are subject to general management within a hierarchy, the purchaser is not a person but an agency. Similarly, providers too are organisations and not individual, professional practitioners. It is for this reason that the move to this system of social welfare should be seen as a form of work control. The emerging constraints on the staff of the purchasing units in practice therefore appear to be that the limitations of resources lead to new forms of service-directed, rather than needs led, assessment and decision making (Cochrane, 1994, p. 126; Hadley and Clough, 1996, pp. 185–6). Confidentiality may come to include keeping information from service users in order for this resource-led system to continue to maintain the ideology of consumerism (see Chapter 6, below).

One possible exception to this view of the purchaser/provider split is the role of the general medical practitioner (GP). As some of the work undertaken by a GP can involve diagnosis and prescription in the one event, as a purchaser the GP must be able also to provide. The UK model has been to allocate resources direct to GP practices, called fundholding. It is then the responsibility of the GP to allocate the available funds among the needs of patients.

Hoggett (1994, p. 43) comments that rather than controlling professionals by managers this variation of the purchaser/provider model converts professionals into combined manager-practitioners and cuts them off from the bureaucracies through the device of quasi-autonomous business units. To an extent this is the case, although it is limited by the small number of professionals who might actually work in such an independent form of practice. In addition to GPs there are possibly a small number of nurses, occupational therapists and social workers acting as brokers to whom this would apply. However, the vast majority of caring professionals are employed in some form of agency.

What would seem to be the more common structure that is emerging is that of professionals becoming the managers of quasi-autonomous business units within which are employed junior professional colleagues who undertake the actual welfare practice. Rather than seeing this as a new form of organisation, this outcome represents a return to an earlier strategy which has defined the caring professions as bureau-professions (Cochrane, 1994, p. 127). That is, within the process of professionalisation in nursing, the remedial therapies and social work, the colonisation of organisational hierarchies by professions was a common strategy, so that the two hierarchies came to be synonymous (Hugman, 1991). It must be questioned, therefore, how new the underlying structures of post-Fordist social welfare are, or how much they represent a continuation of a development from the preceding forms. Indeed, it may be that the quasi-autonomous business unit becomes the more favoured option for the caring professions, who may find it more acceptable to exercise self-control than be controlled by general managers. This seems unlikely in the larger organisations, such as hospitals, although even there some degrees of autonomy may be obtained.

At the same time it is necessary to be cautious, in that the limitations to resources may ultimately determine any freedom of action, and these are set by governments. Quasi-autonomous business units may simply be the occupational equivalent of the electronic tagging of offenders in the community. As such they would indeed be the epitome of post-Fordist welfare work. It is also important that the impact of such changes on labour-market segregation are considered. Although at present there is scant evidence, previous knowledge would suggest that the most likely outcome is that oppressed and disadvantaged groups are unlikely to fare any better (Williams, 1994). At best these changes may represent a move sideways rather than forwards. The numbers moving out of the system suggest that for many it may be experienced as a move backwards (Pollitt, 1993).

Professions as Producers: Coda

As a response to the cultural shift towards the valuing of industry over service and its related impact on the caring professions, the portrayal of social welfare as production clearly is interwoven with wider developments in advanced industrial society. It is tied to economic and political changes and to that extent the formulation of professionals as producers may be representational of an era. The contradictions which are emerging include an apparent decentralisation to increase central control, and the restriction of service availability to target groups in the name of choice. In such circumstances, for caring professions to seek to demonstrate that they do contribute something to society is both necessary and understandable. It may be that to make use of what is happening is therefore a better strategy than outright opposition.

Yet there is an anomaly between the enhanced power of the state over the lives of citizens through the commodification of welfare (among other changes) which is couched in the language of the consumer market, and the professed purposes of nursing, the remedial therapies and social work. To some extent this is not new, as they have all struggled with the contradictions of care and control over long periods of time. What is highlighted in the process of commodification, however, is the way in which the language of inclusion and responsiveness can be used to exclude and limit response. This is nowhere clearer than in the phenomenon which has accompanied the industrial-production metaphor in social welfare, namely the remodelling of the service user as 'consumer'. Production is for consumption in late capitalism, and welfare as production must have its customer. Therefore it is to that issue that the discussion turns in the following chapter.

6

Service Users as Consumers

Consumerism in Social Welfare

Accompanying the commodification of health and welfare, in which professionals are to be seen as producers, is the reformulation of service users as consumers. Indeed, it could be seen as axiomatic that if the service in question becomes a product (a good or commodity) then the user of the service must become a consumer of that product. So the claims which have been made about consumerism frequently make reference to the desirability of seeing the relationship between services and service users in this way, not as an outcome but as an integral part of the process of commodification. That is, unless both professionals and service users themselves see service users as consumers, with attendant expectations about rights to standards of service, then the project of reformulating social welfare as production will be incomplete. Therefore, consumerism is a necessary part of the overall reconstruction of social welfare (Walsh, 1994).

However, there are different ways of understanding the role of consumer. The possible variations in this role can be seen as a continuum which stretches from the passive receipt of a service by individuals, through the active participation of individual users in the delivery of a service, the participation of individual users in the formulation of services, to collective participation of service users in defining service goals and structuring actual provision. Of course, even in the first of these the service user (or another person on their behalf) must take the active step of defining a need and seeking a service to meet it. This point differs from the others on the continuum in that it does not envisage the service user having any more active role than that of selecting between possible sources of need satisfaction. The other three points share an understanding that the service user will, in different ways, participate in both the definition of need and the means by which this need will be satisfied. It is in the type and extent of envisaged participation that they differ.

For the individual person who participates in the delivery of a social welfare service the extent of active involvement may be in relation to *how* the service is provided at the point of use. This may be achieved by professionals ensuring that they are responsive to feedback from users about the way in which services are provided, through formal or informal consultations (Cambridge, 1992, pp. 504–5). Whether formal means for consultation are built into the structures and processes of services can affect the extent to which professionals are obliged to listen to users and therefore whether consultation is a right or a contingent benefit of good practice. For example, Cambridge (p. 504) notes that actual practices may differ, from the expectation of users being involved in certain types of discussions (such as case reviews) but not in others (such as inter-agency meetings), to users being represented in formal meetings by keyworkers who consult with the users informally outside meetings.

Although the former version does provide the user with a more concrete expectation of being heard in service processes, both forms of consultation make assumptions about the separation of service users from service provision. Reference is made by some professionals to the need for this limitation. It may be judged that the service user is unable to participate more fully (such as in situations of dementia) or it may be that the service user does not wish to take part (perhaps because the person feels the formal setting of a meeting is intimidating) (Cambridge, 1992, p. 505). Critics of this consultation approach to consumerism argue that the social relationships which it implies still give considerable power to the professionals (Hadley and Hatch, 1981; Croft and Beresford, 1990; Brandon, 1991b). Whether the user exercises any power of influence or control over services depends on the willingness of the professionals to be open to it. Therefore it is and remains contingent.

Participation, as opposed to consultation, is the next point on the continuum. The major difference between the two is in the extent to which the service user has a role, as of right, in the definition of service goals as well as means. The objective is to set a 'floor' in the balance of power between users and professionals below which it is not possible to go (Cambridge, 1992, p. 510). Behind this approach is the assumption that as professionals have considerable power then it is necessary for some structured limits to be established so that service users can exercise countervailing power (Hugman, 1991). Much of the literature on case (or care) management, for example, either assumes or makes explicit this issue (Moxley, 1989; Onyett, 1992; Orme and Glastonbury, 1993).

Yet participation of this kind seems to be extremely difficult to achieve in practice. In part this may be seen as a consequence of professionalism as such (as discussed in the previous chapter). The very existence of occupations which make claims to expertise in areas of health and welfare may be said to have been founded on the exclusion of users from the definition of need or appropriate responses to its remedy. At the individual level it may also be the effect of paternalistic professionalism over time, as service users have been denied the opportunity to participate (Brandon, 1991a). Attempts to create greater participation therefore may be constructed as challenges to existing services rather than as the restructuring of services in dialogue with service users. The floor may turn out also to be a ceiling, above which the level of participation is not able to rise. Yet the nature of this problem lies not in the idea of participation as such but in the historical limitations within which it is being developed.

Possibly the most radical approach to user participation has been the growth of formal structures in which a collective voice for service users has been created. This may be seen in forms of social welfare which are controlled by service users themselves, or in self-help provision which totally excludes professionals. Although varying in the extent to which they are based on existing forms of organisation, these two strands are part of a similar approach, namely one in which the service user is to be seen as the source of authority and legitimation. Examples of services in which such developments have taken place include disability services, children's services, services for older people, mental health services, women's services and services for Black people (Collins and Stein, 1989; Chinnery, 1990; Johnson, 1990; Oliver, 1990; Hiscock and Weeks, 1995; Timor and Wilson, 1995). In each instance the gain for service users is not only in the quality of the service received but in the fact of being able to exercise some control over decisions to be made about one's own life. Indeed, it is frequently shown that, without a sufficient degree of control, not only is the value of service provision undermined but that even the objectives of orthodox practices impossible to achieve because professionals provide the wrong services in the wrong way.

How the points on this continuum of participation are seen in relation to each other depends on the criterion used to make a comparison. If we are concerned primarily with the difference between passivity and activity of role, then only the first point (passive receipt of services) can be seen as failing to provide a degree of consumerism. If the involvement of service users in the definition of welfare objectives is the key issue, then a division occurs between passive receipt and consultation on the one hand, and participation and user control on the other. However, if a judgement between the two is to be made on the basis of social autonomy then only the latter arrangement will achieve the objective of enabling the service user, as a consumer of welfare services, to exercise power. It is necessary, therefore, to examine contemporary policies and practices in relation to these distinctions and to explore the way in which claims to consumer focus and to empowerment actually constitute quite different measures of the way in which the role of the service user has shifted within the commodification of social welfare.

Models of Consumerism

Beresford (1988) makes a clear and decisive distinction between the neo-liberal vision of the consumer and that expressed by the service user movement. The former is based on the free-market vision of social relations. That is, to the extent that it is concerned with the power to exercise choice and take control in one's own life it seeks to replicate for social welfare the social relations which pertain when purchasing any other good. To make the usage of services as like buying a washing machine or a car as possible is regarded as a virtue. The reason for this is not that a difference between goods and services is not recognised, but that because in the neo-liberal framework *to exercise choice is to have power*, goods and services can and should be treated in exactly the same manner. The service user movement, in contrast, sees the situation in entirely the opposite way. From this perspective, service users must gain power *as the means of exercising choice*. Without appropriate forms of social power it is simply not possible for service users to make any meaningful choices about the type of services they wish to use or how these services should be provided. In an historical context where professions and the state exercise power over (and against) disadvantaged and disempowered sections of society, to treat service users as consumers is simply to compound their exclusion from real decision making.

This analysis leads Beresford (1988) to conclude that there is a major cleavage between the two approaches to consumerism informing time-bound debates in social welfare in the 1990s. These cannot simply be reconciled, even though they may both make reference to choice and empowerment. The market definition is based on an instrumental view of social relations, while the democratic approach seeks to involve people directly in the decisions which affect their lives. Indeed, while both are congruent with formal political democracy, the former is parallel to Marshall's definition of 'political citizenship' while the latter reflects a 'social citizenship' perspective. It is for this reason it has been argued that consultation, as defined above, is insufficient to ensure that paternalistic bureaucracy is not simply replaced by an equally paternalistic market. Consultation as a means of reforming the relationships between professionals and service users is seen by Beresford (1988) as little more than a form of market research, in which the questions are set by the producers, so determining the range of possible answers obtained. In these circumstances, choice in social welfare resembles the choice between different makes of car or brands of washing machine, in which the goods basically are the same but have slight variations in trim and finish. The model of democratic consumerism which Beresford proposed is radically different. It would require a shift in the social relations between the state, the professions and service users, such that the former two were responsible and accountable to the latter, both individually and collectively.

Problems with Consumerism

Notwithstanding the critique of consumerism, and the development of dialogue between professionals and service user groups, there has also been a sense that neither the market nor the democratic model is fully applicable to the contemporary form of social welfare. For example, neither type of consumerism can fully take account of situations in which the service user is forced by statute to receive a service, or where a wide range of people have an interest in decisions about services (and whose interests may be in conflict) (Huxley, 1993; Aldridge, 1996; Powell and Goddard, 1996). Indeed, it may be that these aspects of services reveal the extent to which it is implausible to apply the concept of the consumer to social welfare.

It has long been a part of the debates in social work as to whether the use of the term 'client' revealed a devaluing of the service user (see, for example, Hadley and Clough, 1996, p. 1). In part this is not a consequence of lexical essence (lawyers do not have the same problem with the word) but of the way in which (some) social workers and others have negatively stereotyped the people who use their services (see, for example, Pithouse, 1987). Similarly, it is not without irony that some community-based nurses have sought to abandon the epithet 'patient' for precisely the same reason, that it connotes dependence and the superiority of the professional, only to replace it with the same term, client, that social workers have sought to change (for example, Weir, 1995, p. 5). Even those who choose to retain the term patient may feel the need to justify this usage (for example, Williamson, 1992, p. 13). Yet in much of the contemporary literature there is almost no such uncertainty about using the term 'consumer' in a non-problematic way. Some commentators (Strong and Robinson, 1990; Hadley and Clough, 1996) may also reject this on grounds of its market ideology implications, and seek to replace this with the more neutral 'service user' (also see Brandon, 1991b; Onyett, 1992, p. 4), but these are relatively few. It would seem, therefore, to the extent that language reflects and shapes reality, the social relations of consumerism have permeated much of the thinking among health and social welfare professionals and policy makers. However, in order to analyse these developments it is necessary to question the links between the language used and the practices and policies which are implemented, if the changes in social welfare are to be fully understood.

The impact of consumerism has been felt in all aspects of social welfare, although it has not taken exactly the same form everywhere. To illustrate what has happened, four areas of policy and practice will be discussed briefly and some common threads drawn together.

Pensions

A primary strategy for responding to the perceived demographic crisis (discussed in Chapter 4 above) has been for those countries which had extensive state provision for retirement pensions to transfer responsibility to the non-state sector. This has been achieved through the promotion of occupational pensions and private pension schemes (Papadakis and Taylor-Gooby, 1987). Such a move has not been confined to countries which already had a 'residual' welfare state, such as the USA or Greece, but even those which had an extensive corporate welfare state structure, such as the UK or the Scandinavian countries (Daatland, 1992; Robolis, 1993). Jones (1996, p. 130) notes that the primary aim of these changes is to create funding for pensions through investment of accrued payments, rather than through the transfer payments that have been the main feature of the twentieth century. The levels of benefit available are thus tied to levels of investment.

This shift to occupational or private pension arrangements brings together the economics of neo-liberalism and its central values. Not only is it intended that the resources available for pensions will reflect the level of payments made, but also the role of the state is reduced from the primary provider to that of secondary regulator. Dominance shifts from direct welfare to fiscal and occupational welfare (Papadakis and Taylor-Gooby, 1987). Consumerism underpins the neo-liberal emphasis on personal responsibility through appeals to choice and flexibility, as well as to a greater sense of certainty that future pensions will be viable. Notwithstanding some crucial difficulties (notably problems in the arrangements for regulation: see Jones, 1996), such developments may well be seen to advantage large sections of the populations in advanced industrial countries. However, it will do so at the expense of a minority for whom residual state provision will continue to be a necessity (Wearing, 1994). In an era of high levels of unemployment such a minority may not be as small as the rhetoric assumes, at least in the near future.

Acute Health Care

A move from direct to fiscal and occupational welfare can be seen also in the area of acute health. Personal choice and the reduction of waiting times have been used as the rationales for attempts to encourage individual service users to favour private health provision (Barr et al., 1989; Johnson, 1990; Scotton and Macdonald, 1993; Papadakis, 1994; Petersen, 1994). Critiques of bureaucracy and the power of professionals have been utilised, by inference, in appeals to private health care as providing the capacity to choose when, where, how and by whom one is to be treated. Quality of service, most especially privacy when in hospital, have also been used to some effect as factors to influence the choice to purchase private health cover. However, the effect has not been as widespread or extensive as governments would wish (Strong and Robinson, 1990; Scotton and Macdonald, 1993; Papadakis, 1994).

There are two reasons why the privatisation of public acute health care has not been as successful as it was envisaged by policy makers. The first is that most private health care is not purchased directly by patients from health providers, but indirectly through insurance companies. The types and amounts of cover are determined contractually in advance so that the individual patient is not able to exercise the degree of choice that policy statements or government advertisements might imply. The power of the consumer is limited by individual contract, so that the terms are set by private (for-profit) companies rather than by professionals or government. Second, evidence that, in the area of health, positive public opinion has not fully swung away from professionals or the state as the appropriate judges of health needs and providers of care suggests that campaigns to create new public opinion have not been successful in this regard (Taylor-Gooby, 1991; Papadakis, 1994). So, the result appears to be that the public sector remains the first choice for most health service users faced with major needs, in countries where a strong public sector had been established. (The USA is probably the main exception to this.) Even Margaret Thatcher herself recognised that she would have used the NHS for 'complicated and costly surgery' (a remark which, perhaps predictably, attracted a hostile response) (Johnson, 1990, p. 70).

The other major weakness in the privatisation of health care has been the marginalisation of the very social groups who are seen as the largest users of services. Private health schemes tend to favour younger and healthier people, who are, after all, the better risks in actuarial terms. Older people or people with chronic health difficulties find it extremely difficult to obtain health insurance cover at rates they can afford and so are obliged to use state services. There is an accompanying risk, therefore, in the moves to privatise health care that people who are widely seen as needy become marginalised (Petersen, 1994), and this has the effect of undermining the very consumerist ethos on which such policies are based (Jones, 1996). At most, the privatisation of public health care can be said to have created a limited form of quasi-market consumerism (Hugman, 1994b).

Community Care

Services for people with long-term difficulties in health or who require assistance in taking care of themselves have in recent decades moved from being predominantly located in large institutions to more ordinary settings. This pattern of service provision has come to be known as community care or home care (Challis and Davies, 1986; Howe et al., 1990; Henrard, 1991; Jamieson, 1991). Although there is some debate as to whether the defining feature of such developments is of care provided in the person's own home, or whether it is not in an institution (and so in the community), this trend can be seen in services for people with disabilities, people with mental health problems and older people (Hugman, 1994a, p. 136). As in many countries residential care facilities of up to 50 people can be seen as 'not an institution', the concept must be regarded as both relative and flexible.

Community care services may be separated from acute health services for several reasons. That they are oriented towards caring rather than curing gives such services a different ethos. This is expressed in many countries by such services being provided through agencies which are distinct from acute health care. In some countries health professionals, particularly nurses, are the main providers of care, while in others occupational therapists or social workers may predominate. In many instances, therefore, there has been a growing orientation towards a social rather than medical model of the care provided. Taken together, these factors have influenced developments in approaches to the relationship between services and their users that move away from the quasi-medical model that permeated the former institutions. It is in the move away from institutions and towards community (or home) care that case management, advocacy and brokerage have been developed. These practices have been supported by policies of locating care in situations which as far as possible are those of ordinary living.

Because of the long-term nature of the problems faced by people who use community care services there has been much less possibility of governments relying on market mechanisms than, for example, in acute health care. The people who use these services tend to have difficulties in gaining employment, or are retired and have limited resources. The area which has the largest private sector is that of residential care for older people. Yet, even in this, massive state subsidies have been necessary either to create or sustain the sector. Again, it may be said that direct welfare gives way to fiscal welfare (as in Australia or many parts of Europe) as tax incentives and other government support is given to individual service users. In the UK in the 1980s substantial direct government financial intervention was used to create a large private market (Henwood, 1986). In the early 1990s the government was obliged to shift direction as the costs spiralled out of control (Wistow et al., 1994). Case management (now called care management) was harnessed to operate as a rationing mechanism, thus severely curtailing the form of state-funded market consumerism which had developed. In this, the UK (re)joined the countries which also have case-managed systems, which (like brokerage and advocacy) work within recognised resource limits. Practices which assume a democratic consumerist position in the relationship between service users and professionals thus at the same time face the same limitations of market consumerism in relation to other goods and services: that choice is determined by price in relation to funds available.

The other aspect of community care which is difficult to fit into a consumerist framework is that of compulsory intervention (Fisher, 1990). In certain instances, such as severe mental ill-health, there may be legislative powers or requirements on which service use is based and over which the service user exercises little or no choice. Under these circumstances attempts to mirror the notion of the service user as customer or consumer rely on concepts of service standards as the basis for a quasi-consumerism. In other words, procedures are established, by which professional practices can be judged, that construct definitions of acceptability *as if* the service user were able to exercise choice and to seek the service elsewhere. As a form of accountability the use of standards in this way blurs the boundary between professionalism and the market rationale. What it cannot do is to place someone who is statutorily obliged to receive the service in the same social position relative to the service as the person making a purchase of goods is in relation to a shop. Civil and legal rights thus substitute for a full consumer status; even these rights may be couched in general terms within codes or charters rather than laws, and so be difficult to enforce.

Children's Welfare

Consumerism has also tended to emphasise the divide in children's services between those which are provided at the request of families and those which are statutorily imposed. In other words, it further opens up the split between child *care* and child *protection* policies and practices (Parton, 1991; O'Connor et al., 1995). The impact of consumerism in these two spheres is quite different, at least on the surface.

In child care services, as in acute health care, consumerism and privatisation are closely tied together. The benefits of choice and flexibility of provision, it is asserted, come from payment at the point of usage. This principle supports an emphasis on private provision of pre-school facilities, child care for working parents and, to a lesser extent, private school education. The neo-conservative reluctance to support mothers working outside the home is harnessed to the neo-liberal belief in the moral value of the market. Yet it is precisely in those social classes where it is important for family incomes that either both or the only parent work/s that the ability to pay full costs for such services is lowest. It has been recognised for some time that the effect of these policies is to create a divide in which women and families with lower incomes are disadvantaged (Castles, 1985; Bryson, 1992; Wearing, 1994; O'Connor et al., 1995). Yet, unlike health care, residual provision is often stigmatised and may be restricted to those families who are subject to forms of statutory intervention.

Child protection policies and practices are not easily to be understood within a consumerist frame of reference. By definition they represent a removal of choice and individual autonomy through the control, on behalf of the state, of those who have been judged to be inappropriately exercising child-care responsibilities. While child protection fits clearly with both neo-conservative and neo-liberal social philosophies, being focused on the exercise of personal responsibility, it is more difficult to construct it within a free-market model of the service user as a consumer. Yet there are two ways in which these principles have been applied in an indirect manner. The first is in the incorporation of the idea of rights into child protection policies and practices; the second is in the separation of the needs and rights of children and their parents, accompanied by a parallel definition of the rights of parents in respect of professionals and state bureaucracies (Allen, 1990; Fox Harding, 1991).

The rights of children and young people when in the care of the state, to appropriate privacy and to their view being listened to in decision making, represent a form of limited consumerism. It is limited to the extent that the notion of contract on which the free-market ideology is based cannot be held to apply, although there are some similarities with the notion of standards to which reference may be made in resolving disputes, such as also applies in consumer protection legislation (Hugman, 1994b). In some countries this has been extended to include legal powers for children to initiate action against their parents, as well as vice versa (Harrison, 1995, p. 72), although the exact terms of such legislation vary considerably between countries (or states and provinces within countries). In these developments, neo-liberal ideas, which favour the rights of children, clash with the neo-conservative emphasis on the family as the primary social unit, in which parents' rights are paramount (Chamberlayne, 1992; van Every, 1992).

Legally defined rights for parents in child care and child protection can be seen in other spheres as well. For example, the UK policies to strengthen parents' rights in respect of education in state schools has at times been framed as 'giving back' to 'the family', from teachers, control over curriculum content and hence the socialisation of children (van Every, 1992). However, even in child protection intervention the rights of parents increasingly are provided for in law in a similar way and often phrased in a like manner, so that the rights of parents are set against the power of professionals (Walton, 1993). This individualises the relationship between the parties and obscures the role of the state, which continues to be that of mediating between professionals (as producers) and citizens (as consumers) (see above, Chapter 5). It also obscures the in herent contradictions between the potential interests of parents, children, professionals and the state. For example, the neo-conservative and neo-liberal mix of New Right governments can be seen to be enthusiastic about the rights of parents largely because it supposes that ordinary parents are more likely to share their social values than those of the professionals. Professionals, from this perspective, are frequently seen as a threat to the family as well as being the appropriate agents of the state in the protection of children (Parton, 1991). However, professionals are, in effect, a threat only to 'good' families, so procedures serve a primary purpose in ensuring that intervention is directed only at those families who have 'failed'.

In this process civil rights become fused (even confused) with consumerist attention to quality. The rights of the consumer citizen, idealised as freedom from interference collapse into state managerialist control over professionals through devices such as quality assurance systems (Dalley, 1992; Hugman, 1994b). Paradoxically, such controls also strengthen the powers of state agencies in certain instances (such as child abuse investigations) in which the following of correct procedures can in itself be taken as evidence of ensuring the maintenance of civil rights (Calder, 1995). Bureau-ethics are thus manipulated into a pseudo-business framework.

Charters, Contracts and the Consumer Citizen

Common to each of these four areas of social welfare has been the move from the social democratic welfare state, with its assumptions of the collective basis of entitlement and responsibility grounded in citizenship, to individualistic models which are based on a contractual approach (Yeatman, 1996). The nature of the contract as this has developed in European law (and its derivatives) is that of an agreement between free individuals. Notions of contractual obligation are based on consent; it is because each party freely chooses to be bound by the terms of an agreement that any sense of liability is created (p. 42). Indeed, the presence of coercion or deceit may lead to a contract being declared null and void by a court. The acceptance by neo-liberal governments of the reshaping of social welfare provision around the needs of individual service users is, therefore, consistent with this view of rights as formal contracts (p. 40). The rights of the social welfare consumer, seen in this way, are those of being able to determine all aspects of a service in free negotiation with service providers. However, as has been shown above, there are crucial limits to the way in which private individuals can exercise choice in social welfare.

The first of these limits lies in the extent to which it is possible for the individual to pay for a service. As has been discussed in previous chapters, part of the agenda of New Right governments has been to move to a user pays system as far as possible, both because of the supposed freedom this brings for individuals but also because it enables the costs of welfare to be apportioned privately rather than through taxation. Yet in each of the areas of pensions, acute health care, community care and children's services (in which education might be included), the capacity of most people to pay at the point of use cannot be assumed across all sections of advanced industrial societies. This leads, quite reasonably, to the conclusion that contractual consumerism in social welfare advantages the wealthier sections of society (Wearing, 1994).

Second, the capacity for private individuals to be given sufficient information in order to make an informed choice cannot be assumed. Some information is better understood as propaganda, in the sense that it promotes one position rather than the possible range in relation to choices which individuals might make about their own health or welfare (Beattie, 1991). Even where a full range of choices can be and is presented, the overall objectives of the service may still be controlled by the nexus of the state and the professions. In other words, information is not neutral. How it is constructed and presented will be subject to exactly the same social processes as advertising in any other consumer field. That is, it conveys both fact and value. An example, common to Australia, New Zealand and the UK, is the promotion of private health care in television advertisements which replicate the style of advertisements for cars, banks and foreign holidays.

Third, significant aspects of social welfare (in health, community care and children's services) contain elements of social policing which are inimical to consumerism. Heward (1994) makes the point that even the police themselves have been subject to the pressures of a consumerist focus. This has included, for example, an attempt in Greater London to change the identity of the police *force* into a police *service* (p. 246). Yet this use of terms as a rhetorical device cannot resolve the contradiction that the work of the police, and like it the statutory work of doctors, nurses or social workers (for example in child protection or mental health), cannot be subject to the free individualist contract on which consumerism is built. That those people who are obliged to receive such services are members of the same public as those who are not does not of itself remove the conflict of interest between groups inherent in such actions. Indeed, the work of doctors, nurses or social workers, like the work of the police, may be to coerce some citizens in the perceived interest of others.

Ability to pay at the point of use, ability to access and make use of information and the limits of law are all factors that affect consumerism outside the social welfare sphere. Buying a house, a car or a foreign holiday are just as restricted to those with certain income levels, manipulable by manufacturers and suppliers through the control of information, and subject to legal constraint on the purchaser as well as the manufacturer and supplier. What therefore makes the notion of consumerism problematic in relation to social welfare? In one respect, of course, it is possible to argue that it is problematic in social welfare because it is also problematic elsewhere. The flaw lies in the inability for a fully free market actually to develop in the economic as well as in the social spheres of society (Plant, 1986). However, a more important limitation lies in the inability of the social welfare field to become fully developed as a free market, for the reasons outlined above. What is achievable is the quasi-market (Bartlett and Le Grand, 1993; Wistow et al., 1994), which brings with it the *quasi-consumer*.

Just as the quasi-market represents the way in which the organisational principles of the free market have been introduced in sectors which remain funded (at least at their core) as well as regulated by the state, so the quasi-consumer can be seen as an extension of this organisation into the relations between producer and user of services. As with the quasi-market, the quasi-consumer is constructed not on the legally defined contractualism of the free market, but around a reworking of the citizenship on which the social democratic model of social welfare was founded. Political citizenship and social citizenship have, in this respect, been pushed aside for consumer citizenship.

Consumer citizenship is expressed in term of charters rather than legal rights, in which are enshrined statements of obligation by which the quasi-consumer can evaluate services. In the UK the government issued a series of service-specific charters under the umbrella of the Citizens' Charter (HMSO, 1991). This latter document was a statement of what the (quasi-consumer) citizen could expect from the government as the funder and regulator of welfare services, social infrastructure and social regulation (armed forces and police). In this sense a charter can be seen as a statement of intent. It outlines what the quasi-consumer citizen can reasonably expect from services in relation to quality, choice, standards and value (Walsh, 1994, p. 193). While this appears to be wholly reasonable (who would want to deny their fellow citizens access to such information?), there is actually no legally enforceable guarantee that such criteria will be met (see, for example, Hadley and Clough, 1996, pp. 137–8). In this sense the neo-liberal ethos that lies behind the idea of charters is itself contradicted. Citizenship is reduced to a 'loose amalgam of consumer roles' which are not grounded in a sense of either community or society (Walsh, 1994, p. 194).

Bartlett and Le Grand (1993) conclude that the move towards the quasi-market has had little impact on the social relations of consumption in social welfare, compared to production. While much has been made of the disaggregation of previous bureaucracies, what can be observed to be emerging is that this has often only been at the level of detail. The National Health Service in the UK has been sub-divided into purchaser and provider functions, and a similar model has been applied in community care and children's services. It may well be that schools have opted out of local government control, that hospitals have gained trust status and that general practitioners (always independently contracted) have started to be fund-holders. Yet very little has changed for the service user (Hadley and Clough, 1996).

In so far as a customer is a person who has the power to effect choices by expending resources, then these developments have succeeded in creating a society in which consumers are not customers. While the former are the citizens using or trying to access services, the latter must be seen as the professionals who control budgets. The quasi-consumer can only be empowered as much (or as little) as the person with the purse-strings will permit. Where the professional is willing and able to share this power then the relationship could be described as that of the multiple consumer. Examining this logic one may be left with the sense that a great deal of time and talent has been devoted to creating the image of change behind which core social relations have been less affected than the image suggests.

Restoring Professional Power: Old Wine and the Emperor's New Clothes

Does this mean that the changes which have taken place in the relationship between the state, professionals and citizens is simply illusory? To some extent the analysis offered here supports such a conclusion. Hirschman's (1979) distinction between 'exit' and 'voice' as strategies for exercising power in organisations is useful here. This is the difference between being able to have an effect on decision-making and action through being able to contribute to the discourse, and through removing oneself from a situation which is unacceptable. However, the opportunity for exit implied by a genuine market relationship (the consumer can freely move to another manufacturer or supplier) cannot be created by the quasi-market. At the same time there is little opportunity for the voice of the consumer to be heard beyond a complaint about a specific individual service. There may be no alternative service (or access may be blocked), information may be partial or packaged as advertising, and participation may be only through a complaints procedure. Information and an accessible complaints procedure may be necessary to the exercise of voice, but they are not sufficient in themselves. Moreover, Hirschman's concept of voice was tied to loyalty, a commitment to the institutional arrangement of which social actors are part. This is as lacking in the quasi-consumerist models of social welfare as in the state bureaucracies which the quasi-market was intended to replace.

This situation leads Marquand (1992) to argue that what has happened is that public social welfare has been remodelled to fit within the disorganised capitalism (compare Lash and Urry, 1987) that predominates at the end of the twentieth century. The ideology is still the ideology of capitalism and the market, but it has been adapted along with the logic of post-Fordism and the deregulated global economy. It is 'old wine in new bottles' (Marquand, 1992, p. 70). Central to Marquand's argument is the view that perhaps even more than the move from the public to the private sector, the consumerism now infused through social welfare masks the way in which, in public, private and mixed-sector organisations, power has shifted even further towards the top (p. 69). In other words, quasi-consumerism obscures a strengthening both of the state and of senior managers and professionals. From this perspective, the new clothes of the corporate social welfare 'emperor' (the state and senior executives) begin to look suspiciously transparent.

Consumerism *versus* Professionalism?

In terms of abstract logic, if consumerism is based on the power of the purchaser and citizenship is based on the power of formal legal rights combined with social obligation, then the ideology of the service user as a consumer should result in empowerment. Yet the preceding analysis argues that this has not happened, nor can it under present arrangements. The language of consumerism in social welfare presupposes that the state acts as an impartial mediator between the professions and their clientele. However, as I have argued elsewhere (Hugman, 1991, Ch. 1), the relationship between the three parties is more complex. The professions can also be seen to mediate the relationship between the state and its citizens. The outcome within the social democratic welfare state was a corporate bond between the state and the professions from which the citizen-as-service-user was excluded. Not only is the state therefore not impartial, but also there are limits to the extent to which professionals can claim independence from the state.

Even within a consumerist social welfare professionals continue to exercise power and authority on behalf of the state in relation to the provision of services. The issue of social control which has been discussed above is an important aspect of this, but there are also elements of social management in the role of the caring professions that continue in the quasi-market. For example, assessments that establish eligibility for services continue to be undertaken by professionals who, as was shown in the previous chapter, have added to their repertoire the skills of budgeting and resource management at the level of individual service users. The fund-holding general practitioner or case/care manager is required to adopt the same stance to a service user as that of the salesperson of consumer goods to a customer, offering what is available at prices over which neither has immediate influence or control.

However, unlike the salesperson, the professional also continues to exercise considerable authority to determine the needs of the consumer. In the free-market model the customer might seek the advice of the salesperson but, ultimately, advice can be ignored. The difference in the social welfare quasi-market remains the extent to which caring professionals will expect, and be expected by the state, to exercise some constraint over the expression of needs as demands by service users, *unless the person has the individual capacity to pay directly for the service they want.* It is this logic that was brought to the fore in the UK government's attempts to restrict access to residential care for older people by way of community-care policies (Hadley and Clough, 1996, p. 15). It is this logic also that informs similar developments in other countries with diverse social welfare histories, such as Australia, Greece and Sweden (Daatland, 1992; McCallum and Howe, 1992; Stathopoulos and Amera, 1992).

What is at issue in these policy developments, which affect all age groups, not only older people, is the wish to control the level of government spending on social welfare that has been discussed in previous chapters. The rights of the citizen are not to a specified outcome, but the right to a fair and competent assessment to determine eligibility. That it is the professionals who are constructed as the customer (in the sense of being the budget holder) is neither accidental or unforseen. It is built deliberately into the relevant legislation, policies and organisational arrangements. In this way the interests of the consumer may be quite divergent from the caring professionals through whom access to services remains the only route for those who cannot make a purchase on the open market.

Consumer Orientation in Professionalism

Various forms of professional practice have been developed to create an alternative manner of relating to service users. In the field of community care these include advocacy and brokerage as well as some case-management projects (Brandon, 1991b; Lawson, 1991; Onyett, 1992). Each of these, the forms originally intended, requires a change from the previous orthodox relationship between professional and service user towards one which is more equal. Each, to different degrees, has had an impact in health (including medical) and social (or human or community) services.

Advocacy can be summarised as the representation of the views and wishes of the service user by a person who is independent of the individual user (Lawson, 1991). The importance of this role can be seen in situations where, because of disability or illness, the service user is unable to speak for her- or himself. Either a professional who does not have any other interest in the services provided to the user or else a non-professional person (known as a citizen advocate) can fulfil the role. The advocate's role is to work with the service user to enable the formulation and presentation of such views and wishes. Increasingly there has been an emphasis on helping people to speak for themselves, known as self-advocacy (Gould, 1986). The advocate role is not tied to a specific form of service delivery, but was originally developed in the USA to counter the power of caring professions in traditional services (including institutional care). The person who acts as advocate, by making use of a social role outside the direct professional/service user relationship, can exercise a balance which empowers the service user. Advocacy schemes operate in many countries (Onyett, 1992).

Brokerage, which originated in Canada, also separates the representation of the service user's needs and wants from the provision of services (Brandon, 1991b). The role of the broker is to provide the service user with information about the range of services available, assist the service user in making a choice and negotiate between service users and services. In some ways this role can be compared to that of a travel agent, although a broker can also assist the service user to employ carers directly. As with advocacy, the strength of the role lies with the separation of representation and decision making about eligibility to public funds or access to services. In Canada the calculation of state benefits is relatively straightforward, which is an additional aspect in favour of this practice in that context (Hugman, 1994b, p. 218). In other countries there may be problems arising from the state benefits system, but even in a country such as the UK, with a highly complex arrangement of entitlements and discretionary benefits, there have been successful schemes based on the brokerage model (Onyett, 1992, pp. 65–8). The other key feature in Canada is the management of brokerage by service users themselves.

Case (or care) management, unlike advocacy and brokerage, brings together advice-giving, decision-making and negotiation with the holding of public funds by the professional rather than the service user (Orme and Glastonbury, 1993). Although some schemes may be structured to enable the service user to participate in decision making (Onyett, 1992, pp. 65–6), there is not the same direct control of funds by service users as that normally seen in brokerage models. Case management, indeed, can be seen as a process which is defined in terms of the requirements of service organisations (Huxley, 1993). The stages described (case finding, assessment, planning, intervention, monitoring and reviewing – Challis and Davies, 1986; Department of Health, 1991) are categorised usually as a series of professional actions. The role of the service user may be referred to as that of consumer or customer, but this is not necessarily built into such practices *per se*. Indeed, the growing criticism of the implementation of the system of care management in the UK is that it has quickly reverted to being resource- rather than needs-led, with assessment forming a barrier controlled by professionals on behalf of the state (Hadley and Clough, 1996). The administrative model, anticipated without enthusiasm by Challis (1992) and Huxley (1993) (as against decentralised and participatory, or even clinical models), has marginalised any possibility of democratic consumerism forming part of the case/care management development. The same criticism could be applied in acute health services where general practitioners are budget holders. It is in these situations that the professional is the person who becomes the real customer (able to exercise choice through control over resources) and the empowerment of service users is supported or undermined by the practice of the budget-holder.

Although the terms 'advocacy' or 'brokerage' may be used to describe the activity of professionals within a case management framework (Dant and Gearing, 1993; Huxley, 1993), others would prefer to see these concepts reserved for the support provided for people with care needs operating outside formal professional/ user relationships (for example, Brandon, 1991b; Onyett, 1992; Henderson and Armstrong, 1993). What is at issue here is that for the service user to be an effective consumer requires more than a re-ordering of current professional practices within existing arrangements for the distribution of power and authority in decision making, especially that which concerns access to resources. Where professionals continue to exercise power over service users, without a counterbalancing direct accountability, they may seek to promote the views of service users or they may negotiate for services, but this does not go as far as advocacy or brokerage were originally intended.

Moreover, there may be connections between the situation of willing service users in community care and those who are in receipt of the statutory functions of social welfare. Fisher's (1990) point that not all users of community care services receive services willingly connects problems of consumerism in community care with its application in statutory child protection and criminal justice. It may also relate to situations where the user of state services does not have an effective choice even though the service may be desired. It is because concepts of compulsion are incompatible with the ideals of consumerism that advocacy and brokerage were initially developed. The opportunities to exercise power that they create for service users stem from their location outside the structures of service provision. For this reason, although Challis (1990) is correct to warn of the dangers of separating administrative tasks from the interpersonal dimensions of case/care management (Hugman, 1994c), this does not mean that advocacy and brokerage must be seen as administrative practices. The risk of them being reduced to forms of administration becomes apparent when professionals or the state co-opt such practices to legitimate quasi-consumerism while at the same time effectively excluding service users from decisions affecting their own lives. Advocacy and brokerage represent a democratic consumerism only when practitioners are accountable directly to service users and not solely to managers in their employing agencies.

Customer Care and Social Management

Part of the strategy of consumerism is a concern with whether or not an organisation (or profession) has appropriately identified and responded to the needs and wants of its clientele. From this the phrase 'customer care' has now permeated health, education, social or community services and even the police (Williamson, 1992; Heward, 1994; Walsh, 1994). This chapter has examined the difficulties of understanding such a concept and some ways in which this has developed in practice. The argument presented here is that the model of consumerism that has actually emerged (except in a few instances) is that of the quasi-market type, rather than the more democratic approach outlined by Beresford (1988). The reason for this is that the quasi-market is a *social* rather than an *economic* structure, no matter how much it is modelled on the latter. The relationship between professionals (as producers) and service users (as consumers) may be based on a genuine fee-paying arrangement at point of service in some situations, but for the most part this is a minority circumstance and for the majority of situations the history of the welfare state continues to exert limitations (Strong and Robinson, 1990, p. 149). The quasi-market is prevented, by political control over budgets, from behaving like the economic free market and, as a consequence, there is a balance between quality and spread of service to be sought (Hadley and Clough, 1996, p. 195). Free markets are assumed to allow for supply to respond to demand, but where the rights of consumerism are exercised by way of access to public (state) funds then cash limitations set by governments actually produce a situation where professionals act as rationers and gate-keepers. What emerges is a reframing of the social management role of social welfare, cast in the mould of disorganised capitalism (Lash and Urry, 1987). It is at this point the connections between post-Fordist organisation of professional work and consumerism becomes clear.

Democratic and empowering aspects of advocacy and brokerage as service-user-oriented practices thus become subverted by their incorporation into services controlled by professionals accountable through managers to the state. Other alternatives, such as voucher schemes in which all members of society would be eligible for a set amount of a given service on the basis of explicit criteria of entitlement, have been ignored as unworkable, despite neo-liberal and social democratic support (Walsh, 1994, p. 196). Only service-user-controlled or self-help services can be said to have escaped this problem (Chinnery, 1990; Segal, 1991, pp. 105–6). Indeed, such services often represent those groups facing discrimination and include women's groups, Black groups, disabled people and older people (Cornwell, 1993). Yet even this approach can be marginalised by limited access to funds and as a consequence operate outside the mainstream of social welfare.

The situation is not monolithic. Within more orthodox mainstream services some professionals are attempting to open up possibilities for creating different relationships with service users, that expand the choices available and share decision making and responsibility with service users (Ross, 1995). Examples include services for people with learning disabilities (McGrath, 1993, p. 26), mental health problems (Huxley, 1993), children and young people (Barbier with Clough, 1994) and services for older people (Ellis, 1993). Strategies have included structuring services so that users are included in the decision-making processes and the formulation of rights of inclusion. Such rights are social rather than legal, but they do create a context in which service users can make claims on the accountability of professionals in such a way that the balance of power in relationships begins to shift.

In acute health Williamson (1992, p. 113) notes that doctors, nurses and therapists may work on the basis of sharing as much information as possible with service users so that participation can occur. Such information includes the availability and constraint of resources as well as alternative forms of intervention. Williamson suggests that this practice, previously common in the USA, would develop elsewhere as professionals became unwilling to accept responsibility for the necessity of rationing. This appears to be what has transpired in the UK as health and social welfare reforms have been accompanied by large reductions in the scale of resources relative to community expressions of need (Hadley and Clough, 1996). The British Association of Social Workers (1990) took the step of advising its members (and others) that acting as apologists for government financial decisions was not a professional task. There is evidence that other caring professions have responded in a similar manner, in practice if not formally (Bagguley, 1992).

Such developments reveal the potential for different approaches to the question of the relationship between service users and the services they use. In particular, a redefinition of the values of social welfare, based on the mutual participation of service users and professionals that goes beyond the limitations of market consumerism, could be seen to be possible. However, in order for this to be achieved it would be necessary to accept explicitly the reasons for such limitations, the difficulties faced in empowering service users to participate and the importance of the development of power sharing through information giving and joint decision.

A Future for Consumerism: New Values for Old?

The values which underpin the participatory, power-sharing approach are relational rather than contractual (Gilligan, 1982; Held, 1993). Such a view of rights and obligations, it is argued, provides a means of moving away from the restrictions of an abstract view of these concepts. The neo-liberal idea of contract, based on notions of free and independent actors making agreements that are binding solely because of the commitment of will expressed in the agreement, has been shown to be inapplicable in situations where care of some type is the outcome. Not only is this the case in motherhood (defined as a social construct rather than simply a biological fact) but in situations where professionals provide care the lack of tangible alternatives, the imbalance of power (through knowledge and access to resources) and the (often) involuntary dimensions to the relationship provide parallels with the role of professionals. An ethic of the good professional could be seen to be comparable to that of the good parent, in that the use of power should be directed towards the achievement by the other of as great a degree of selfhood as possible. With this goal is a corollary, that power should be used only for mutual interest or the interest of the other and not for self-interest.

As both Walsh (1994) and Yeatman (1996) recognise, there are inherent problems with this concept. It points away from the individualistic privatised person to the *social* nature of care. At the same time it provides the basis for an ethical understanding of the professional that is no more privileged that that of a family carer or a concerned neighbour. Yet the emphasis in Held's concept of a move 'from society to greater individuality' (1993, p. 208) allows neo-liberal individualism to retain its influence. The point is that the inter-dependence of society is not recognised in a consumerism based on markets, whether free or quasi. It is this *social* dimension that is missing from the neo-liberal consumer vision of social welfare. Moreover, the very weaknesses of parenting as a basis for rights and obligations has increasingly been cast in the contractarian mode of consumerism through child protection and related legislation (Harrison, 1995). Finally, there is a practical and political difficulty, in that the struggles by service users to rid themselves of paternalism (of states or professions) would seem to be contradicted by reference to 'maternalism' as an ethical alternative. If the underlying logic of this concept is to be used, then it must be rethought in terms of its point of reference. This point will be pursued in the following chapter.

So, does consumerism have a future in social welfare? Clearly it is now embedded in the thinking of governments, managers and professionals. Yet, as this chapter has argued, the inherent weaknesses of the concept can be recognised. If the goal of maintaining *social* welfare is to be achieved, then it must be founded not on private individualism but on an understanding of the common bonds of social citizenship. It is on this objective that the final Part of this book is focused.

PART III
THE PROFESSIONS IN SOCIAL WELFARE

Introduction

In the preceding Parts of this book the focus has been on the value implications of the reconstruction of social welfare in terms of neo-liberal and neo-conservative ideas, and its effect on the caring professions (especially nursing, the remedial therapies and social work). These final chapters explore the possibilities and challenges which face these professions as part of the continued development of social welfare. In particular, the place of the professions in contemporary social welfare and the nature of professionalism as a way of understanding their role are crucial to these issues.

In Part I the importance of social values as an element of the nature of debates about social welfare was demonstrated. It was argued that the attention paid by caring professions to such questions arises from the contested nature of social welfare and the meaning of professionalism for these occupations. Part II argued that the neo-liberal and neo-conservative reconstruction of social welfare through processes of commodification, in which professionals are seen as producers and service users as consumers of welfare as a commodity, has challenged the basis of professionalism claimed by nursing, the remedial therapies and social work.

In the concluding Part the prospect of reshaping the relations of social welfare is explored. It is argued that if this is to happen, then it cannot represent a maintenance of (or return to) older forms of professionalism, but the development of new ideas and practices. Forms of practice which are seen as indirect rather than direct (in the extent to which the professional actually works with the service user face to face) are now shaping the caring professions. Indirect practice, which is, in effect, the management of service provision, has increasingly been impacting on the way in which caring professions undertake their work. In many ways, this change in orientation is experienced as a challenge to previous concepts of professional practice. Not only does it require the development of new skills and knowledge, as well as that which existed previously, but it is often seen as a negation of the core of caring professionalism *per se*. Issues of ethics and the social value of health and welfare are not resolved by these changes, but thrown into a new focus, as they emphasise control and responsibility on the part of nurses, remedial therapists and social workers.

Addressing the problems of professional power (inherent in the possession of knowledge and skills) which was claimed as a value by neo-liberalism must be a central focus of a new professionalism. However, this cannot plausibly be done on the ground established by neo-liberalism, in which the relationship between service user and professional is perceived on the basis of an abstract quasi-market economics. It must be seen as part of the more complex web of social relations, in which social values are expressed through the mutual obligations and responsibilities of people, including all potential stakeholders in social welfare, as members of families and communities, and as citizens.

7

Reshaping Relations in Social Welfare

The Problem of Welfare Values

The work of nursing, the remedial therapies and social work is value-laden because it is directed towards the enhancement of human well-being in addition to the more technical accomplishment of skilled practices. Indeed, the understanding of professionalism on which these occupations draw portrays the use of such skilled practices, combined with expert knowledge, as means to the ends of an increase in the welfare of service users. This leads these occupations to orient their work towards particular views of service users as fellow citizens (for example: BASW, 1980; Scully, 1995) and to be concerned with questions of the social origins of disadvantage as well as personal distress. Such an approach is embedded in the structures of the caring professions, as evidenced by the ethical basis on which they have been developed.

The patterns of employment and labour-market relations in which caring professions are now being employed reflect the wider post-Fordist tendencies of strong central control of the labour process accompanied by fragmentation in the structures of employment. Aspects of deprofessionalisation, even proletarianisation, can be seen increasingly in the highly specified regulation of practice. In some areas there can be said to be an exchange, in that technical autonomy may remain while the ideological dimensions of professionalism are denied; in others there has been simply a growth in the controls exerted by general management over professionals constructed as skilled workers.

As a consequence of these changes the welfare states of the mid-twentieth century have been eroded. Moreover, this is not only at the concrete level of the institutions delivering health and social services, but also in respect of the social value attached to welfare as a shared, social entity. Privatisation as an ideal as well as a practice has impacted to such an extent that in various countries the election of governments committed to reducing welfare has continued, despite the strong continued support expressed for social welfare in general (Taylor-Gooby, 1991). Barry (1990) notes that such support may be for social welfare in general and not for a specific institutional form. Nevertheless the outcome of New Right policies has been both a change in the institutional forms of social welfare and a reduction in the extent of *public* commitment to a welfare society (limited though that may ever have been – see Robson, 1976). The services may still be there, but unless in some way constituted as a private good they are increasingly seen as a worst option. The principle of 'less eligibility' has returned along with other Victorian values, in the form of 'workfare' and the increasing marginalisation of health and social services (Barry, 1990, p. 112; Nicholls, 1992, p. 233; Wiseman, 1996, p. 309). The problem of social welfare values is that they are no longer congruent with the dominant economic and political values and this is a major reason that caring professions themselves feel under attack.

Quasi-market and Welfare Mix

The emergent institutional form of privatised social welfare in countries such as Australia, Canada, New Zealand and the UK has been that of the quasi-market (Bartlett and Le Grand, 1993; Cochrane, 1994). This is most highly developed in New Zealand and the UK, with reference (perhaps deference) to the United States' model of contractual relations between the state and service providers. As we have seen in the previous chapter, caring professions also take on a role as gatekeepers of public funds with which eligible service users may access privately provided services. However, in countries which have had a tradition of unitary state agencies, it has often been possible only to separate them. Although the underlying logic is to create a system of private provision to which access by public funds is restricted, the practical effect has been to have both purchasers and providers located within state organisations, albeit different agencies, with some providers also located in a slowly growing private sector (some for-profit, some not-for-profit). This could be seen, for example, in the expectation in the UK that the role of local government agencies in community care would include the active creation of an independent (that is, non-government) sector in services for older people or people with disabilities (Department of Health, 1991).

In this way the purchaser/provider split in health and social services is the institutional expression of an attempt to create the quasi-market in practice. Attacks on the caring professions can thus be seen as part of the strategy for promoting a 'cultural revolution' which was necessary for the creation of such a market (Marquand, 1992, p. 68; Rudman, 1996b, p. 387). In Australia and Canada the move to purchaser/provider models and quasi-markets is following the same pattern, with similar problems and lack of clarity (Huston, 1991; Degeling and Thomas, 1995).

Quasi-markets are part of the wider shifts in the pattern of welfare states. Recent analysis has suggested that rather than seeing variations in terms of different structures (as in Esping-Andersen, 1990) the concept of the welfare mix should be used to explain the diversity of arrangements and to understand specific patterns (Svetlik, 1991; Evers, 1993). The concept of the welfare mix is used to describe the pattern of arrangements between four different sectors in social welfare provision. These sectors are the state, the private market (for profit), independent or voluntary (non-government, not for profit) and informal (personal, individual households). As noted briefly in Chapter 4 above, a welfare mix has always existed in some sense, irrespective of the scale of state welfare provision. Even in the most extensive welfare states some forms of voluntary, informal and market provision contribute to the overall range of services (Kraan et al., 1991; Hugman, 1994a). This is illustrated by reference to services for older people and their families. It has always been the case that family care for older people has been the main welfare provision (Finch, 1989; Hashimoto and Kendig, 1992). Recent statements about the need to 'return' care to the family therefore must be seen as political rhetoric to support the restructuring of public (state, market and voluntary) provision.

However, there are differences between the limited mix contained within the extensive welfare state models discussed by

Esping-Andersen (1990) and the pluralism which is described and advocated by Svetlik (1991) and Evers (1993). In the former the direct provider role of the state was central, whereas in the latter not only does the role of the state increasingly become one of regulator rather than direct provider, but also at the same time is strengthened. For this reason in countries such as Germany or the USA the role of the state has become stronger, while in Denmark, Sweden or the UK it is becoming less direct. So, the convergence between countries is not of the movement of the state out of social welfare altogether, but towards a form of welfare state which is both indirect and strongly centralist. The quasi-market of the welfare mix is a highly regulated market, which can be said to embody the contradiction between the neo-liberalism and neo-conservatism of the New Right. Libertarian liberalism is tempered with mechanisms to ensure that state control is maintained over the social and moral implications of welfare provision. Indeed, it is partly to ensure the exercise of this power that the New Right has been concerned to challenge the ideological legitimacy of caring professions and others (Laffin, 1988). Contracting for service provision, the purchaser/provider split and other post-Fordist measures to implement the welfare mix are a central aspect of this process (Lawson, 1993).

To what extent is it possible to understand the welfare mix as a *social* market? The concept assumes that there is a plurality of actors, who must interact in order for the mix to operate. For example, the provision of health and welfare to an older person may arise from negotiations between formal state services (community nurse, physiotherapist, social worker), independent services (a local church-based day centre), private provision (a cleaner) and family (daughter and son-in-law). The pattern of health and welfare provision for such an older person includes all these people and their input to the situation. This implies both interconnectedness and flexibility in the range of alternatives available and the way in which individual people may utilise them (Kraan et al., 1991, pp. 193–4). It requires co-ordination and planning. Moreover, the form of exchange which may constitute this complex set of relationships is not solely economic. The transactions between family members, for example, may in themselves be emotional and psychological. Services provided by the voluntary (or non-government) sector may also include a component of nonmonetary exchange, for example where residential care is provided by independent organisations and fees are set according to the service user's means (supported by charity), or family members contribute practically to care provision. Beyond this understanding of the social element of care transactions, the welfare mix concept assumes that no one sector will be the sole provider. The balance between them (the mix) is not only a matter of public policy, it also occurs at the level of individual service use. At that level it is a negotiated order, in which the actors work together to achieve the most appropriate mix which is possible.

However, the overwhelming body of evidence is that such mixed systems are no better, or may even be worse, at responding to the issues of family care *in situations where the need for care is very high* (Finch, 1989; Twigg, 1989; Bryson, 1992; Baldock and Ungerson, 1993). Put simply, the welfare mix as it has been developed in many countries assumes the continuing presence of large numbers of family carers, especially in services for older people. Despite the continuing predominance of the family as the source of care, such assumptions in policy do not accord with other changes in families in recent decades, most especially regarding the role of women. Nor does the idea of a pluralist mix itself challenge this assumption. It presumes that no one sector will necessarily be the sole provider, but at the same time contains implications of family care as the natural mode of care, and that it will form the foundations of welfare. As a consequence other sectors (especially those paid for by public funds) are targeted to people who are deemed to be in most need. As it is defined in ways which come to mean people without families, or those whose families cannot or will not any longer provide direct care, it often means that family care is put under enormous pressure (or collapses) before other sectors intervene. This logic is not new. It applied in the practices of the traditional state welfare services (Ungerson, 1987). The pluralism of the welfare mix does not of itself address this issue, and as a deliberate strategy may therefore simply represent a new technology with an old content.

Pierson (1991) suggests that the development of new social movements distinct from class-based politics, expressing the interests of groups disadvantaged by gender, race, ethnicity, disability, sexuality and age, questions the legitimacy of the state as the arbiter of their needs or wishes and therefore as the main provider of services. A pluralistic approach would, on this basis, allow for greater independence from the state and the possibility for such groups to create their own services. To some extent this has happened. However, the extent of such services is limited and the efforts of governments in promoting the welfare mix has focused on mainstream services. As Baldock and Ungerson (1993, p. 310) observe, markets work better the more standardised the commodity. Catering for social diversity is potentially less economic in terms of sheer cost. It is also fraught with social and political hazard in that the contested nature of social welfare is amplified by the contentions of social divisions and associated disadvantage. The simple remedy of making cash payment is not an easy substitute if the grounds of eligibility cannot be agreed and are experienced as racist or sexist (Bryan et al., 1985; Ahmad, 1990). For members of marginalised or disadvantaged groups, therefore, the market cannot be social in the sense of being inclusionary but remains a point of exclusion from society.

Service User and Citizen: Inclusion or Exclusion

As was shown in the previous chapter, the translation of the service user into a consumer is fraught with intellectual and practical difficulties. Baldock and Ungerson (1993, pp. 293–312) point to five factors implicit in market principles that raise questions about its effectiveness or appropriateness as a model of social welfare. They argue that on its own terms the social impact of the market approach may have failed so far to have been any better than state bureaucracies at meeting need. These factors are that:

- sufficient buyers and sellers are required so the market is not distorted;
- sufficient and equal knowledge of the market on the part of users and suppliers is necessary;
- there should be ease of access to the market for both suppliers and users;
- willingness and ability to participate in the market on the part of both suppliers and users is required;
- markets function better if commodities are standardised.

These are elements of market principles, they argue, which are missing from crucial parts of pluralist social welfare (also see Hoyes and Means, 1993). For those who are able to purchase services to meet their social welfare needs (including health, education, pensions and so on) a market model may work reasonably well. Yet even this is not guaranteed, as the experience of private pensions in the UK has shown, in a debacle where substantial mistakes have been made at a direct cost to the customers (Hutton, 1995, pp. 201–2). For those groups who are dependent on public funds these principles are frequently breached.

First, the balance between suppliers and buyers is not equal. There are not sufficient of the former to ensure an undistorted market. However, there is no shortage of consumers of social welfare, even if this is understood only in its most restrictive sense of services for people with substantial needs in relation to poverty, disability, long term ill-health or old age (Baldock and Ungerson, 1993, p. 294). For those who are able to buy social welfare in the private (for-profit) market there may be at least sufficient competition between suppliers to create some choice. For those who are reliant on state-funded services the quasi-market is still, in effect, a monopoly (Hadley and Clough, 1996). Even where the state, voluntary (non-government, not-for-profit) and informal sectors are combined in a 'package of care', the power to make choices effectively rests with state agencies. Moreover, in practice the range of alternatives to the state sector may simply not be there for a market as such to operate, even where government injunctions have directed a proportion of budgets to be spent on external provision (Department of Health, 1991; Baldock and Ungerson, 1993).

Second, many people who remain eligible for public services in targeted systems do not have access to necessary information. Without this knowledge a service user or an informal carer is effectively excluded from the market, both in principle and in practice. It is at this point the role of caring professions in the mixed welfare economy comes to the fore. The practices of advocacy, brokerage or case (in the UK, care) management, described previously, in varying degrees contain a core element of information sharing. Where it has been possible to open caring professions up to be responsive to service users in this way then the charge of paternalism may effectively be countered. In contrast, the way in which care management has been implemented in the UK illustrates the way in which such practices cannot simply be assumed *in themselves* to be a means of facilitating service users to exercise choice and make decisions about their own care (Hadley and Clough, 1996). With restrictions on how information can be shared with service users and an emphasis on the management of resources, such practices can become another means of exercising state power over citizens. The way in which this may be avoided is to make professionals directly accountable to service users (Chinnery, 1990; Brandon, 1991b; Sines, 1996b), but this has not, as yet, been the predominant mode of organising professional work.

Third, the market (for-profit) sector often serves to exclude the most needy (Papadakis and Taylor-Gooby, 1987). Private health, education and pensions can replace public provision for people in middle-income groups (while few upper-income earners have been users of public provision anyway). Chronic ill-health and disability tend to be associated with poverty, so in an insurance model people who face these challenges may be excluded as bad risks and unable in any case to pay for premiums. Furthermore, poverty is experienced disproportionately by people who are marginalised in terms of gender, race, ethnicity and age (see for example, Williams, 1989). As a consequence the opportunities for those people whose needs are greatest to access the full range of the welfare mix may be limited both by their inability to obtain private market provision and by endemic discrimination.

Fourth, whether service users are willing participants in the social welfare market depends on what type of needs are to be met and how they are to be met. Education, acute health and retirement pensions again are examples where service users may be willing customers of the market. The reason why these areas have a favoured status among service users is that they are utilised by *all* sections of society. Of these three forms of social welfare, only retirement pensions were ever completely subject to the logic of less eligibility, and they rapidly became accepted as necessary for most of the population early in the twentieth century (Stearns, 1977). It is in these areas, too, that the middle-classes have utilised public services (Le Grand, 1982), so it is these services which have received the attention of policies to privatise provision. In corollary, public services for people with chronic health problems or major disabilities, as well as care for elderly people, were for a long period of time the focus of less eligibility and have to some extent remained residual because they are not used by everyone. Thus they have been less easily turned into a private market.

Fifth, if markets work best when there is a standardised commodity, it seems to be a contradiction that personalised, needs-based care will fit well to market principles (Baldock and Ungerson, 1993, p. 310). Yet again, those forms of social welfare which can be standardised in this way are education, acute health and retirement pensions. This is not because such services are uniform, but because the large number of potential users and suppliers means that a sufficient degree of choice can be offered to satisfy a large enough proportion of the market. For the other, that is the care, services this principle does not easily hold. The reason for this is that it is based on the very notion of caring (Finch, 1989; Ward, 1991). As Parsloe and Stevenson (1993, cited in Baldock and Ungerson, 1993, p. 311) note, the basis of this type of social welfare is the personal relationship, which is the epitome of caring. This is so whether the service user is resident in a nursing home or social care home, or is receiving nursing or social care in their own home. An approach to social welfare that is based on the standardisation of personal relationships does not accord with contemporary notions of the person. Indeed, it is on precisely this point that monopoly state provision has so often been criticised as resource-focused, institutional and unresponsive to the individual service user.

Only the private market would appear to be able to meet all these five criteria. The state, voluntary and informal sectors cannot, for various reasons, respond in this way. Yet, at the same time, it is not all forms of *social* welfare which can be delivered by the private market. As has been noted, where problems requiring assistance are chronic then the capacity of the person to pay for services, either directly or through insurance mechanisms, reflect on the type, level and quality of services available. Quite simply, social class remains a key dimension to the construction of social welfare. The more market forces are brought to bear then the more social class will affect the outcome, albeit affected by the social divisions of gender, race, ethnicity and sexuality (Bryson, 1992; Sargent, 1994). Those people who might be deemed to be most eligible for *social* welfare support on a needs-based analysis (Doyal and Gough, 1991) are precisely those people who are unable to access a private market. Targeting, in this way, amplifies rather than removes the 'moral hazard' of public provision. It is not that these services encourage people to incompetence or indolence but that they stigmatise and marginalise the recipient. A quasi-market does not avoid this effect unless it is accompanied by citizenship rights to benefits and to patterns of professional support that are derived from such rights.

Reconstructing the service user as a consumer in the forms of quasi-market which have been created therefore fails to empower the person. State-dominated social welfare, in which the caring professions were the arbiters of need, have been found wanting because they effectively sacrificed personal choice for equality of citizenship (Gray, 1996). At the same time they were not very efficient in promoting equality. The market, however, does not resolve this dilemma because it simply turns the formula around and sacrifices equality of citizenship for personal choice, while only being able to deliver the latter in limited measure and only to some social groups. For those who can choose whether to buy private education, acute health care or retirement pensions personalised welfare has been enhanced. For those who cannot it is not only their welfare which may be under threat but also their standing as citizens.

The Role of Caring Professions: New Practices

As the primary point of contact for many service users with the welfare state or the welfare (quasi-)market, members of the caring professions have a crucial role to play in the reconstruction of social welfare. Of particular note in recent years has been the rapid change from the importance of direct practice, in what is widely known in these occupations as 'hands on' work, to forms of what may be termed 'indirect practice' (Hugman, 1996b). Examples of the former in nursing include traditional patient care such as providing injections and medication, changing dressings, advice-giving about self-care. In the remedial therapies, direct practice focuses on assessment and the application of therapy. In social work it includes casework with individuals and families, groupwork and community action. For all these occupations direct practice includes counselling (although each might approach this work in different ways).

The shift to the quasi-market conception of health and welfare has been accompanied by the growth of practices which are less direct, in that they may involve the caring professions working through others, including ancillary workers. As such, these new roles are based on co-ordination and the management of information and resources to achieve the provision of health and welfare services for service users. Case management is probably the most well-developed approach to 'indirect' work (Ozanne, 1990; Rubin, 1992; Orme and Glastonbury, 1993). The indirect practices which it involves can be seen as removed from the actual service received by the user. Key roles are assessment, planning, co-ordination, monitoring and evaluating (DoH, 1991; Rubin, 1992). Although some of these tasks may involve meetings with service users, the provision of the care tasks will be undertaken by someone else. The case manager (or care manager in the UK: DoH, 1991; Orme and Glastonbury, 1993) forms the practice of the purchaser side of the purchaser/provider relationship discussed above in Part II. It may be argued that case management is, therefore, managerial rather than professional (Wolk et al., 1994). However, it is the management of the care process rather than necessarily of staff or resources.

Not all members of the caring professions are or will become case managers. Some are part of the provider side of the equation. Whether they are in the state or the non-government sectors of the welfare mix, these members of the caring professions can thus be seen as those who remain more in touch with the established practices of their occupations. However, these areas of work too are becoming defined through less direct practices. The implementation of 'casemix' in health has implications for nurses in different sectors (such as surgery or psychiatry) (Kingsland et al., 1994; McCrone, 1995; Fanker, 1996), for remedial therapists (Williams and Shah, 1995), and for social workers (Shera, 1996). Casemix is the use of planning in the provision of care to match the needs of service users, so that a comparable mix of services is provided for people with similar needs. This also can be seen as managerial, in so far as it focuses on making the best use of the range of resources available by targeting these to service users who can be seen as forming 'diagnostically related groups' (McCrone, 1995). The intention is to match the level of service provided (inputs) with the need and the probable outcome (outputs) which can be achieved.

Case management and casemix differ, in that the orientation of the former is to the management of access to services through assessment of individual need, while the latter is a way of managing the services to ensure maximum spread for people with comparable needs. However, both require the same sets of skills and knowledge development on the part of the caring professions. These are in need assessment, planning care, negotiating with a wide variety of providers across the welfare mix (sometimes equated with brokerage, not always correctly), advocacy, budgeting, monitoring and evaluating, and sometimes the management of ancillary colleagues (Hugman, 1996b). As Williams and Shah (1995) and Fanker (1996) note in relation to occupational therapy and psychiatric nursing respectively, these approaches require the development of entirely new sets of skills and knowledge, and a rethinking of the use of more established practices. They have implications for the training of new entrants to these professions as well as for the retraining of professionals now in practice.

Not all those who propose case management as a useful direction for the caring professions regard it as administrative in its implications for practice. Biegel et al. (1994), for example, argue that some of the indirect work to be undertaken is very close to more established practices, such as the promotion of community networks, the negotiation between family members and the connection of individuals with local services that form part of traditional community nursing or social work. However, others, such as Challis (1992) and Cnaan (1994), caution that the move towards administrative and managerial practices is the likely outcome from a resource-rather than a need-focused context. It is just such a context, that of the quasi-market, in which these new practices have been developing.

The Role of Caring Professions: Empowerment

It is at this juncture that the forms of practice which are oriented towards the facilitation of what has come to be known as 'empowerment' are crucial. Advocacy, brokerage and case management were each, in different ways, built on the enhancement of the service user's status as a citizen. Each aimed to create opportunities for service users to exercise their civil, political and social rights, through professionals (and others) acting as advisors, representatives and sources of information. There are clear implications for the balance of power in the relationship contained in these models, as each was intended to make the professional accountable directly to the service user. That these forms of practice have been co-opted within the market model does not in itself deny their capacity to achieve their aims. It is not so much that they have been tried and found wanting, but that they have not been sufficiently tried in many countries. Any transformative potential is not inherent in technique as such, but comes from the application of practices in particular contexts. In other words, it matters how such practices are used, the ends to which they are put, and the constraints placed on them. In those countries where these practices have been most widely implemented, such as brokerage in Canada, they may be under threat from the same shift to a market model. Ultimately, any social welfare which might change the central relationships of society is inimical to capitalism (Mullaly, 1993).

The common thread of these forms of practice is that they seek to change the social power relations between service users and professionals. Some critics have tended to discuss this in terms of the potential for professions to build their power over service users through the development of esoteric knowledge and skills (Chinnery, 1990; Croft and Beresford, 1990; Brandon, 1991a; Simes, 1996b). The exclusion of service users is part of the process of professionalisation. Strategies such as the separation of the role of advocate from decision making and service provision, and the employment of brokers by service users, were both intended to create a dynamic of accountability by professionals to service users. It was this structuring of the social relationships in service provision that had the potential to enable service users to exercise power in relation to their own welfare. Most importantly, such models of service provision are based on the personal relationship which lies at the core of professional, as well as informal, caring (Parsloe and Stevenson, 1993).

The creation of a quasi-market model, with the accompanying commodification of services, and the remodelling of professionals as producers and service users as consumers, introduces a different dynamic. In terms of Johnson's (1972) three types of professionalism, collegiate, patronage and mediative (discussed above in Part I), the appearance is of a shift from professional as mediator between state and citizen to a more equal and direct relationship between professional and patron (service user). Yet this is illusory, because the state has not withdrawn from the relationship, but rather has sought to relabel the actors while remaining in control through policy and management. Contracts, charters and service specifications are examples of how this is achieved, in which the type and standard of the welfare commodity is set not by response to a multiplicity of consumers (service users) but by a different 'invisible hand', namely that of the strong central state (Marquand, 1992). In practice this can come to be seen in a collapsing of empowerment into consumerism, so that it is not clear whether the objective is to create real opportunities for service users to exercise power, or simply to control the actions of professionals (North, 1993, quoted in Rudman, 1996b, p. 387).

There is a contradiction in this development, as empowerment for service users cannot be supported or facilitated by professionals who are themselves disempowered. Power sharing, which is effectively what empowerment requires within a social citizenship model, cannot take place if the state is exerting greater power, towards different goals, and seeking to cover this with a smokescreen of market principles. In these circumstances, what has begun to develop is not a market in a social sense, as in the set of relationships between independent actors envisaged by neo-liberal theory, but rather a highly structured and managed market in which the state retains the major controlling role. Under such circumstances it is not surprising that the model of professionalism which prevails for nurses, remedial therapists, social workers or other comparable occupations, in those areas which cannot 'enjoy' complete privatisation, is that of mediating between state and citizen.

What has changed markedly is that, under the previous social democratic structures of the welfare state, the relationship between the state and the caring professions could be described as corporate (Hugman, 1991, pp. 26–8); this is increasingly not the case. Corporate in this sense means that there was a degree of mutuality in this relationship, in the benefit derived by both sides and in the trade-off of expertise and co-operation for favourable policies and re-sources (Cawson, 1982). In so far as the agenda of the New Right has included the sharp reduction of resources and shifts in policies away from those favourable to the caring professions, then this relationship could not continue. Its demise was initiated not by radical critiques from within the professions, but from the disjuncture between the social democratic assumptions of orthodox professionalism and the direction of New Right policy. In so far as this is based on the assumed *value* base of market principles, which are consistent with neo-liberal philosophy, then only those professions which can fully engage with the private market can have such a corporate relationship with the state. Even medicine and law have been subject to this attack on their corporate power relationship with the state (Hutton, 1995).

The impact of post-Fordism as a means of radically reconstructing social welfare through the professions which deliver services may thus be seen as a logical development. The metaphor of professionals as producers takes on concrete form through variants of deprofessionalisation and proletarianisation. Yet this is not a uniform development, as the connections with the processes of managerialism show. In so far as professionals can seek to recolonise organisational hierarchies in the guise of managers (Hoggett, 1994), then other divisions of the professional labour market can be seen to re-emerge.

This is demonstrated by reference to the 'thirty, thirty, forty' society described by Hutton (1995, pp. 105–10). Hutton demonstrates that contemporary, post-Fordist employment patterns are creating societies in which the proportion of the population who can be said to have a major stake in the labour market is now a minority. 30 per cent are 'disadvantaged', including those who are unemployed and those who can only find casual labour. 'Paid volunteers' would potentially fit in this category. The next 30 per cent are 'marginalised' or 'insecure' in their employment. This includes the large numbers of part-time women workers (many of whom are in the ancillary sections of social welfare or lower echelons of the caring professions). There are also the growing numbers of people who have been 'contracted out', in situations where there is effectively only a limited market of purchasers of their labour power (p. 107). The third group within this 30 per cent are those people, including an increasing number of professionals, who are on fixed term contracts. Finally, the other 40 per cent, the 'privileged' workforce (p. 108), are those with full-time long-term jobs. It is in this section of the workforce that the managers of social welfare and the senior caring professionals are located and to whom a government will be responsive in any remaining vestiges of the corporatist legacy.

What Hutton's model reveals for the caring professions is that the historical labour-market divisions within them have not been resolved but have been reshaped. There is a considerable body of evidence that gender forms a major category around which a dual labour market developed in nursing, the remedial therapies and social work (for example: Game and Pringle, 1983; Howe, 1986; Mills, 1989; Nicholls, 1995; Marsland et al., 1996; Ratcliffe, 1996). Women tend to be located in the lower echelons, the less well-qualified, less permanent or the less 'expert' areas of work, while men tend to be located in those which are the opposite (including entering management or professional education in greater proportion than their numbers in these professions as a whole). A similar effect can be seen to operate in relation to race and ethnicity (Colston, 1994; Foolchand, 1995; Cortis and Rinomhota, 1996). In the 'thirty, thirty, forty' post-Fordist labour market of social welfare the same divisions are still evident (Williams, 1994). As Hutton notes (1995, p. 108) the primary divide is between the sixty and the forty, along which lines in the caring professions gender and racial labour-market cleavages can still be seen. In particular, it is women who, as family carers, paid or unpaid volunteers, ancillary or assistant staff or in the junior ranks of the qualified professionals, make up a very large proportion of the social welfare workforce, between 65 and 95 per cent depending on which type of work is being considered (see, for example: Kelly, 1996; Valentine, 1996).

Those areas of social welfare which were identified in the discussion above as the least favoured by market principles are those which in this sense can be understood as 'women's work'. The claim to the definition of 'caring' professions is based in a wider social definition of caring. In nursing, the remedial therapies and social work this has been widely accepted as combining those elements of care which can be seen as the performance of tasks (attending to physical needs) and those which are based on personal relationships (attending to social and emotional needs) (Abbott and Wallace, 1990; MacPherson, 1991; Grimwood and Popplestone, 1993; Mattingly and Fleming, 1994). It is for this reason that the observation by Parsloe and Stevenson (1993) of the importance of *social* relationships in these aspects of social welfare, with implica-

tions for the emotional and intellectual demands placed on professionals, reveals an important dimension of the professional role.
Commodified, quasi-market social welfare therefore appears to
create a new contradiction for the caring professions. They must be
responsive to service users as consumers, but the very nature
of their work is based on principles that are at odds with
market relationships. As Hutton (1995, p. 99) asks, 'what, in short,
if . . . people are not commodities?' The neo-liberal reconstruction
of social welfare seeks to treat people's welfare needs in just this
way, along with many other areas of life. Hutton's answer to his
own rhetorical question is that if people are not commodities then
the New Right agenda is mistaken and will fail to achieve its goal of
increasing individual liberty in 'freeing' people from decision-
making by the state. This strategy in practice required a change in
the relationship between consumer-citizens and the agents of the
state, which in most aspects of social welfare are the caring professions. It was necessary, therefore, to bring the caring professions
within the market structures as a means of control over their work.
By linking to their self-critiques of social-power relations, and a
growing acceptance that empowerment for service users should be
a professional goal, the objectives of the market ideology could be
made to appear congruent with those of providing service-user-
centred care. So, in the next section of this chapter the question of
how the value of empowerment relates to this situation will be
examined, before looking at the contemporary prospects for these
areas of social welfare as a whole.

Social Relations and Social Welfare: the Reality of Empowerment

Commitment to empowerment as a goal for the caring professions
is now apparently widespread. The notion is drawn on by a range of
approaches which includes both orthodox and radical practices
(see, for example: Barber, 1991; Orme and Glastonbury, 1993;
Mattingly and Fleming, 1994; Thomas and Ingham, 1995; Rudman,
1996b). The common thread to the different usages of the concept
are that professionals should seek to facilitate and promote decision making by service users with regard to their own needs and
ways of meeting them, and that this is to be achieved through

indirect rather than direct forms of practice, unless the latter is controlled by and accountable to the service user. Advice and information giving is an essential part of such roles, probably the centre. In so far as knowledge is the basis of power, then putting knowledge at the disposal of service users does constitute power sharing. This may include giving the service user information about financial benefits, or housing or employment opportunities; it may involve assisting the service to identify other professionals whose service users might assist. Advising and supporting a service user in planning and managing their own use of a co-ordinated welfare mix would, in this sense, be the goal.

The importance of empowerment as an issue for the caring professions is the recognition that they do exercise considerable power, usually on behalf of the state, even when as individuals they feel relatively powerless (Cousins, 1987; Hugman, 1991; Ramon, 1991; Mullaly, 1993). However, it is precisely because of the crucial role of the state in social welfare that empowerment can be very problematic (Ward and Mullender, 1991). Both Ramon (1991, p. 17) and Walker (1993, pp. 221–3) point to the way in which empowerment can be portrayed as a form of consumerism, which they both argue is a travesty of the concept. Drawing implicitly on Beresford's (1988) distinction between consumer research and participatory democracy (discussed in Chapter 4 above), Walker (1993, p. 222) argues that the important difference is between choice of a service from a pre-given range of alternatives and the socially structured capacity to define the nature and form of services, including the assessment of need (also see, for example, Rudman, 1996b).

It is at this juncture that the struggles between the caring professions and the state (in the form of governments) can be seen to continue (Aldridge, 1996). If they are able to move into the arena of free-market self-employment then their customers will be those who have access to resources and who are likely to require a technical service. Apart from education and acute health care the provision of residential care for well-off elderly people is the most obvious contender for consumerist empowerment. It is in services for people who are reliant on public funds that the importance of empowerment takes on its clear relationship to ideological commitment and the caring professions come into conflict with the state (in the form of governments and general managers).

The End of Welfare?

In Chapter 3 above, the argument by Parton (1994) – that the end of welfarism (the fragile social-democratic consensus on welfare) has brought with it a new role for the caring professions in the management of social risks – was discussed briefly. This was connected to the processes of deprofessionalisation which have also been examined in more detail above. Social management in this sense is a new gloss on social control, which, it may be said, has always formed part of the nature of the caring professions. It is the personal welfare aspect of the more general role of the professions in the management of risk (Beck, 1992). For Beck the necessity of such a role could only have become possible in circumstances where the majority of a population have achieved sufficient personal wealth not to be reliant on public welfare structures (1992, p. 96). The separation of the privatisable parts of social welfare from those which cannot be so treated, and the marginalisation of the remainder, thus can be seen as part of this development of late capitalist society. The emergent role of social management (for example, in child protection or support of people with long-term mental health problems) is in this way a recapitulation to the 'control of the disorderly poor' which is part of the heritage of nursing and social work (Dingwall et al., 1988; Rojek et al., 1988; Cheek and Rudge, 1994).

Social management in this sense can thus be seen as the technicalisation of caring in its task orientation. What is managed is access to and use of those caring services which perform tasks. The ideological dimensions, including arguments for access to services not otherwise allocated through policies and procedures, are excluded. Even the voluntary (or non-government) sector has been faced with the choice between concentrating on the provision of concrete, task-focused services or losing public funding. As one of the key sectors, in countries such as Australia and the UK, from which arguments to promote welfarism have often emerged, this shift has the effect, sometimes intended, of diminishing public debate on needs, rights and social citizenship in the welfare field (Hadley and Hatch, 1981; Wearing, 1994). This formerly dominant role of the voluntary sector could have been seen as exactly what Aldridge (1996, p. 191) suggests in the notion of a 'social education' version of health education. Yet the problem for social education would be that, like health education, there are ideological difficulties in choosing between individualist and collective explanations of problems and how they might be resolved (Beattie, 1991). The pressure on the voluntary sector to focus on concrete service provision is precisely the requirement to choose the individual level of action (and by implication of analysis). Social education that seeks to educate the policy makers is deemed to be illegitimate because it is seen as professionals entering the political arena inappropriately. This was a challenge that faced nursing in the early part of the twentieth century (Baldwin, 1995) and is continued in work relating to HIV/AIDS (Bell and Williams, 1991).

In connection with the idea of social education, Aldridge (1996, p. 191) also asks why criticisms of consumerism usually focus attention at the level of individual service users. What is wrong with seeking to satisfy the aggregate consumer, she asks, by providing clear information about what nursing, remedial therapy or social work services can do and what they could achieve? Yet there is an irony revealed here, in that the discourse of rights is founded in liberal individualism (Barry, 1990, pp. 78–9). It is, therefore, difficult to talk about the rights of service users or consumers without talking about individuals (Gray, 1996). To speak of rights for communities or groups is more problematic, because rights have to be exercised or claimed on an individual basis, although they can be applied through community membership, as is the case in equal opportunity legislation or in statutes affecting racial or ethnic communities such as Aboriginal people in Australia (Barbalet, 1996). Nevertheless, in Western law it is the individual who must seek redress if rights are not upheld. (The implications of this point in social welfare practice will be developed further in the next chapter.) Empowerment, which aims to enable people to exercise their welfare rights and to speak for themselves must, therefore, draw on the same individualist value base as market consumerism which seeks to meet welfare preferences (the expression of choice rather than rights). Thus, in so far as they seek to promote the empowerment of service users, the caring professions also find themselves engaging with an individualist frame of reference.

What is at issue is not the end of welfare, but that the demise of welfarism heralds the end of *social* constructions of welfare. Privatisation as a process relates not only to the provision or the resourcing of welfare services, but also to the explanation of the causes of need. If there is 'no such thing as society' (Heelas and Morris, 1992, p. 2) then clearly this is a logical conclusion. If, however, the network of relations between people, which constitute groups and communities, can be said to operate (just as the 'invisible hand' of the market is said to) then a *social* dimension to our understanding of need and the means to alleviate it is required.

It is in so far as they base their claims to expertise (knowledge and skills) on this social approach that caring professions have been attacked and delegitimised by the New Right; where they have made claims to individualised technical expertise their role in the residual neo-liberal and neo-conservative vision of welfare is retained, at least in that part which can be controlled through quasi-market mechanisms. It is in this way that autonomy in the instrumental sphere has been maintained while autonomy in the ideological sphere has become highly contested.

Some writers speak of the 'social market' (Hutton, 1995). By this is meant that, although it is accepted that monopolist state services as the remedy for welfare needs have effectively disappeared, individuals are still seen in their social context. In other words, such a perspective recognises that the market has social dimensions. Unless all sense of commonality is to be reduced to the Hobbesian problem of order, in which the likely outcome would be dictatorship, then some level of shared investment in fellow citizens will be sought by a sufficient proportion of society. The sense of paradox in such a view would not be lost on the neo-liberal whose rejection of social welfare has been precisely because it is seen as a form of moral dictatorship.

In addition it must be remembered that the early development of the caring professions in the later part of the nineteenth century was coincident with, even contingent upon, a very similar debate. On the one side is the stated importance of a market-driven social order, in which people are motivated by acquisition and possession, and on the other are claims to a social view of humanity, in which people are motivated by a sense of being tied together by mutual interests. This was the situation of the nineteenth century, in Australasia, Europe and North America, which inspired various campaigns and struggles to promote welfare and the growth of the caring professions at both a socio-political and an individual level (Baly, 1987; Rojek et al., 1988; Nicholls, 1992). Although there is a risk of sliding into a teleological view of history, or suggesting that past forms are bound to repeat themselves, a recognition of the dynamic nature of society suggests that the argument against social welfare should not, even yet, be seen as conclusively successful.

To the evidence that has been discussed in previous chapters (such as the general support for actual welfare service shown by research findings, in Taylor-Gooby, 1991) can be added the observations that some of the arguments successfully used by the opponents of social welfare come from sections of society who nevertheless continue to use the services provided by the caring professions (Chinnery, 1990; Lawson, 1991). These critical service users ally themselves with those practices that achieve (or seek to achieve) a more open exchange between professionals and themselves. Such practices are those where professionals use whatever potential is available, even if limited, to share social power with service users. Even where this may be reduced to a recognition of what is non-negotiable, such as in the criminal justice field (Barber, 1991, p. 53), an open and accountable professionalism is more likely to be seen as a possible ally by service users than one which is defensive and exclusionary.

What of the realities of marginalisation? One of the potential gains to be made for women, people in Black or ethnic minority communities, disabled people, or gay men and lesbians from the fragmentation of social welfare has been to be able to develop arguments for appropriate services. In some instances this has resulted in the creation of separate services for designated communities (Williams, 1994, p. 70; Jang, 1995). In most services, especially those provided by mainstream state agencies or agencies contracted to the state, there remains a considerable gap between the demands and aspirations of marginalised groups and the reality of social welfare provision (Ahmad, 1990; Rhodes, 1991; Williams, 1994; Foolchand, 1995). Indeed, Williams demonstrates that it is in the arena of social diversity where the neo-conservative dimensions most clearly dominate the uneasy alliance with neo-liberalism, where social welfare is used as a vehicle for the assertion of a particular view of what is socially desirable. This is particularly the case with respect to views about the family (also see van Every, 1992).

Any continued drive for professionalism in social welfare must seek to achieve several related objectives. It is clear that without the support of service users, and those in the wider society who are generally concerned about these aspects of society, the legitimacy of any claims to a continued role for the caring professions will sound extremely hollow. As Gray (1996) notes, the monopoly social welfare institutions did not, and could not, provide the degree of personal autonomy that has become a basic expectation in Western culture (also see Beck, 1992, p. 130). Even though the alternative, radical liberal individualism, cannot provide either equality or connectedness (community), there seems little possibility that the process of history can simply be rolled back. Nor could this be expected to receive any widespread support, as these qualities were not necessarily seen by everyone to have existed in the previous structures. The caring professions likewise must be prepared to construct a new professionalism that enables them to overcome the class, gender, racial, cultural and other biases that have marked their development to date (O'Neill, 1993). What is required is the reformulation of the role of these professions in the welfare mix that seems likely to define the field in the medium term. So, it is to an exploration of this task that the discussion will turn in the next, and final, chapter.

8

The Future of Professionalism

Restating the Problem of Professionalism

A central element of the dilemma facing the caring professions with respect to their role in social welfare is the question of professionalism itself. As has been argued in the preceding chapters of this book, any claims which nursing, the remedial therapies and social work might have to a voice in determining the objectives of their work are based on a particular interpretation of profession alism. Reference to bodies of skills and knowledge in themselves have been demonstrated to be insufficient to support the more traditional views of professions as independent in their internal organisation or their relations with service users (Johnson, 1972; Friedson, 1983; Cousins, 1987; Hugman, 1991). The classic professions, having made much of self-government or responsiveness to patrons, also find themselves under similar threat where they too are involved in social welfare which is paid for by public funds, through the state. All professions can be seen as being sustained by the social relations of contemporary forms of democracy. Independence is a relative concept which has to be understood as socially grounded. To paraphrase John Donne, 'no profession is an island entire of itself, but each a part of the continent'. This continent is comprised of service users and other fellow citizens, other professions and the state. As has been argued throughout the above discussion, it is from this (inevitable) location within social structures that the challenges to professionalism emerge.

This conclusion should not in itself be surprising, for two reasons. The first is that all professions draw on ideas about their social role from sets of ideas which contain contradictions, between autonomy and responsiveness, between exclusivity and openness, and between status and service. The second reason why challenges to professionalism should not be surprising is that the matters with which they deal, which concern the well-being of persons (considered very broadly), have always been contentious. So, this final chapter will consider the future for professionalism in the context of social welfare by examining these contradictions and contentions in relation to ways in which caring professions might respond and actively seek to restate their role. In this way it will look at the grounds for these professions to pursue such a place in contemporary society.

Revisiting Core Values of Professionalism

If a central facet of professionalism is autonomy, then it is necessary to ask what autonomy is intended to achieve. Why should professions seek to be independent in this way? The analysis offered by Larson (1977) or Friedson (1983) is that autonomy is a key ingredient in professionalism as status, which in turn is a foundation for the capacity to maximise remuneration and other controls over resources. This combination of material and ideological elements in professionalism as status can be traced to the social-class origins of the early professions (Perkin, 1989). Status is thus linked to class, and autonomy is seen as a means to ensuring a particular position for a given occupation.

It is this linkage between professionalism, class and status that has fuelled the radical criticisms of professionalism in nursing, the remedial therapies and social work, from within and without (Galper, 1975; Simpkin, 1979; Salvage, 1988; Storch and Stinson, 1988; Mullaly, 1993; Parkin, 1995). Consequently, proletarianisation is not simply accepted as an historical inevitability, but advocated by some critics as the ideal as well as the reality for these occupations (Simpkin, 1979; Parkin, 1995). If professionalism is necessarily tied to class and status, then the only way to identify and ally with the less powerful and the marginalised groups with whom these occupations work is to jettison professionalism itself.

However, others who begin from the same radical analysis reach a different conclusion in order to avoid the apparent risk of accepting the pressure to deprofessionalise which comes from more powerful social groups who are not concerned to promote the greater exercise of power by social welfare service users. It may be that the classic 'full' professionalism could never have been achieved by nursing, the remedial therapies and social work (Salvage, 1988). Nevertheless, it may be argued that to abandon *all* vestiges of professionalism may simply be to give up any claim to be able to exercise more than a limited voice about technical matters in debates set by other, more powerful sections of society (Hugman, 1991; Mullaly, 1993).

To what extent, therefore, could the ideal of service be the basis for a different approach to professionalism? Mullaly (1993, p. 192) notes that the primary problem with the notion of service is that it has been seen as apolitical. In contrast, the understanding of social welfare that has been developed in this book is that it is inherently political because it is about social power. Apolitical approaches to the ideal of service may thus be regarded as a smokescreen for the exercise of political interests. For the status-conscious profession these interests are those of the occupation, and for the mediated profession they must also be those of the state. An apolitical service ideal may also then become a status device in itself, emphasising the capacity of those who serve against the incapacity of those who are served. In these ways it may become the basis of exclusionary closure.

A different view of service, however, would be seen in practices which made occupational skills and knowledge open and available to service users. It is this which practices such as advocacy and brokerage have sought to achieve in different ways. Case (or care) management has failed to become this type of open practice where it has been absorbed as part of large welfare bureaucracies or has been framed within contractual obligations defined by the state (Hadley and Clough, 1996). From a structural perspective, therefore, it is the state which is the primary customer. Paying the piper still calls the tune.

There is a congruence between openness and other older professional values. For example, it would be difficult to imagine a profession which would not subscribe to honesty, which is a basic presupposition of openness, as consistent with their own code of ethics. Nevertheless, as recent discussions of the principle of self-determination have demonstrated, where such values are taken out of context then they can easily become pious platitudes (McDowell, 1991). Such debates occur in nursing (Elander et al., 1993; Browne, 1995; Kendrick, 1995b), in the remedial therapies (Adamson et al., 1994; Sachs and Labovitz, 1994) and in social work (Rhodes, 1986; O'Connor et al., 1995). Openness in work at the individual level may require that a caring professional makes clear what is not negotiable, as much as helping the service user to be aware of the full range of options available (Barber, 1991; Wise, 1995). At a more structural level it may be based on ensuring that service users have a voice in the definition and development of the skills and knowledge used in the provision of services, through having a voice in the design of professional curricula (Rudman, 1996a) or in debates within relevant professional associations (Hugman, 1991; Mullaly, 1993).

In so far as orthodox professionalism did not (perhaps could not) recognise the limitations on self-determination, then it was inevitable that it would fail to succeed in its own terms. However, a more critical perspective must also avoid this pitfall, because a commitment to empowerment is equally prone to the same problems of decontextualisation. Being clear about power relations is a necessary but not in itself a sufficient condition for empowerment to be achieved by service users (Ward and Mullender, 1991; Rudman, 1996b). This is something which has to be grasped and worked through in direct practice, although it cannot be dealt with by service users or professionals alone. It is for this reason that critical or radical professionalism tends to draw on structural analysis and to promote collective practice responses. Service user groups and professional organisations are both part of this approach to practice. (The implications of this point will be discussed below.)

Recognising such limitations to the autonomy of caring professionals in this way certainly conflicts with the classic mode of professionalisation (Jolley, 1989). Full professionalism was built around the interplay between autonomy, status and class. Yet an outcome in which these are accepted as both impossible and undesirable could only be seen as a 'half-profession' if the apolitical assumptions discussed above were to be accepted. An alternative position would be to accept that the object of the work of nursing, the remedial therapies or social work not only is inherently contested but will remain so, as will the forms of skill and knowledge used in that work. Such a position is not to reject the claims which these occupations have to appropriate skills and knowledge to address the social issues that have become their work (Aldridge, 1996, p. 191). Expertise can be ascribed to these occupations, but it must work in conditions of uncertainty (which even in physics has been elevated to a principle). It could be argued also that the more established professions would regain some public standing by being more open about the lack of certainty with which they too deal.

A professionalism in which skills and knowledge were based on responsiveness, openness and service could not accrue and exercise the same degree of social power as that based on autonomy, exclusion and status. Yet to the extent that the New-Right attacks on the professions have been successful it is because they have been based in part on widespread public perceptions of the professions which attached themselves to the latter group of characteristics as an ideal. Trust, a value of which much is made by professionals in their relationship with service users, can only exist as part of an interpersonal relationship (Richards, 1995, pp. 172–3). Yet trust is often assumed to operate only one way: the service user must trust the professional. Without the reciprocating openness it is perhaps inevitable that trust disappears as the wider public comes to see that indeterminacy means uncertainty, and not simply that issues are too difficult for the lay person to understand. While not everyone wants to hear blunt facts harshly expressed, the opposite, deception, destroys trust (Brandon, 1991a, p. 87). A profession that is confident in dealing with uncertainty will seek ways to share information so that it can be heard and responded to by service users.

A genuinely critical and reflexive professionalism would, therefore, not abandon its skills and knowledge, but seek ways to make these more openly available to service users. Accepting the implications of social power relations means that ways must be found to overcome the divisions which exist. It is to this task that much of the critical practice literature of the last two decades has been directed. Empowerment as an objective has in many ways become the focus of this strand in the caring professions, and has been variously applied in work with individuals, families, groups and communities.

Critical, or radical, professionalism has, at the same time, also sought to examine practices from a technical point of view. The struggle not to be confined to the technical dimension of their work does not equate with abandoning concern about how work is undertaken. It remains the case that if an occupation cannot say how it is to meet its objectives, then to have the capacity to establish those objectives is either of no consequence or else is potentially very dangerous. The issue in question is that of accountability, but not the accountability which is developing in the contractual post-Fordist welfare state. The accountability which would accompany a critical and reflexive professionalism would be that in which the caring professions are accountable to all stakeholders, including current and potential service users.

In order to take an active role in the reconstruction of social welfare the caring professions must adapt and respond to these pressures. In so far as the option of continued struggles to professionalise in the classic mode are no longer plausible, even from the most orthodox perspective, then new strategies must be developed. As demonstrated in the foregoing discussion, there are two dimensions to such strategies, the material and the ideal. So each of these will be examined in turn before, in conclusion, the connections between these two dimensions and the implications of them for relations between service users and the caring professions are examined.

Remaining Contested: Professionals in Social Welfare

In the material relations of social welfare, as has been shown, the state remains a strong central actor in the control of resources and arbitration of objectives. In order to control the costs of social welfare it may very well be that the only option available to advanced industrial countries in economic decline is to move towards a two-tier welfare system (Hoggett, 1994, pp. 45–6). However, because of the relatively low level of wealth controlled by the primary labour sector (Hutton's 40 per cent, see Chapter 7 above) in countries such as the UK or Australia, compared to the USA, it is just as likely that no one pattern emerges around the world. Local differentiation between countries seems just as possible. The majority of those members of the caring professions who form part of this primary sector are in the category of relatively not-wealthy. There are also many members of these professions who form part of the 30 per cent in insecure employment, who likewise do not constitute part of the wealthy echelons of society. The material interests of the members of the caring professions are therefore already allied to those of others who cannot or would not choose to be part of an exclusionary upper tier of social welfare. At the same time, actively to choose the route of explicit proletarianisation is not appropriate. To argue this position is not simply elitism. It is because nurses, remedial therapists and social workers *do* possess knowledge and skills which, it has been argued, should not be solely controlled by employing agencies or directed by state policies, that there is a degree of social power pertaining to their structural position. A possible alternative to the abandonment of any vestige of professionalism would be to begin to construct a new professionalism alongside the other aspects of post-Fordism in the organisation of welfare. Rustin (1994), in a discussion of university education, observes that, paradoxically, the flexibility of relations between quasi-autonomous service providers may actually create spaces for the creation of responsive services. The important element of this possibility would be to develop co-operative competition. In the social welfare field this could be illustrated by the example of a group of independent residential care facilities joining together in an association. Without removing all vestiges of competition, a sufficient degree of co-operation could enable each separate service provider to tailor their own service to the needs of sufficient service users to obtain a niche within the larger 'market'. Such associations already exist in many places and are beginning to fulfil this type of function. As well as forming the basis for communication with centralised state purchasers, they may also provide a focal point in dialogue with service users and informal carers (Wagner, 1988).

What is being suggested here is that the role of collective organisations can provide a basis for new professionalism. The debate about proletarianisation has often been accompanied by arguments concerning the mutuality or incompatibility of trades unions and professional associations in the health professions and social work (Simpkin, 1979; Parkin, 1995). From the point of view of the anti-professional perspective, the only form of collective organisation that could be seen as plausible is the trade union. Professional associations, by definition, are based on concepts of occupational coherence which is anathema to this approach. Trades unions, it is argued, enable the health or social service worker to engage collectively with those who share a common employer. It is wage employment in this perspective that defines the material circumstances of the work, so it is this which should form the orientation of collective effort to exercise occupational power.

In contrast, the other side of the debate stresses the way in which nurses, remedial therapists or social workers do constitute part of those groups whose 'means of production are [partly] carried in their heads' (Siiriäinen, 1996). As such the continued development of the skills and knowledge on which these occupations base their work are their own responsibility. That the qualifying training of these professions is now provided through universities in many instances underlines the extent to which this part of the professionalisation process has been successful. Recognising the commonality of a knowledge and skill base, those who are critical of orthodox professionalism may still argue for professional associations as an appropriate form of collectivity (Salvage, 1988; Hugman, 1991; Mullaly, 1993). Those who share these particular bodies of knowledge and skills are often employed across sectors, and in the post-Fordist welfare mix this will increasingly be the case. Collectivities based on occupation (profession) rather than employment can span the sectors and bring together people who have different labour market positions.

Mullaly (1993, pp. 193–4) makes the point that professional associations can be vehicles for collective action to promote social welfare and to defend health and social programmes. He cites the Canadian Association of Social Workers as an example, in a variety of actions to lobby government and to work for positive social policies that sustain social welfare. The associations of other professions, and those in other countries, have also been similarly active. These examples suggest that the position of professions on such issues is not a foregone conclusion. Although Mullaly (1993, p. 194) observes that such actions may often be reformist rather than dealing with structural causes, he also notes that trade unions increasingly are caught by the same difficulties. The alternative is to abandon this type of collective voice to sectional interests that would simply accept the emerging orthodoxy of the market model.

A further way in which collectivities such as trade unions and professional associations can act to promote social change is through caucuses for marginalised groups (Mullaly, 1993, p. 194). Women's sections, Black and ethnic minority sections, and gay and lesbian groups are instances of the way in which caucuses can work

(Dominelli and McLeod, 1989; Ahmad, 1990; Cooper, 1993). These groups provide a space for people in the caring professions who identify themselves as sharing an experience of marginalisation, and to work together to develop common approaches to problems around structural social divisions but across sectors. Unions may enable such links to be made between occupations which have a common employment position. Both may also potentially enable professionals to make links with external groups that have shared experience, including service users groups and caucuses in other professions. It must be recognised that such groups are not spread across all caring professions in the same way, being more prevalent in some parts of nursing and social work than the remedial therapies, for example (Millsteed, personal communication). Nevertheless, where they do exist they have the potential to be the basis for constructive change.

A role for service users 'internalised' within professional structures and practices has also been advocated (Hugman, 1991, pp. 218–22; Mullaly, 1993, p. 195). These suggestions draw on Wilding's (1982) argument that caring professions have to find structural ways of responding to accusations of elitist exclusion. Of course, lay representation is a model which has long been utilised by the more established professions. However, in many instances these practices are open to the criticism that the way in which laypersons are selected tends to exclude people from disadvantaged or marginalised backgrounds. Some modest attempts have been made by professional associations in nursing and social work to develop in this way. However, the practical problems of how people representing service users' views might be effectively included have often seemed to be too great. Indeed, notions of representation imply that there are appropriate mechanisms for making a choice and that it is known who will make the decision. The idea that an effective starting point could be to make use of connections with existing service users' groups has begun to have an impact, although it tends to be in the form of dialogue at a local level rather than across these associations nationally.

Examples of the effective development of dialogue at a local level can be seen in links between associations and service user groups on joint committees and in professional support for service user committees (Brandon, 1991a; Lawson, 1991; Croft and Beresford, 1992). These ideas have also permeated more orthodox practices, such as the increasing existence of residents' groups in residential or day-care settings and their possible role in setting and monitoring standards of service (see, for example, Cook and Gentry, 1994, p. 59). Where such developments are part of greater control and participation by service users, then opportunities to create genuine exercise of power by service users could be said to be possible. However, where service-user groups exist within services controlled only by professionals then such committees may be unsuccessful in terms of empowerment because they are caught in the social relations of market consumerism.

It is because of the pressures of the employment relationship (whether direct or contracted), and the dynamics of social welfare organisations, that some external reference point must be maintained by those in the caring professions who seek to exercise their ideological discretion. Indeed, it may only be possible in circumstances of managerialism and post-Fordist 'labour market flexibility' (that is, job insecurity) that strong collective groups can provide the arena for caring professionals to exert any influence in the realm of social welfare values and debates about the objectives of social welfare provision. After a great deal of discussion around participatory approaches it may seem that not much has been achieved. The realist position would be to accept that the countervailing pressures are enormous. At the same time it is possible to see grounds for optimism in the form of local initiatives and modest successes.

Rethinking Professional Ethics

In Part I it was noted that the philosophical basis of Western moral thought may be seen as 'modernist' (Lyon, 1994). The rationalist, humanist, empiricist and logical positivist foundations of this tradition were shown to have created particular approaches to ethical values in professionalism, and hence in the caring professions. Ethical and value debates have tended, therefore, to be couched in terms of the conflict between two approaches to moral philosophy: Kantian (deontological, in other words based on essence or absolute standards) and Utilitarian (teleological, that is based on aims and outcomes). Because the origins of both perspectives are in modernism, the implicit tendency is for the liberal and conservative aspects of each to dominate such discussion. However, the Utilitarian ethical view of collective responsibility over individual right has found resonance also with critical or structural theories. Kant, on the other hand, as has been examined in Chapter 3, had a marked influence in the construction of orthodox individualist professional ethics (Hugman and Smith, 1995; Hussey, 1996).

In so far as the end of the welfarist era is also associated with a reappraisal of modernist ethics, then the reconstruction of the caring professions will also necessitate a renewed attention to talk about values (Shardlow, 1989). In order to shed the modernist baggage of both absolutist (deontological) and relativist (teleological) ethics a range of other approaches may be considered. O'Connor et al. (1995, pp. 221–2) identify four other perspectives which might be used in this way:

- rights-based ethics;
- Marxist-based ethics;
- intuitive ethics;
- virtue-based ethics.

The first two derive from a structural analysis, and as has already been noted may have some aspects in common with Utilitarianism. The differences are in the extent to which the rights-based approach, which draws on the work of Rawls (1972) that was discussed in earlier chapters, represents an attempt to reconcile deontological and teleological theories, while Marxist-based ethics in effect requires a choice to be made for the primacy of the rights of those who are less powerful socially.

Intuition as a basis for ethics is highly subjective and individualist. If the postmodern viewpoint, that there are no objective standards of truth or even reliability, holds, then this perspective may be plausible. However, as the basis for the shared, social action which is required of a professional, it could not be said to appear very useful. Although intuition may play a role in the day-to-day lives of people in the caring professions it seems weak as a vehicle for developing a general statement of principles in practice.

Virtue-based ethics might appear to have more relevance for professions (Rhodes, 1986; Hugman and Smith, 1995, p. 11; O'Connor et al., 1995, p. 222). We can speak of the 'good' nurse, remedial therapist or social worker and have some sense of what practices and values would be appropriate to the nature of the traditions of these occupations. However, here too the discussion is prone to conflict over which part of a tradition might have a primary claim to our attention. To *which* definition of the 'good' caring professional are we to refer?

In answer to this question, Fry (1992) points to the importance of the work of Noddings (1984), building on Gilligan (1982), to establish the meaning of 'caring' for professions such as nursing (applicable also to the remedial therapies and social work). This approach does not begin from moral *reasoning* (as do both deontological and teleological approaches) but from moral *being* in the relationship between cared-for and care-giving persons (Fry, 1992, p. 98). In that sense this can be said to be a feminist ethics. Caring is the basis for ethics because it can only, by definition, be said to occur in conditions of mutual respect, consent, commitment and, hence, responsibility between the parties involved. In this sense, it appears to be a virtue-based approach, in that it presupposes that the parties involved can agree on what would constitute 'the good' within such a relationship. It is more than an obligation, because it is based on the common humanity of the cared-for and care-giving persons (Fry, 1992, p. 100). Most importantly, such an approach is regarded as sensitive to context and dynamic (Thomasma, 1994). So, for example, what would constitute confidentiality in this approach is based on responsibility in the relationship to the good of the service user and of the relationship itself. This bridges the use of abstract principles or outcomes as determinants of ethics. Confidentiality is what the parties to the relationship would agree in that situation it should and could mean, which in most instances is what actually happens.

A weakness of caring as the basis for ethics is in the very culture-bound definition of what constitutes 'the good' in relationships (Hussey, 1996). Recent debates about modernity lead to the conclusion that, in the pluralist global society, ethical reasoning is fragmented by social divisions (Lyon, 1994), and there is no reason to suspect that ethical being would not similarly be experienced as a plurality. Although some elements of common humanity may be assumed cross-culturally, as in the meaning of respect (Browne, 1995), there are also many nuances which may render an ethic of caring problematic. Because the post-modernist critique proposes that the limits of the modernist era have been reached, and that modernism is giving way to a recognition that knowledge is always partial, then we may be left with no single generalisable way of speaking about values and ethics. Ultimately this might lead to the position that nothing is fully knowable, therefore everyone must make what they will of the world (Bauman, 1994). An ethic of caring, based on relationship, would thus be contextualised within the limits of the possibility of sustaining relationships across various social divisions, including culture, gender, race, sexuality, age or disability.

This understanding is of particular significance for the caring professions, because it relates to the growing awareness of and response to the diversity within society (McBeath and Webb, 1991; Hussey, 1996). As this diversity is reflected in social divisions around issues of gender, race, culture, age, sexuality, disability and so on, professional codes of ethics, still formulated in the Kantian mode, have tended to responded with categorical imperatives towards anti-discriminatory and anti-oppressive values (CCESTSW, 1991; Mullaly, 1993; AASW, 1994; Dominelli, 1996). In Chapter 1 the debate between Webb (1991) and Dominelli (1991) was discussed. Webb criticises this trend on the grounds that the categorical nature of the anti-oppressive practice approach conflicts with the idea of the professional as moral agent and the legitimacy, in Western democracy, of diverse ethical positions. In reply, Dominelli argues that the classical liberal ethics on which Webb's position is based can also be shown to be partial. Because the liberal position lacks an awareness of this partiality, it may itself be unjust and therefore unethical because it may produce (albeit unintended) inappropriate or even discriminatory practice.

Dominelli's (1991) critique reiterates the recognition within radical social work of its Utilitarian moral foundations (Simpkin, 1983). It also demonstrates the extent to which radical social work, as much as orthodox social work, remains situated within the modernist paradigm, in that the appeal both make to the moral purpose of social work is the rectification of need. The distinction lies in the structural analysis of the origins of social need on which radical practice has been based since the late-1800s (Woods, 1987; Forsythe, 1995).

At the same time, the connection of radical practice with an explicit anti-discriminatory and anti-oppressive analysis does provide hints of the post-modern (McBeath and Webb, 1991). Each social class, group or movement may be said to relate to a different ethical discourse, even where there is common ground (as in the over-arching concepts of discrimination and oppression). Sometimes they may even be in conflict. (See, for example, the discussion of contradictions between race and gender in Bryan et al., 1985.) It is this sense of diversity and difference which provides the link with post-modernity, pointing as that notion does to the many voices of which society (local and global) is comprised.

The caring professions are faced with a considerable challenge in this respect, because their professional foundations lie in particular ethical traditions. That is, although codified in Kantian terms, the professions uneasily embrace the conflict between Kant and the Utilitarians. There is a further challenge also, arising from the recognition that when Western (modernist) professionalism is adapted to other parts of the world there may be quite explicit value clashes (Midgely, 1981; Ngan, 1993; Browne, 1995; Silavwe, 1995; Hugman, 1996a). Therefore, it appears pertinent to ask whether the caring professions should hold to their modernist roots, or seize the post-modernist moment and be remoulded ethically according to context and subject (client).

In their study of human need, Doyal and Gough (1991) argue against an unmediated relativism. As discussed in Chapter 2 above, their theory is based on the principle that in any society two human needs may be observed: physical health and autonomy. These principles assume that a person should not be prevented by circumstance from participation in society. The lack of basic health or autonomy is, for Doyal and Gough, the primary cause of need. This is so whether people are in need of food and shelter or in need of social justice or personal fulfilment. As a *theory*, a framework for analysis and understanding, this model may be applied in different cultural contexts. Clearly, the empirical definition of adequate shelter or social justice may vary between cultures. Nevertheless, Doyal and Gough argue that there will be a minimum basic level of social, political and economic participation necessary in any situation in order for primary human need to be satisfied (1991, pp. 298–300).

Using this approach as a model, it is possible to construct an ethical position for the caring professions which addresses the many voices of the post-modern situation, while at the same time relating to the broader professional discourse (whether radical or orthodox). This is not to deny that there are, at least at times, several 'nursings', 'remedial therapies' or 'social works' as these professions contain many perspectives. This is especially true if the development of more distinctive non-Western practice is considered (see, for example, Browne, 1995; Silavwe, 1995).

Ethics for the caring professions, which have integrity both with their history and the contemporary context, might be constructed around the theory of human need and caring in relationship outlined above. These would provide a moral base for professionals to seek to support and promote health and autonomy. There are two important dimensions to such an ethical framework:

1. it would not be categorical but rather conditional, seeking to create the ethical environment for professional practice in diverse situations, and open to debate, revision and reformulation; consequently,
2. it would not be codified but rather discursive, requiring a degree of elaboration which is impossible in a categorical approach.

The elements of such an ethic would appear quite congruent to those now being proposed in some Western countries. It would include a commitment to the promotion of social justice, notions of working from an understanding of the service user's own knowledge and respect for the service user's identity. It would also include seeking to change those aspects of a society which create human need (through forms of oppression). As such it represents a shift from, while still being articulated to, modernist professionalism.

This approach suggests a move beyond the divide between Kantian and Utilitarian perspectives. It seeks to value both the individual and the social context. To the extent that this was Rawls' (1972) achievement, then it is intended to move in the same direction. However, it is not possible to construct such an ethical framework without being able to show how it would be grounded in context, and Rawls' work has been criticised on this very point (Barry, 1990). This necessitates a structural understanding of social welfare problems defined as need and of the conditions for relationships between cared-for and care-giving persons. Yet at the same time it avoids the Utilitarian pitfall, which Doyal and Gough (1991, p. 295) identify as a key issue in the failure of State socialism, because the person (as cared-for or care-giver) is not subordinated to an imposed centralist view of the collectivity in either the definition of need or the conditions for caring relationships. Moreover, it shows, contrary to Webb (1991) among others, that attention to issues of diversity, anti-discrimination and anti-oppression are not essentially totalitarian, but the basis for contemporary professional ethics.

Finally, it could be asked why a rethought professional ethics should be based on needs rather than rights, especially as Rawls (1972) remains one point of reference. The concept of need, as with the ethic of service, has in the past provided the basis for the caring professions to become paternalistic in their relation to service users. Yet just as it is not the ethic of service in itself, but applied in the context of orthodox professionalism, that generated paternalism, so too an ethic constructed around the promotion of health and autonomy would also have to be set within social relations based on power shared with service users and not used against them. It is in this respect that the ethic of caring in the sense developed by Fry (1992) is a crucial aspect of such a possibility. The importance of a radical concept of needs is that it enables an ethical framework to avoid any individualist liberalism inherent in the idea of rights (as discussed above) because it sets the actors in a social context. The primary needs of health and autonomy, understood socially in this way, are that to which service users have the rights which caring professions might seek to support and enable, and so be caring.

The notion of the morally active practitioner (Husband, 1995), discussed in Chapter 3 above, now becomes central. To meet the requirements of conditional and discursive professional ethics it is necessary for each member of a caring profession to be actively and reflexively engaged with the moral dimensions of their work. By this is meant that professionals should be seeking to develop moral fluency (Sellman, 1996). The capacity to make judgements between the demands of different approaches to service delivery is to be seen as a vital element in professionalism. Unless this is achieved then it is not possible to extend the support for and promotion of health and autonomy that constitutes empowerment for service users.

Of course it will be objected that any caring profession is embedded in a particular social welfare institution. Nurses, remedial therapists and social workers do not make moral judgements in a social vacuum. Indeed, but it is because of the social context of practice that members of these professions have an ethical choice to make. The distinction between the ethics of bureaucracy and business made by Bauman (1994), examined in Chapter 3, suggest that modernism has only a distorted choice to offer the morally competent person. Our justification is either that we were obeying orders or that we were maximising resources in the most materially rational manner possible. Bauman (1994) and Husband (1995) are in agreement that this is not an easy path to follow. For Bauman (1994, p. 14) this will at times mean the uncomfortable situation of being at odds with one's colleagues and managers. For Husband it means the maintenance of 'that anguish in the social regulation of caring which must be nurtured and valued, rather than eliminated through professional ethical certitude' (1995, p. 99). In other words, it should not be expected that the assertion of moral responsibility will be easy or comfortable. This means caring professionals, and their collective groups, must be prepared to take risks (of which whistle-blowing might be just one example, see Purtilo, 1993, and Jan and De Maria, 1997).

There are two issues of context that must be considered in thinking how these claims might appear in practice. The first context is the profession. For a collective expression of values to be made, both the pluralism of society and the complexities of practice must be accommodated. To avoid the opposing problems of the absolute and the relative positions is difficult. Codes of ethics, in being less absolute, must be more discursive. This is not equivalent to unbridled individual autonomy, which would simply collapse into neo-liberalism. What is being advocated here is that statements of ethical principles in caring professions must be just that, principles. They cannot be set in terms of legislative regulation. The role of local associations in this respect is to promote debate and to struggle with these issues. It is in this type of forum also that service users might more easily join the debate and be part of the moral dialogue. Such a form of accountability would also begin to address the power relations discussed above.

From this approach the values of anti-oppressive practice can also be seen not as a prescription but as a framework for ethics-in-practice. Working against the structural oppressions of society can be seen as a moral endeavour as much as political action because it rests on an explicit value orientation. A prescriptive approach satisfies neither the opponents of anti-oppressive practice (Webb, 1991a and b) nor its proponents (Dominelli, 1991). Indeed, the overly enthusiastic grasp of such practices in some quarters has reduced what is a complex set of social analyses and responses to a mechanical set of techniques (Dominelli, 1996). It is thus possible for a contradictory mix of deprofessionalisation and anti-oppressive practice to appear. However, it is only when the demands of anti-oppressive practice are integrated by members of the caring professions for themselves in their own work that more appropriate practices working against discrimination and marginalisation can develop (Torkington, 1983; Thompson, 1993; Browne, 1995).

The other issue of context is that of organisation. In the contemporary climate it may at times appear that the worst of bureaucratic and business ethics are applied by managers and policy makers in social welfare agencies. The discussion of whistleblowers in Chapter 5, above, points to a situation where obeying orders and maximising the use of material resources are combined in an attitude of 'do as you're told or you're out' (see, for example, Hutton, 1995, p. 106). Yet an open democratic society should allow for dissent and debate. This is not to argue for the arbitrary rule of individual whim. What is required, however, is the capacity of managers and policy makers (and, ultimately, politicians) to recognise that it is not a weakness to be challenged by colleagues and to listen and respond to alternative points of view.

Neither bureaucracy nor business appear to have been able to deliver this type of open participative form of organisation in full. For this reason it seems plausible, even desirable, that social welfare services should be located in a variety of organisations. The welfare mix, despite the problems associated with its use to reduce public commitments to social welfare, may also have some positive effects on the further development of diversity in the means of service delivery and professional practice. The organisational near-monopoly of employment for nurses, remedial therapists and social workers of state services in the UK has produced caring professions which for a time enjoyed a rising value dominance (hegemony). Subsequently, however, this has also made them very vulnerable to the forces of post-Fordist reconstruction. They now appear more insecure than colleagues in many other countries. A greater mix of employment could be grasped as an advantage, but this will not happen without a conscious effort and collegial alliance within and between professions, as well as collective support from service users.

It is in this context that professional associations have an important role to play as the basis for a network across the various sectors. Without an over-arching forum for sharing ideas, developing strategy and taking action the opposite to monopolistic control by an employer will be post-Fordist 'divide and rule' (Hoggett, 1994). Nor can such a suggestion ignore the variety of social identity and value perspectives contained within each caring profession. It would be impractical to expect that a consensus can or even should be achieved on each and every issue in order for professional associations to fulfil this type of role. Yet where a sufficient level of agreement can be reached then it will be possible for voices to be raised independent of the demands of specific employment and service structures. Such a position places emphasis on the *social* role of professional organisations and the shared responsibilities they have towards supporting and promoting the physical health and personal autonomy of all fellow citizens.

Professionals and Service Users

Unless caring professions are prepared to work to create open democratic forms of professionalism then claims of any right to a voice in the wider society will not be heard. Indeed, as has been argued above, the support gained by the New Right for attacks on social welfare, which included the caring professions, were in many ways strengthened by criticisms of the exclusionary strategies which these occupations adopted in the struggle to professionalise. With the wisdom of even a short historical gap this approach now seems to have been flawed because instead of working to develop their own stance on professionalism, the caring professions were caught up by the past successes of the 'classic' professions. These, however, did not and could not provide a model for occupations whose practices and structures were appropriately different. What could not have been foreseen, however, was that all such occupations would become subject to the same forces against that type of professionalism.

The service ethic, if considered in plain language, might constitute a way of seeing a reconstituted participatory form of professionalism. That the idea of service to others has had a history of paternalism (Mullaly, 1993, p. 193) does not of itself invalidate the notion entirely. (The word 'client' has had a similar fate in social work – it is not the word itself but the meaning which it has developed in practice that is at issue.) An orientation of service to others does not in any essence have to be patronising. It has become so because the reference point of professionalism has been in knowing 'that which others do not'. The outcome, telling *others* about the causes of and solutions to *their* problems, rather than engaging in a dialogue with people on the basis of shared citizenship, is a consequence of the structural context rather than a service ethic as an abstract ideal.

So, in another context 'service to others' might mean just that, namely that knowledge and skills are placed at the disposal of those who require them (without any false occupational self-deprecation). A different ethic of service would necessitate a more reflexive development of knowledge and skills, through experience and careful study combined with the commitment and capacity to engage in dialogue with service users. This in turn would require structures that support the accountability of caring professions to service users and at the same time do not permit this to be an option controlled by the professionals. For example, within professional associations the structures that scrutinise practice and set standards could be reworked so that 'lay' representation actually included the voice of service users and not only other professionals (Wilding, 1982; Hugman, 1991; Mullaly, 1993). That attention must be given to ensuring power imbalances are not perpetuated does not invalidate the idea. This can be addressed through the right to participate being based around membership of service-user groups. This also begins to deal with problems of representation. In addition, multiple representation may be a useful development to enable service users to support one another. Although this approach to professional associations has been attempted in some instances, it remains a largely unrealised potential.

In practice, citizen advocacy, user-managed brokerage schemes, patients' councils, local area committees and community groups employing professionals are all examples of the ways in which this type of development has been achieved (see, for example:

Chinnery, 1990; Brandon, 1991a; Lawson, 1991; Croft and Beresford, 1992; Macfarlane, 1993; Rudman, 1996b). The uncertainties created by the neo-liberal and neo-conservative attacks on social welfare and the caring professions can be addressed by looking at these detailed forms of services. Finding an answer to the logic of the question 'would they use us if they *could* pay?' does not of itself demand the establishment of pseudo-markets. These other, social means of providing choice for service users create opportunities for people to have a 'voice', and not simply to exert power through the choice to 'exit' (Hirschman, 1979). In situations of great power imbalance the option of 'exit' can be a euphemism for 'take it or leave it'.

It is notable that all the practical examples of service-user empowerment are from particularised instances (Aldridge, 1996). That is, they all operate at the level of creating opportunities for *individual* service users to exercise power, albeit sometimes as members of groups; they are also all examples of developments at the local level (as compared to those of national policy, such as community care in the UK). The debate about individualisation and collectivism which has taken place between orthodox and radical professionalism has, at times, confused issues of the cause or origin of need, the responsibility for resources to meet need, the social identity of those who experience need and relevant approaches to meeting need (compare Smith and Harris, 1972; Smith, 1980). Nurses, remedial therapists and social workers undertake direct practice with people, whether individually or as members of families, groups or local communities. Yet it is feasible to address the needs experienced by individuals, and to find ways of responding that recognise their individuality, without at the same time ascribing the origin of need or responsibility for resources to the individuals concerned (see, for example: Fook, 1993; Purkis, 1994; Butterworth and Rushforth, 1995; Timor and Wilson, 1995). In other words, responding to people as people does not have to be a matter of blaming victims. It does require that all aspects of the person, including the *social* nature of personhood, be recognised in theory, policy and practice. Strategies for empowerment, for the exercise of rights to the meeting of basic needs, therefore have to encompass both the individual and the community.

The importance of finding a balance between individual identity and group membership parallels that of finding equity between different social groups. That individuals and groups have different needs and different values means that equity cannot be seen as a general and uniform equality. Social justice as an ideal may serve well as an ethical orientation (for example, Australian Association of Social Workers, 1993), but it is extremely problematic to define in practice (Grace, 1994). It is this realisation that leads Gray (1996) to propose the struggle for 'complex fairness in local justice' as a more reasonable objective. By this Gray means that a single blueprint may not be possible, but rather principles may be outlined that could be applied to a variety of social welfare structures and practices. What is required is a framework capable of 'generating a sense of fairness that can be shared even by people with very different substantive moral outlooks' (Gray, 1996, p. 48). It is this which forms the central challenge of social welfare in a pluralist society, not simply the technical questions of achieving the right balance in the welfare mix. The welfare mix provides the means, but it is directed towards accomplishing complex fairness.

In practice, appropriate services for people with mental health needs will not be exactly the same as those for people with disabilities, or for children who have been non-accidentally injured, or for people with acute physical health needs, and so on. Across these distinctions run differences of appropriateness in social welfare for Black and ethnic minority people, women, people from different socio-economic classes, gays and lesbians, people with disabilities (including where need is not related to disability) and older people. Between countries, also, there are differences as well as similarities, exemplified by the situation of indigenous peoples in Australasia and North America compared with black settlers in Europe. These complexities require that everyone concerned, policy makers and managers, professionals and service users, live increasingly with the uncertainties that pluralism creates. Flexibility of thought and practice, especially between the general and the particular, have become a necessity. Parallels can also be seen in discussions about poverty and income maintenance based on distinctions between the absolute nature of poverty locally and the relative nature of poverty on a global scale (Pieretti, 1994). Ife (1995, p. 87) likewise draws on the environmentalist dictum to think globally and act locally in his proposals for community development. The forms empowering services take must differ between local contexts, as they attempt to deal with issues of complex fairness, but must at the same time be recognisable in relation to wider social values and principles. Where previous forms of social democracy sought equality at the cost of autonomy, the neo-liberal market seeks individual autonomy and resource efficiency at the cost of equity and fairness. It is the balance between these objectives which defines the values and principles which should be sought for contemporary social welfare.

Social welfare is not a free market, nor can it be reduced to one, because it is grounded in *social* relationships. Autonomy, equity and fairness as values can only be established through the processes of society. While the previous certainties of Marshall (1950) or Titmuss (1958, 1970) cannot simply be restored, the alternative, seen in the individualisation of responsibility, can only lead to a process of atomisation in which the idea of welfare itself is reduced to personal self-interest. In so far as complex fairness demands an exchange relationship then it might be said to be a social market, but this is one which is not defined in relation to use value expressed in monetary terms. It is one which must be seen as a question of social value.

Bibliography

Abbott, P. and C. Wallace (1990) 'Social work and nursing: a history' in P. Abbott and C. Wallace (eds) *The Sociology of the Caring Professions*, London: Falmer Press.

Adamson, B. J., G. Sinclair-Legge, A. Cusick and L. Nordholm (1994) 'Attitudes, values and orientation to professional practice' in *British Journal of Occupational Therapy*, 57(12), pp. 476–80.

Ahmad, B. (1990) *Black Perspectives in Social Work*, Birmingham: Venture Press.

Airaksinen, T. (1994) 'Service and science in professional life' in R. Chadwick (ed.) *Ethics and the Professions*, Aldershot: Avebury.

Aldridge, M. (1994) *Making Social Work News*, London: Routledge.

Aldridge, M. (1996) 'Dragged to market: being a profession in the postmodern world' in *British Journal of Social Work*, 26(2), pp. 177–94.

Allen, I., D. Hogg and S. Peace (1992) *Elderly People: Choice, Participation and Satisfaction*, London: Policy Studies Institute.

Allen, N. (1991) *Making Sense of the Children Act 1989*, London: Longman.

Ashworth, P. D. and J. Saxon (1990) 'On competence' in *Journal of Further and Higher Education*, 14(2), pp. 3–25.

Atkinson, D. (1995) *The Common Sense of Community*, London: Demos.

Australian Association of Social Workers (1993) *Code of Ethics*, Fisher, ACT: AASW.

Australian Association of Social Workers (1994) *Australian Social Work Competency Standards for Entry Level Social Workers*, Fisher, ACT: AASW.

Australian Bureau of Statistics (1994) *Labour Force Projection Australia 1995–2011*, Canberra: AGPS.

Australian Physiotherapy Association [APA] (no date) *Code of Ethics*, Sydney: APA.

Azmi, S. (1997) 'Professionalism and social diversity' in R. Hugman, M. Peelo and K. Soothill (eds) *Concepts of Care: Developments in Health and Social Welfare*, London: Edward Arnold.

Babyar, S. R., M. Sliwinski, G. Krasilovsky, E. Rosen, M. Thornby and J. R. Masefield (1996) 'Survey of inclusion of cultural and gender issues in entry-level physical therapy curricula in New York State' in *Journal of Physical Therapy Education*, 10(2), pp. 53–62.

Bagguley, P. (1992) 'Angels in red? Patterns of union membership among UK professional nurses' in K. Soothill, C. Henry and K. Kendrick (eds) *Themes and Perspectives in Nursing*, London: Chapman & Hall.

Bailey, D. M. (1996) 'Closer to home . . . gay and lesbian clients' in *Occupational Therapy Practice*, 1(6), pp. 34–8.

Baldock, J. and C. Ungerson (1993) 'Consumer perceptions of an emerging mixed economy of care' in A. Evers and I. Svetlik (eds) *Balancing Pluralism*, Aldershot: Avebury.

Baldwin, D. (1995) 'Interconnecting the personal and the public' in *The Canadian Journal of Nursing Research*, 27(3), pp. 19–37.

Baldwin, S. (1993) *The Myth of Community Care*, London: Chapman & Hall.

Balogh, R. (1992) 'Performance indicators and changing patterns of accountability in nurse education' in K. Soothill, C. Henry and K. Kendrick (eds) *Themes and Perspectives in Nursing*, London: Chapman & Hall.

Balogh, R., A. Beattie and S. Beckerleg (1989) *Figuring Out Performance*, Sheffield: English National Board for Nursing, Midwifery and Health Visiting.

Baly, M. E. (1987) 'The Nightingale nurses: the myth and the reality' in C. Maggs (ed.) *Nursing History: the State of the Art*, London: Croom Helm.

Bamford, T. (1990) *The Future of Social Work*, Basingstoke: Macmillan.

Barbalet, J. (1996) 'Developments in citizenship theory and issues in Australian citizenship' in *Australian Journal of Social Issues*, 31(1), pp. 55–72.

Barber, J. G. (1991) *Beyond Casework*, Basingstoke: Macmillan.

Barbier, A. with R. Clough (1994) 'Learning from children and young people' in R. Clough (ed.) *Insights into Inspection: the Regulation of Social Care*, London: Whiting & Birch/SCA (Education).

Barbour, R. (1995) 'Responding to a challenge: nursing care and AIDS' in *International Journal of Nursing Studies*, 32(4), pp. 373–85.

Barr, N., H. Glennester and J. Le Grand (1989) 'Working for patients? The right approach?' in *Social Policy and Administration*, 23(2), pp. 117–27.

Barry, J., K. Soothill and C. Williams (1992) 'Managing nursing wastage' in K. Soothill, C. Henry and K. Kendrick (eds) *Themes and Perspectives in Nursing*, London; Chapman & Hall.

Barry, N. (1990) *Welfare*, Buckingham: Open University Press.

Bartlett, W. and J. Le Grand (1993) 'The theory of quasi-markets' in J. Le Grand and W. Bartlett (eds) *Quasi-Markets and Social Policy*, Basingstoke: Macmillan.

Bauman, Z. (1988) *Freedom*, Milton Keynes: Open University Press.

Bauman, Z. (1989) *Modernity and the Holocaust*, Cambridge: Polity Press.

Bauman, Z. (1992) *Intimations of Post-Modernity*, London: Routledge.

Bauman, Z. (1994) *Alone Again: Ethics After Certainty*, London: Demos.

Beattie, A. (1991) 'Knowledge and control in health promotion: a test case for social policy and social theory' in J. Gabe, M. Calnan and M. Bury (eds) *The Sociology of the Health Service*, London: Routledge.

Beck, U. (1992) *Risk Society: Towards a New Modernity*, London: Sage.

Beilharz, P., M. Considine and R. Watts (1992) *Arguing About the Welfare State*, Sydney: Allen & Unwin.

Bell, P. and A. K. Williams (1991) 'AIDS: knowledge and attitudes of student nurses in Australia and Canada' in *The Canadian Journal of Nursing Research*, 23(1), pp. 15–26.

Beresford, P. (1988) 'Consumer views: data collection or democracy?' in I. Allen (ed.) *Hearing the Voice of the Consumer*, London: Policy Studies Institute.

Beresford, P. and S. Croft (1986) *Whose Welfare?* Brighton: Lewis Cohen Urban Studies Centre.

Bianchi, M. (1991) 'Policy for the elderly in Italy: innovation or modernization?' in A. Evers and I. Svetlik (eds) *New Welfare Mixes in Care for the Elderly (vol. 3)*, Vienna: European Centre for Social Welfare Policy and Research.

Biegel, D. E., E. M. Tracy and K. N. Corvo (1994) 'Strengthening social networks: intervention strategies for mental health case managers' in *Health and Social Work*, 19(4), pp. 206–17.

Biestek, F. (1961) *The Casework Relationship*, London: George Allen & Unwin.

Blom-Cooper, L. (1985) *A Child in Trust: Report of the Inquiry into the Death of Jasmine Beckford, Wembley*: London Borough of Brent.

Borland, A., N. B. Whyte and L. Maxwell (1995) 'Hospital nurses and health promotion' in *The Canadian Journal of Nursing Research*, 27(4), pp. 13–31.

Boyce, R. (1997) 'Health sector reform, profession power, autonomy and culture: the case of Australian allied health' in R. Hugman, M. Peelo and K. Soothill (eds) *Concepts of Care*, London: Edward Arnold.

Bowie, N. E. (1985) *Making Ethical Decisions*, New York: McGraw-Hill.

Bracegirdle, H. (1991) 'Occupational therpay students choice of gender-differentiated activities for psychiatric patients' in *British Journal of Occupational Therapy*, 54(7), pp. 47–53.

Bradshaw, J. (1972) 'The concept of need' in *New Society*, 19, pp. 640–3.

Brandon, D. (1991a) *Innovation Without Change? Consumer Power in Psychiatric Services*, Basingstoke: Macmillan.

Brandon, D. (1991b) 'Implications of normalisation work for professionals' in S. Ramon (ed.) *Beyond Community Care*, Basingstoke: Macmillan.

Braverman, H. (1974) *Labor and Monopoly Capital*, New York: Monthly Review Press.

Bridges, J. M. (1991) 'Literature review of the image of the nurse and nursing in the media' in *Journal of Advanced Nursing*, 15(7), pp. 850–4.

British Association of Social Workers (BASW) (1980) *Clients are Fellow Citizens*, Birmingham: BASW.

British Association of Social Workers (BASW) (1990) *Whose Choice?*, Birmingham: BASW.

Brockett, M. (1996) 'Ethics, moral reasoning and professional virtue in occupational therapy education' in *Canadian Journal of Occupational Therapy*, 63(3), pp. 197–205.

Browne, A. J. (1995) 'The meaning of respect: a First Nations perspective' in *The Canadian Journal of Nursing Research*, 27(4), pp. 95–110.

Bryan, D., S. Dadzie and S. Scafe (1985) *The Heart of the Race*, London: Virago.

Bryson, L. (1992) *The State and Welfare*, Melbourne: Macmillan.

Bucknall, T. and S. Thomas (1995) 'Critical decision making in critical care' in *The Australian Journal of Advanced Nursing*, 13(2), pp. 10–17.

Bunting, S. M. (1996) 'Sources of stigma associated with women with HIV' in *Advances in Nursing Science*, 19(2), pp. 64–73.

Burnham, J. (1945) *The Managerial Revolution*, Harmondsworth: Penguin.

Butcher, H. (1992) 'Community work: current realities, contemporary trends' in P. Carter, T. Jeffs and M. K. Smith (eds) *Changing Social Work and Welfare*, Buckingham: Open University Press.

Butrym, Z. (1976) *The Nature of Social Work*, London: Macmillan.

Butterworth, T. and D. Rushforth (1995) 'Working in partnership with people who use services' in *The International Journal of Nursing Studies*, 32(4), pp. 373–85.

Bytheway, B. (1995) *Ageism*, Buckingham and Philadelphia: Open University Press.

Cahill, M. (1994) *The New Social Policy*, Oxford: Blackwell.

Calder, M. (1995) 'Child protection: balancing paternalism and partnership' in *British Journal of Social Work*, 25(6), pp. 748–66.

Callahan, D. (1987) *Setting Limits: Medical Goals in an Aging Society*, New York: Simon and Schuster.

Cambridge, P. (1992) 'Case management in community service: organizational responses' in *British Journal of Social Work*, 22(5), pp. 495–517.

Campbell, B. (1988) *Unofficial Secrets*, London: Virago Press.

Carr-Saunders, A. M. and P. M. Wilson (1933) *The Professions*, London: Oxford University Press.

Carter, J. and Jackson, N. (1993) 'Modernism, postmodernism and motivation, or why expectancy theory failed to come up to expectation' in J. Hassard and M. Parker (eds) *Postmodernism and Organizations*, London: Sage Publications.

Castle, J. (1987) 'The development of professional nursing in New South Wales' in C. Maggs (ed.) *Nursing History: the State of the Art*, London: Croom Helm.

Castles, S. (1985) *The Working Class and Welfare*, Sydney: Allen & Unwin.

Cawson, A. (1982) *Corporatism and Welfare*, London: Heinemann.

Central Council for Education and Training in Social Work (CCETSW) (1991) *Rules and Requirements for the Diploma in Social Work (Paper 30)*, 2nd edition, London: CCETSW.

Chadwick, R. (1992) 'Nursing, advertising and sponsorship: some ethical issues' in K. Soothill, C. Henry and K. Kendrick (eds) *Themes and Perspectives in Nursing*, London: Chapman & Hall.

Challis, D. (1990) 'Case management: problems and possibilities' in I. Allen (ed.) *Care Managers and Care Management*, London: Policy Studies Institute.

Challis, D. (1992) 'State of the art' in S. Onyett and P. Canbridge (eds) *Case Management: Issues in Practice*, Canterbury: University of Kent.

Challis, D. and B. Davies (1986) *Case Management in Community Care*, Aldershot: Gower.

Challis, D. and S. Missiakoulis (1988) 'Heineken and matching processes in the Thanet community care project: an empirical test of their relative importance' in *British Journal of Social Work*, 18(supplement), pp. 55–78.

Chalmers, K. I. and I. J. Bramadat (1996) 'Community development: theoretical and practical issues for community health nursing in Canada' in *Journal of Advanced Nursing*, 24(4), pp. 719–26.

Chamberlayne, P. (1992) 'New directions in welfare? France, West Germany, Italy and Britain in the 1980s' in *Critical Social Policy*, 11(3), pp. 5–21.

Cheek, J. and T. Rudge (1994) 'The panopticon revisited?' in *The International Journal of Nursing Studies*, 31(6), pp. 583–92.

Chinnery, B. (1990) 'The process of being disabled' in *Practice*, 4(1), pp. 43–8.

Clarke, J. (ed.) (1993) *A Crisis in Care? Challenges to Social Work*, London: Sage Publications.

Cnaan, R. (1994) 'The new American social work gospel: case management of the chronically mentally ill' in *British Journal of Social Work*, 24(5), pp. 533–57.

Cochrane, A. (1993) 'Challenges from the centre' in J. Clarke (ed.) *A Crisis in Care? Challenges to Social Work*, London: Sage Publications.

Cochrane, A. (1994) 'Restructuring the local welfare state' in R. Burrows and B. Loader (eds) *Towards a Post-Fordist Welfare State?* London: Routledge.

Collins, S. and M. Stein (1989) 'Users fight back: collectives in social work' in C. Rojek, G. Peacock and S. Collins (eds) *The Haunt of Misery*, London: Routledge.

Colston, H. (1994) 'Occupational therapy courses and applicants from minority groups: attitudes and feelings' in *British Journal of Occupational Therapy*, 57(10), pp. 398–400.

Cook, A. and E. Gentry (1994) 'Listening to the views of the service user' in R. Clough (ed.) *Insights into Inspection: the Regulation of Social Care*, London: Whiting & Birch/SCA (Education).

Cooper, D. (1993) 'Off the banner and into the agenda: the emergence of a new municipal lesbian and gay politics' in *Critical Social Policy*, 12(3), pp. 20–39.

Cornwell, N. (1993) 'Assessment and accountability in community care' in *Critical Social Policy*, 12(3), pp. 40–52.

Cortis, J. D. and A. S. Rinomhota (1996) 'The future of ethnic minority nurses in the NHS' in *Journal of Nursing Management*, 4(6), pp. 359–66.

Cousins, C. (1987) *Controlling Social Welfare*, Brighton: Wheatsheaf.

Cox, D. (1991) 'Health service management – a sociological view: Griffiths and the non-negotiated order of the hospital' in J. Gabe, M. Calnan and M. Bury (eds) *The Sociology of the Health Service*, London: Routledge.

Croft, S. and P. Beresford (1989) 'User involvement, citizenship and social policy' in *Critical Social Policy*, 9(2), pp. 5–17.

Croft, S. and P. Beresford (1990) *From Paternalism to Participation: Involving People in Social Services*, York: Joseph Rowntree Foundation.

Croft, S. and P. Beresford (1992) 'The politics of participation' in *Critical Social Policy*, 12(2), pp. 20–44.

Culley, L. (1996) 'A critique of multiculturalism in health care' in *Journal of Advanced Nursing*, 23(3), pp. 564–70.

Curtin, L. L. (1994) 'Collegial ethics of a caring profession' in *Nurse Management*, 25(8), pp. 28–32.

Daatland, S. O. (1990) 'What are families for?' in *Ageing and Society*, 10(1), pp. 1–15.

Daatland, S. O. (1992) 'Ideals cost? Current trends in Scandinavian welfare policy on ageing' in *Journal of European Social Policy*, 2(1), pp. 33–47.

Dalley, G. (1992) 'Quality management: lessons from the NHS' in I. Allen (ed.) *Drawing the Line: Purchasing and Providing Services in the 1990s*, London: Policy Studies Institute.

Dalton, T., M. Draper, W. Weeks and J. Wiseman (1996) *Making Social Policy in Australia*, St. Leonards: Allen & Unwin.

Dant, T. and B. Gearing (1993) 'Key workers for elderly perople in the community' in J. Bornat, C. Pereira, D. Pilgrim and F. Williams (eds) *Community Care: a Reader*, Basingstoke: Macmillan.

Davies, B. and D. Challis (1986) *Matching Resources to Needs in Community Care*, Aldershot: Gower.

Davies, B. and M. Knapp (1988) 'The production of welfare approach: some new PSSRU argument and results' in *British Journal of Social Work*, 18(supplement), pp. 1–12.

Davies, B. and S. Missiakoulis (1988) 'The Heineken and matching effects' in *British Journal of Social Work*, 18(Supplement), pp. 55–78.

Davies, J. (ed.) (1993) *God and the Marketplace*, London: Institute of Economic Affairs.

Davies, M. (1994) *The Essential Social Worker*, 3rd edition, Aldershot: Arena.

De Maria, W. (1996) 'The whistleblower: in praise of troublesome people' in *Australian Social Work*, 49(3), pp. 15–24.

Degeling, P. and D. Thomas (1995) 'Health policy' in M. Laffin and M. Painter (eds) *Reform and Reversal*, Melbourne: Macmillan.

Dent, M. (1994) 'Professionalism, educated labour and the state: hospital medicine and the new managerialism' in *Sociological Review*, 41(2), pp. 244–73.

Department of Health (1989) *Caring for People: Community Care in the Next Decade and Beyond*, Cm. 849, London: HMSO.

Department of Health (1991) *Care Management and Assessment (The Managers' Guide)*, London; HMSO.

Department of Health and Social Security (1988) *Report of the Inquiry into Child Abuse in Cleveland 1987*, (The Butler-Sloss Report), London: HMSO.

Derber, C. (1983) 'Managing professionals: ideological proletarianization and post-industrial labor' in *Theory and Society*, 12(3), pp. 309–41.

Dingwall, R., M. Rafferty and C. Webster (1988) *An Introduction to the Social History of Nursing*, London: Routledge.
Dominelli, L. (1988) *Anti-Racist Social Work*, London: Macmillan.
Dominelli, L. (1991) ' "What's in a name?" A comment on "puritans and paradigms" ' in *Social Work & Social Sciences Review*, 2(3), pp. 231–5.
Dominelli, L. (1996) 'Deprofessionalising social work: anti-oppressive practice, competencies and postmodernism' in *British Journal of Social Work*, 26(2), pp. 153–76.
Dominelli, L. and E. McLeod (1989) *Feminist Social Work*, London: Macmillan.
Donzelot, J. (1988) 'The promotion of the social' in *Economy and Society*, 17(3), pp. 395–427.
Doyal, L. and I. Gough (1991) *A Theory of Human Need*, Basingstoke: Macmillan.
Drury, E. (1992) 'Employment and retirement in Europe' in L. Davies (ed.) *The Coming of Age in Europe*, London: Age Concern England.
Early, M. B. (1987) *Mental Health Concepts and Techniques for the Occupational Therapy Assistant*, New York: Raven Press.
Edgar, D. (1995) 'Sharing the caring: rethinking current policies' in W. Weeks and J. Wiseman (eds) *Issues Facing Australian Families Today: Human Services Respond*, (2nd edition), Melbourne: Longman.
Elander, G., K. Dreschler and K. W. Persson (1993) 'Ethical dilemmas in long term care settings: interviews with nurses in Sweden and England' in *The International Journal of Nursing Studies*, 30(1), pp. 91–7.
Elliot, P. (1972) *The Sociology of the Professions*, London: Macmillan.
Ellis, H. (1992) 'Conceptions of care' in K. Soothill, C. Henry and K. Kendrick (eds) *Themes and Perspectives in Nursing*, London: Chapman & Hall.
Ellis, K. (1993) *Squaring the Circle: User and Carer Participation in Assessment*, York: Joseph Rowntree Foundation.
England, H. (1986) *Social Work as Art*, Hemel Hempstead: Allen & Unwin.
Ernst, J. (1994) *Whose Utility?* Buckingham: Open University Press.
Esping-Andersen, G. (1990) *The Three Worlds of Welfare Capitalism*, Cambridge: Polity Press.
Estes, C. (1986) 'The aging enterprise: in whose interests?' in *International Journal of Health Services*, 16(2), pp. 243–51.
Etzioni, A. (ed.) (1969) *The Semi-Professions and Their Organization*, Englewood-Cliffs: Free Press.
Etzioni, A. (1995) *The Spirit of Community: Rights, Responsibility and the Communitarian Agenda*, London: Fontana.
Evandrou, M., J. Falkingham and H. Glennerster (1990) 'The Personal Social Services: "Everyone's poor relation but nobody's baby?" ' in J. Hills (ed.) *The State of Welfare: the Welfare State in Britain Since 1974*, Oxford: Clarendon Press.
Evers, A. (1993) 'The welfare mix approach. Understanding the pluralism of welfare systems' in A. Evers and I. Svetlik (eds) *Balancing Pluralism*, Aldershot: Avebury.

Eyles, J. and J. Donovan (1990) *The Social Effects of Health Policy*, Aldershot: Avebury.

Fanker, S. (1996) 'Issues in casemix funding for acute inpatient psychiatric services and their relevance to mental health nursing' in *Australia and New Zealand Journal of Mental Health Nursing*, 5(3), pp. 95–102.

Finch, J. (1989) *Family Obligations and Social Change*, Cambridge: Polity Press.

Finnis, (1980) *Natural Law and Natural Rights*, Oxford: Clarendon Press.

Fisher, M. (1990) 'Defining the practice content of care management' in *Social Work & Social Sciences Review*, 2(3), pp. 204–30.

Flexner, A. (1915) 'Is social work a profession?' in *Proceedings of the National Conference of Charity and Corrections*, London: Hildman.

Fook, J. (1993) *Radical Casework: a Theory of Practice*, St Leonard's, NSW: Allen & Unwin.

Foolchand, M. K. (1995) 'Promoting racial equality in nurse education' in *Nurse Education Today*, 15(2), pp. 101–5.

Forsythe, B. (1995) 'Discrimination in social work – an historical note' in *British Journal of Social Work*, 25(1), pp. 1–16.

Fox Harding, L. (1991) *Perspectives in Child Care Policy*, London: Longman.

Franker, S. (1996) 'Issues in casemix funding for acute psychiatric services and their relevance to mental health nursing' in *Australia and New Zealand Journal of Mental Health Nursing*, 5(3), pp. 95–102.

Friedson, E. (1970) *The Profession of Medicine*, New York: Dodd Mead.

Freidson, E. (1983) 'The theory of professions: state of the art' in R. Dingwall and P. Lewis (eds) *The Sociology of the Professions*, London: Macmillan.

Friedson, E. (1986) *Professional Powers: a Study of the Institutionalization of Formal Knowledge*, Chicago: University of Chicago Press.

Friedman, M. (1962) *Capitalism and Freedom*, Chicago: Unversity of Chicago Press.

Fries, J. F. (1993) 'Medical perspectives on successful aging' in P. B. Baltes and M. M. Baltes (eds) *Successful Aging Perspectives from the Behavioral Sciences*, Cambridge: Cambridge University Press.

Fry, S. T. (1992) 'The role of caring in atheory of nursing ethics' in H. B. Holmes and L. M. Purdy (eds) *Feminist Perspectives in Medical Ethics*, Bloomington and Indianapolis: Indiana University Press.

Galper, J. (1975) *The Politics of Social Services*, Englewood-Cliffs, N. J.: Prentice-Hall.

Gamble, A. (1988) *The Free Economy and the Strong State*, London: Macmillan.

Game, A. and R. Pringle (1983) *Gender at Work*, Sydney: Allen & Unwin.

Gardner, H. and B. McCoppin (1995) 'Struggle for survival by health therapists, nurses and medical scientists' in H. Garner (ed.) *The Politics of Health: the Australian Experience*, Melbourne: Churchill Livingstone.

George, V. and Wilding, P. (1976) *Ideology and Social Welfare*, London: Routledge & Kegan Paul.

Gilligan, C. (1982) *In a Different Voice*, Cambridge, Mass.: Harvard University Press.

Gottlieb, L. N. (1995) 'A blueprint for the development of the profession of nursing: the legacy of F. Moyra Allen and Joan Gilchrist' in *The Canadian Journal of Nursing Research*, 27(3), pp. 5–11.

Gould, M. (1986) 'Self-advocacy: consumer leadership for the transition years' in *Journal of Rehabilitation*, 52(4), pp. 39–42.

Grace, D. (1994) 'Social justice' in M. Wearing and R. Berreen (eds) *Welfare & Social Policy in Australia*, Sydney: Harcourt Brace.

Gray, J. (1992) *The Moral Foundations of Market Institutions*, London: Institute of Economic Affairs.

Gray, J. (1996) *After Social Democracy*, London: Demos.

Graycar, A. and A. Jamrozik (1993) *How Australians Live*, 2nd edition, Melbourne: Macmillan.

Greenwood, E. (1957) 'Attributes of a profession' in *Social Work*, 2(3), pp. 44–55.

Griffiths, R. (1988) *Community Care: Agenda for Action*, London: HMSO.

Grimwood, C. and R. Popplestone (1993) *Women, Management and Care*, Basingstoke: Macmillan.

Hadley, R. and S. Hatch (1981) *Social Welfare and the Failure of the State*, London: George Allen & Unwin.

Hadley, R. and R. Clough (1996) *Care in Chaos*, London: Cassell.

Halmos, P. (1978) *The Faith of the Counsellors*, 2nd edition, London: Constable & Company.

Halsey, A. H. (1992) *Decline of Donnish Domination*, Oxford: Clarendon Press.

Harbert, W. (1988) *The Welfare Industry*, Hadleigh: Holhouse Publications.

Harrison, M. (1995) 'The legal and social status of children' in W. Weeks and J. Wilson (eds) *Issues Facing Australian Families: Human Services Respond*, 2nd edition, Melbourne: Longman.

Harrison, M. J., A. Neufeld and K. Kuster (1995) 'Women in transition: access and barriers to social support' in *Journal of Advanced Nursing*, 21(5), pp. 858–64.

Hashimoto, A. and H. Kendig (1992) 'Aging in international perspective' in H. Kendig, A. Hashimoto and L. C. Coppard (eds) *Family Support for the Elderly*, Oxford: Oxford University Press.

Hassan, R. (1996) 'Euthanasia and the medical profession' in *Australian Journal of Social Issues*, 31(3), pp. 239–52.

Haug, M. R. (1973) 'Deprofessionalization: an alternative hypothesis for the future' in P. Halmos (ed.) *Professionalization and Social Change*, Keele: University of Keele.

Hayek, F. A. (1960) *The Constitution of Liberty*, London: Routledge & Kegan Paul.

Hearn, J. (1982) 'Notes on patriarchy, professionalization and the semi-professions' in *Sociology*, 16(2), pp. 184–202.

Heelas, P. and P. Morris (1992) 'Enterprise culture: its values and value' in P. Heelas and P. Morris (eds) *The Values of the Enterprise Culture*, London: Routledge.

Held, V. (1993) *Feminist Morality: Transforming Culture, Society and Politics*, Chicago: University of Chicago Press.

Helewa, A., H. A. Smythe, C. H. Goldsmith, J. Groh, M. C. Thomas, B. A. Stokes and J. Sugerman (1987) 'The total assessment of rheumatoid polyarthritis – evaluation of a training programme for physiotherpaists and occupational therapists' in *The Journal of Rheumatology*, 14(1), pp. 87–92.

Henderson, A. (1994) 'Power and knowledge in nursing practice: the contribution of Foucault' in *Journal of Advanced Nursing*, 20(5), pp. 935–9.

Henderson, P. and J. Armstrong (1993) 'Community development and community care' in J. Bornat, C. Pereira, D. Pilgrim and F. Williams (eds) *Community Care: a Reader*, Basingstoke: Macmillan.

Henrard, J.-C. (1991) 'Care for elderly people in the European Community' in *Social Policy & Administration*, 25(3), pp. 184–92.

Henwood, M. (1986) 'Community care: policy, pratice and prognosis' in M. Brenton and C. Ungerson (eds) *The Yearbook of Social Policy in Britain 1985–6*, London: Routledge & Kegan Paul.

Heward, T. (1994) 'Retailing the police' in R. Keat, N. Whitely and N. Abercrombie (eds) *The Authority of the Consumer*, London: Routledge.

Hewitt, M. (1992) *Welfare, Ideology and Need: Developing Perspectives on the Welfare State*, Hemel Hempstead: Harvester Wheatsheaf.

Hibberd, J. M. and J. Norris (1991) 'Strike by nurses: perceptions of colleagues coping with the fallout' in *The Canadian Journal of Nursing Research*, 23(4), pp. 43–54.

Hirschman, A. O. (1979) *Exit, Voice and Loyalty – Responses to Decline in Firms, Organizations and States*, Cambridge, Mass.: Harvard University Press.

Hiscock, V. and W. Wccks (1995) 'A hcalthy approach to scrvicc dclivcry: women working with women' in W. Weeks and J. Wilson (eds) *Issues Facing Australian Families: Human Services Respond*, 2nd edition, Melbourne: Longman.

HMSO (1991) *The Citizens' Charter: Raising the Standard*, London: HMSO.

Hobhouse, L. T. (1922) *The Elements of Social Justice*, London: George Allen and Unwin.

Hoggett, P. (1994) 'The modernization of the UK welfare state' in R. Burrows and B. Loader (eds) *Towards a Post-Fordist Welfare State*, London: Routledge.

Holloway, J. (1992) 'The media representation of the nurse: the implications for nursing' in K. Soothill, C. Henry and K. Kendrick (eds) *Themes and Perspectives in Nursing*, London: Chapman & Hall.

Hopton, J. (1995) 'The "political correctness" debate and caring in psychiatric nursing' in *Nurse Education Today*, 15(3), pp. 161–3.

Howe, A., E. Ozanne and C. Selby-Smith (eds) (1990) *Community Care Policy and Practice: New Directions in Australia*, Melbourne: Public Sector Management Institute, Monash University.

Howe, D. (1986) *Social Workers and Their Practice in Welfare Bureaucracies*, Aldershot: Gower.

Howe, D. (1991) 'The shape of social work practice' in M. Davies (ed.) *The Sociology of Social Work*, London: Routledge.

Howe, D. (1994) 'Modernity, postmodernity and social work' in *British Journal of Social Work*, 24(5), pp. 513–32.

Hoyes, L. and R. Means (1993) 'Quasi-markets and the reform of community care' in J. Le Grand and W. Bartlett (eds) *Quasi-Markets and Social Policy*, Basingstoke: Macmillan.

Hughes, E. (1958) *Men and Their Work*, Glencoe, Ill.: The Free Press.

Hugman, R. (1991) *Power in Caring Professions*, Basingstoke: Macmillan.

Hugman, R. (1994a) *Ageing and the Care of Older People in Europe*, Basingstoke: Macmillan.

Hugman, R. (1994b) 'Consuming health and welfare' in R. Keat, N. Whitely and N. Abercrombie (eds) *The Authority of the Consumer*, London: Routledge.

Hugman, R. (1994c) 'Social work and case management: models of professionalism and elderly people' in *Ageing & Society*, 14(3), pp. 237–53.

Hugman, R. (1996a) 'Professionalization in social work: the challenge of diversity' in *International Social Work*, 39(2), pp. 131–47.

Hugman, R. (1996b) 'Health and welfare policy and older people in Europe' in *Health Care in Later Life*, 1(4), pp. 211–22.

Hugman, R. and D. Smith, (1995) 'Ethical issues in social work: an overview' in R. Hugman and D. Smith (eds) *Ethical Issues in Social Work*, London: Routledge.

Hume, C. (1991) 'Occupational therapy with ethnic minority elders' in A. J. Squires (ed.) *Multicultural Health Care and Rehabilitation*, London: Edward Arnold.

Hunt, G. (1995) 'Introduction: whistleblowing and the breakdown of accountability' in G. Hunt (ed.) *Whistleblowing in the Health Service*, London: Edward Arnold.

Husband, C. (1995) 'The morally active practitioner and the ethics of anti-racist social work' in R. Hugman and D. Smith (eds) *Ethical Issues in Social Work*, London: Routledge.

Hussey, T. (1996) 'Nursing ethics and codes of professional conduct' in *Nursing Ethics*, 3(3), pp. 251–8.

Huston, L. (1991) *Shifts in the Welfare Mix: the Case of Care for the Elderly*, Vienna: European Centre for Social Policy and Research.

Hutton, W. (1995) *The State We're In*, London: Jonathan Cape.

Huxley, P. (1993) 'Case management and care management in community care' in *British Journal of Social Work*, 23(4), pp. 365–81.

Ife, J. (1995) *Community Development*, Melbourne: Longman.

Illich, I. (1977) *Disabling Professions*, London: Marion Boyars.

Irvine, R. and J. Graham (1994) 'Deconstructing the concept of profession' in *The Australian Occupational Therapy Journal*, 41(1), pp. 9–18.

Issit, M. and M. Woodward (1992) 'Competence and contradiction' in P. Carter, T. Jeffs and M. K. Smith (eds) *Changing Social Work and Welfare*, Buckingham: Open University Press.

Jackson, D. (1995) 'Nursing texts and lesbian contexts: lesbian imagery in the nursing literature' in *Australian Journal of Advanced Nursing*, 13(1), pp. 25–31.

James, C. (1995) 'Who learns what?' in *Nurse Education Today*, 15(3), pp. 161–3.

Jamieson, A. (1991) 'Home care in Europe: background and aims' in A. Jamieson (ed.) *Home Care for Older People in Europe: a Comparison of Policies and Practices*, Oxford: Oxford University Press.

Jamous, H. and B. Peloille (1970) 'Changes in the French university-hospital system' in J. A. Jackson (ed.) *Professions and Professionalization*, Cambridge: Cambridge University Press.

Jan, C. and W. De Maria (1997) 'Eating its own: the whistleblowers' organization in vendetta mode' in *Australian Journal of Social Issues*, 32(1), in press.

Jang, Y. (1995) 'Chinese culture and occupational therapy' in *British Journal of Occupational Therapy*, 58(3), pp. 103–6.

Jayasuriya, D. L. (1996) 'Citizenship and welfare: rediscovering Marshall' in *Australian Journal of Social Issues*, 31(1), pp. 19–38.

Jessop, B. (1994) 'The transition to post-Fordism and the Schumpeterian workfare state' in R. Burrows and B. Loader (eds) *Towards a Post-Fordist Welfare State?* London: Routledge.

Johnson, M. (1978) 'Big fleas have little fleas – nurse professionalism and nursing auxiliaries' in M. Hardie and L. Hockey (eds) *Nursing Auxiliaries in Health Care*, London: Croom Helm.

Johnson, N. (1990) *Reconstructing the Welfare State*, Hemel Hempstead: Harvester Wheatsheaf.

Johnson, P. and J. Falkingham (1992) *Ageing and Economic Welfare*, London: Sage.

Johnson, T. J. (1972) *Professions and Power*, London: Macmillan.

Jolley, M. (1989) 'The professionalization of nursing: the uncertain path' in M. Jolley and P. Allan (eds) *Current Issues in Nursing*, London: Chapman & Hall.

Jones, A. and J. May (1992) *Working in Human Service Organisations: a Critical Introduction*, Melbourne: Longman.

Jones, C. (1993) 'Distortion and resistance: the right and anti-racist social work education' in *Social Work Education*, 12(3), pp. 9–16.

Jones, M. (1996) *The Australian Welfare State*, St Leonard's, NSW: Allen & Unwin.

Jordan, B. (1987) *Rethinking Welfare*, Oxford: Basil Blackwell.

Jordan, B. (1990) *Social Work in an Unjust Society*, Brighton: Harvester Wheatsheaf.

Jouvenal, H. de (1988) *Europe's Ageing Population*, Paris/Guildford: Futuribles/Butterworths.

Kelly, G. (1996) 'Feminist or feminine? The feminine principle in occupational therapy' in *British Journal of Occupational Therapy*, 59(1), pp. 2–6.

Kendrick, K. (1992) 'Considerations of personhood in nursing research: an ethical perspective' in K. Soothill, C. Henry and K. Kendrick (eds) *Themes and Perspectives in Nursing*, London: Chapman & Hall.

Kendrick, K. (1995a) 'Nurses and doctors: a problem of partnership' in K. Soothill, L. Mackay and C. Webb (eds) *Interprofessional Relations in Health Care*, London: Edward Arnold.

Kendrick, K. (1995b) 'Codes of professional conduct and the dilemmas of professional practice' in K. Soothill, L. Mackay and C. Webb (eds) *Interprofessional Relations in Health Care*, London: Edward Arnold.

Kersbergen, A. L. (1996) 'Case management: a rich history of co-ordinating care to control costs' in *Nursing Outlook*, 44(4), pp. 169–72.

Kingsland, S., P. Smith and S. McKinley (1994) 'Introduction of managed care plans in a cardiac surgery unit' in *Contemporary Nurse*, 3(4), pp. 189–94.

Knapp, M. (1988) 'Searching for efficiency in long-term care: deinstitutionalisation and privatisation' in *British Journal of Social Work*, 18(Supplement), pp. 149–72.

Knowlden, V. (1991) 'Nurse caring as constructed knowledge' in R. M. Neil and R. Watts (eds) *Caring and Nursing: Explorations in Feminist Perspectives*, New York: National League for Nursing.

Koerner, J. E. (1995) 'Professional practice: trangressor or revolutionary?' in *Journal of Professional Nursing*, 11(2), p. 68.

Kraan, R., J. Baldock, B. Davies, A. Evers, L. Johansson, M. Knapen, M. Thorslund and C. Tunissen (1991) *Care for the Elderly: Significant Innovations in Three European Countries*, Vienna: Campus Verlag.

Kruzich, J. M. (1995) 'Empowering organizational contexts: patterns and predictors of perceived decision-making influence among staff in nursing homes' in *The Gerontologist*, 35(2), pp. 207–16.

Laffin, M. (1988) *Professionalism and Policy*, Aldershot: Gower.

Laffin, M. (1989) *Managing Under Pressure: Industrial Relations in Local Government*, Basingstoke: Macmilan.

Lamberston, E. C. (1995) 'The emerging health professions' in *Nursing Forum*, 30(2), pp. 22–6.

Langan, M. and P. Lee (1989) 'Whatever happened to radical social work?' in M. Langan and P. Lee (eds) *Radical Social Work Today*, London: Routledge.

Larson, M. S. (1977) *The Rise of Professionalism*, Berkeley: University of California Press.

Larson, M. S. (1980) 'Proletarianization and educated labor' in *Theory and Society*, 9(1), pp. 131–75.

Laschinger, H. K. S. and D. S. Havens (1996) 'Staff nurse work empowerment and perceived control over nursing practice' in *Journal of Nursing Administration*, 26(9), pp. 27–35.

Lash, S. and J. Urry (1987) *The End of Organised Capitalism*, Cambridge: Polity Press.

Lawson, M. (1991) 'The recipient's view' in S. Ramon (ed.) *Beyond Community Care*, Basingstoke: Mamcillan.

Lawson, R. (1993) 'The new technology of management in the personal social services' in P. Taylor-Gooby and R. Lawson (eds) *Markets and Managers*, Buckingham: Open University Press.

Le Grand, J. (1982) *The Strategy of Equality*, London: George Allen & Unwin.

Le Grand, J. and R. Robinson (eds) (1984) *Privatisation and the Welfare State*, London: Allen & Unwin.

Le Grand, J., D. Winter and F. Wooley (1990) 'The National Health Service: safe in whose hands?' in J. Hills (ed.) *The State of Welfare: the Welfare State in Britain Since 1974*, Oxford: Clarendon Press.

Le Grand, J. and W. Bartlett (eds) (1993) *Quasi-Markets in Social Policy*, Basingstoke: Macmillan.

Levitas, R. (ed.) (1986) *The Ideology of the New Right*, Cambridge: Polity Press.

Lister, R. (1991) 'Citizenship engendered' in *Critical Social Policy*, 11(2), pp. 65–71.

Loewenberg, F. M. and R. Dolgoff (1992) *Ethical Decisions for Social Work Practice*, 4th edition, Itasca: Peacock Publishing.

Lorentzon, M. (1990) 'Professional status and managerial tasks' in P. Abbott and C. Wallace (eds) *The Sociology of the Caring Professions*, London: Falmer Press.

Luker, K. A., K. Beaver, S. J. Leinster, R. G. Owens, L. F. Degner and J. A. Sloan (1995) 'The information needs of women newly diagnosed with breast cancer' in *Journal of Advanced Nursing*, 22(1), pp. 134–41.

Lyon, D. (1994) *Postmodernity*, Buckingham: Open University Press.

Macfarlane, A. (1993) 'The right to make choices' in J. Bornat, C. Pereira, D. Pilgrim and F. Williams (eds) *Community Care: a Reader*, Basingstoke: Macmillan.

Mackay, L. (1989) *Nursing a Problem*, Milton Keynes: Open University Press.

Mackay, L. (1993) *Conflicts in Care: Medicine and Nursing*, London: Chapman & Hall.

MacPherson, K. I. (1991) 'Looking at caring and nursing through a feminist lens' in R. M. Neil and R. Watts (eds) *Caring and Nursing: Explorations in Feminist Perspectives*, New York: National League for Nursing.

Maggs, C. (1987) 'Nursing history: contemporary practice and contemporary concerns' in C. Maggs (ed.) *Nursing History: the State of the Art*, London: Croom Helm.

Marquand, D. (1992) 'The enterprise culture: old wine in new bottles?' in P. Heelas and P. Morris (eds) *The Values of the Enterprise Culture*, London: Routledge.

Marshall, T. H. (1950) *Citizenship and Social Class*, Cambridge: Cambridge University Press.

Marsland, L., S. Robinson and T. Murrells (1996) 'Pursuing a career in nursing: gender differences between men and women qualifying as registered general nurses' in *Journal of Nursing Management*, 4(4), pp. 231–41.

Martin, G. W. (1995) 'HIV/AIDS – an issue in nurse education' in *Nurse Education Today*, 15(2), pp. 106–10.

Maslow, A. (1970) *Motivation and Personality*, 2nd edition, New York: Harper & Row.

Mattingly, C. and M. H. Fleming (1994) *Clinical Reasoning: Forms of Inquiry in a Therapeutic Practice*, Philadelphia: F. A. Davis.

Mauksch, H. O. (1966) 'The organisational context of nursing practice' in *The Nursing Profession: Five Sociological Essays*, New York: Wiley.

McBeath, G. and S. Webb (1991) 'Social work, modernity and post-modernity' in *Sociological Review*, 39(4), pp. 745–62.

McCallum, D. (1990) 'The case in social work: psychological assessment and social regulation' in P. Abbott and C. Wallace (eds) *The Sociology of the Caring Professions*, Basingstoke: The Falmer Press.

McCallum, J. and A. L. Howe (1992) 'Family care of the elderly in Australia' in J. I. Kosberg (ed.) *Family Care of the Elderly: Social and Cultural Chnage*, Newbury Park: Sage.

McCrone, P. (1995) 'Predicting mental health service use: diagnsotic based systems and alternatives' in *Journal of Mental Health*, 4(1), pp. 31–40.

McDowell, B. (1991) *Ethical Conduct and the Professional's Dilemma: Choosing Between Service and Success*, New York and Westport: Quorum Books.

McGrath, M. (1993) 'Whatever happened to teamwork?' in *British Journal of Social Work*, 23(1), pp. 15–29.

McHale, J. (1995) 'Whistleblowing in American health care' in G. Hunt (ed.) *Whistleblowing in the Health Service*, London: Edward Arnold.

McMurray, A. (1993) *Community Health Nursing: Primary Health Care in Practice*, 2nd edition, South Melbourne: Churchill Livingstone.

Means, R. and R. Smith (1994) *Community Care: Policy and Practice*, Basingstoke: Macmillan.

Midgely, J. (1981) *Professional Imperialism*. Heinemann Education.

Midgley, J. and C. Jones (1994) 'Social work and the radical right: impact of developments in Britain and the United States' in *International Social Work*, 37(2), pp. 115–26.

Mills, A. J. (1989) 'Gender, sexuality and organization theory' in J. Hearn, D. L. Sheppard, P. Tancred-Sherriff and G. Burrell (eds) *The Sexuality of Organization*, London: Sage.

Mills, C. W. (1956) *White Collar*, New York: Galaxy Books/Oxford University Press.

Mishra, R. (1984) *The Welfare State in Crisis*, Brighton: Wheatsheaf Books.

Mishra, R. (1987) *The Welfare State in Capitalist Society*, Brighton: Wheatsheaf.

Moxley, D. P. (1989) *The Practice of Case Management*, Newbury Park: Sage.

Mullaly, R. (1993) *Structural Social Work*, Toronto: McClelland & Stewart.

Murray, C. (1984) *Losing Ground: American Social Policy 1950–1980*, New York: Basic Books.

Murray, C. (1990) *The Emerging British Underclass*, London: Institute of Economic Affairs.

Nellis, M. (1995) 'Towards a new view of probation values' in R. Hugman and D. Smith (eds) *Ethical Issues in Social Work*, London: Routledge.

Ngan, R. (1993) 'Cultural imperialism: western social work theories for Chinese practice and the mission of social work in Hong Kong' in *The Hong Kong Journal of Social Work*, XXVII(2), pp. 47–55.

Nicholls, D. (1992) 'The invisible hand: providence and the market' in P. Heelas and P. Morris (eds) *The Values of the Enterprise Culture*, London: Routledge.

Nicholls, D. (1995) 'Equal opportunities – aspects: gender and physiotherapy' in *Physiotherapy*, 81(3), pp. 115–16.

Noddings, N. (1984) *Caring: a Feminine Approach to Ethics and Moral Education*, Berkeley: University of California Press.

Nolan, M., J. Nolan and G. Grant (1995) 'Maintaining nurses' job satisfaction and morale' in *British Journal of Nursing*, 4(19), pp. 1149–54.

North, N. (1993) 'Empowerment in welfare markets' in *Health and Social Care*, 1(2), pp. 129–37.

Nozick, R. (1974) *Anarchy, State and Utopia*, Oxford: Basil Blackwell.

Oakley, A. (1984) 'What price professionalism? The importance of being a nurse' in *Nursing Times*, 80(50), pp. 24–7.

O'Connor, I., J. Wilson and D. Setterlund (1995) *Social Work and Welfare Practice*, 2nd edition, Melbourne: Longman.

Oliver, M. (1990) *The Politics of Disability*, London: Macmillan.

O'Neill, S. (1993) 'The drive for professionalism in nursing: a reflection on classism and racism' in J. L. Thompson, D. G. Allen and L. Rodrigues-Fisher (eds) *Critique, Resistance and Action: Working Papers in the Politics of Nursing*, New York: National League for Nursing.

Onyett, S. (1992) *Case Management in Mental Health*, London: Chapman & Hall.

Orme, J. and B. Glastonbury (1993) *Care Management*, Basingstoke: Macmillan.

Ozanne, E. (1990) 'Reasons for the emergence of case management approaches and their distinctiveness from present service arrangements' in A. Howe, E. Ozanne and C. Selby Smith (eds) *Community Care Policy and Practice: New Directions for Australia*, Clayton: Public Sector Managament Institute, Monash University.

Papadakis, E. (1994) 'Public opinion, redistribution and the welfare state' in M. Wearing and R. Berreen (eds) *Welfare and Social Policy in Australia*, Sydney: Harcourt Brace.

Papadakis, E. and P. Taylor-Gooby (1987) *The Private Provision of Public Welfare*, Brighton: Wheatsheaf.

Parkin, F. (1979) *Marxism and Class Theory: a Bourgeois Critique*, London: Tavistock.

Parkin, P. A. C. (1995) 'Nursing the future: a re-examination of the professionalization thesis in the light of some recent developments' in *Journal of Advanced Nursing*, 21(3), pp. 561–7.

Parry, N. and J. Parry (1979) 'Social work, professionalism and the state' in N. Parry, M. Rustin and C. Satyamurti (eds) *Social Work, Welfare and the State*, London: Edward Arnold.

Parsloe, P. and O. Stevenson (1993) *Community Care and Empowerment*, York: Joseph Rowntree Foundation.

Parton, N. (1991) *Governing the Family: Child Care, Child Protection and the State*, Basingstoke: Macmillan.

Parton, N. (1994) ' "Problematics of government", (post) modernity and social work' in *British Journal of Social Work*, 24(1), pp. 9–32.

Payne, M. (1990) *Modern Social Work Theory: a Critical Introduction*, Basingstoke: Macmillan.

Perkin, H. (1989) *The Rise of Professional Society: England Since 1880*, London: Routledge.

Perkins, R. (1995) 'Meeting the needs of lesbian service users' in *Mental Health Nursing*, 15(6), pp. 18–21.

Petersen, A. (1994) *In a Critical Condition: Health and Power Relations in Australia*, Sydney: Allen & Unwin.

Philp, M. (1978) 'Notes on the form of knowledge in social work' in *Sociological Review*, 27(1), pp. 83–111.

Pieretti, G. (1994) 'From poverty to the poor: implications for social policy' in P. Giudicini and G. Pieretti (eds) *Urban Poverty and Human Dignity*, Milan: FrancoAngeli.

Pierson, C. (1991) *Beyond the Welfare State?* Cambridge: Polity Press.

Pilgrim, D. (1993) 'Mental health services in the twenty first century: the user-professional divide?' in J. Bornat, C. Pereira, D. Pilgrim and F. Williams (eds) *Community Care: a Reader*, Basingstoke/Milton Keynes: Macmillan/Open University.

Pithouse, A. (1987) *Social Work: the Social Organisation of an Invisible Trade*, Aldershot: Gower.

Pittman, L. and T. Rogers (1990) 'Nursing: a culturally diverse profession in a monocultural health system' in *Australian Journal of Advanced Nursing*, 8(1), pp. 30–8.

Pixley, J. (1993) *Citizenship and Employment*, Cambridge: Cambridge University Press.

Plant, R. (1986) 'Needs, agency and rights' in C. G. Stampford and D. J. Galligan (eds) *Law, Rights and the Welfare State*, London: Croom Helm.

Pollitt, C. (1993) *Managerialism and the Public Services*, 2nd edition, Oxford: Basil Blackwell.

Powell, J. and A. Goddard (1996) 'Cost and stakeholder views: a combined approach to evaluating services' in *British Journal of Social Work*, 26(1), pp. 93–108.

Propper, C. (1993) 'Quasi-markets, contracts and quality in health and social care: the US experience' in J. Le Grand and W. Bartlett (eds) *Quasi-Markets and Social Policy*, Basingstoke: Macmillan.

Purkis, M. E. (1994) 'Entering the field: the intrusion of the 'social' and its exclusion from studies of nursing practice' in *The International Journal of Nursing Studies*, 31(4), pp. 315–36.

Purtilo, R. (1993) *Ethical Dimensions in the Health Professions*, 2nd edition, Philadelphia: W. B. Saunders.

Quinn, J. (1995) 'Case management in hone and community care' in *Journal of Gerontological Social Work*, 24(3/4), pp. 233–49.

Ralph, C. (1989) 'Nursing management and leadership – the challenge' in

M. Jolley and P. Allan (eds) *Current Issues in Nursing*, London: Chapman & Hall.

Ramon, S. (1991) 'Principles and conceptual knowledge' in S. Ramon (ed.) *Beyond Community Care*, Basingstoke: Mamcillan.

Ratcliffe, P. (1996) 'Gender differences in career progress in nursing: towards a non-essential structural theory' in *Journal of Advanced Nursing*, 32(2), pp. 389–95.

Rawls, J. (1972) *A Theory of Justice*, Oxford: The Clarendon Press.

Rhodes, M. (1986) *Ethical Dilemmas in Social Work Practice*, London: Routledge & Kegan Paul.

Rhodes, P. (1991) 'The assessment of black foster parents: the relevance of cultural skills' in *Critical Social Policy*, 11(2), pp. 31–51.

Richards, J. (1995) 'Two levels of care – the emergence of the health care assistant and the implications for registered nurses' in K. Kendrick, P. Weir and E. Rosser (eds) *Innovations in Nursing Practice*, London: Edward Arnold.

Rider, B. A. and R. M. Brashear (1988) 'Men in occupational therapy' in *American Journal of Occupational Therapy*, 42(4), pp. 231–7.

Robinson, J. (1989) 'Nursing in the future: a cause for concern' in M. Jolley and P. Allan (eds) *Current Issues in Nursing*, London: Chapman & Hall.

Robolis, S. (1993) 'A view from the south: reforms in Greece' in *Journal of European Social Policy*, 3(1), pp. 56–9.

Robson, W. A. (1976) *Welfare State and Welfare Society*, London: George Allen & Unwin.

Roche, M. (1992) *Rethinking Citizenship*, Cambridge: Polity Press.

Rojek, C., G. Peacock and S. Collins (1988) *Social Work and Received Ideas*, London: Routledge.

Rooney, B. (1987) *Racism and Resistance to Change*, Liverpool: Merseyside Area Profile Group.

Rose, H. (1981) 'Re-reading Titmuss: the sexual division of welfare' in *Journal of Social Policy*, 10(4), pp. 477–502.

Rose, N. and P. Miller (1992) 'Political power beyond the state: problematics of government' in *British Journal of Sociology*, 43(2), pp. 173–205.

Ross, K. (1995) 'Speaking in tongues: involving users in day care services' in *British Journal of Social Work*, 25(6), pp. 791–804.

Ross-Kerr, J. C. and P. Paul (1995) 'Visions realised and dreams dashed' in *Canadian Journal of Nursing Research*, 27(3), pp. 39–63.

Rubin, S. (1992) 'Case management' in S. M. Rose (ed.) *Case Management and Social Work Practice*, White Plains NY: Longman.

Rudman, M. J. (1996a) 'User involvement in the nursing curriculum: seeking users' views' in *Journal of Psychiatric and Mental Health Nursing*, 3(3), pp. 195–200.

Rudman, M. J. (1996b) 'User involvement in mental health nursing practice: rhetoric or reality?' in *Journal of Psychiatric and Mental Health Nursing*, 3(6), pp. 385–90.

Rustin, M. (1994) 'Flexibility in higher education' in R. Burrows and B. Loader (eds) *Towards a Post-Fordist Welfare State?* London: Routledge.

Sachs, D. and D. R. Labovitz (1994) 'The caring occupational therapist' in *American Journal of Occupational Therapy*, 48(11), pp. 997–1005.

Salvage, J. (1985) *The Politics of Nursing*, London: Heinemann.

Salvage, J. (1988) 'Professionalization – or struggle for survival? A consideration of current proposals for the reform of nursing in the Unted Kingdom' in *Journal of Advanced Nursing*, 13(3), pp. 515–19.

'Sammy's Dad' (1996) *News From Sammy's Dad*, issue 2, internet newsletter: intsocwork@nisw.org.uk, downloaded September 1996.

Sandall, J. (1995) 'Choice, continuity and control? Recent developments in maternity care in Britain' in K. Soothill, L. Mackay and C. Webb (eds) *Interprofessional Relations in Health Care*, London: Edward Arnold.

Sargent, M. (1994) *The New Sociology for Australians*, 3rd edition, Melbourne: Longman.

Satyamurti, C. (1979) 'Care and control in child care' in M. Rustin, N. Parry and C. Satyamurti (eds) *Social Work, Welfare and the State*, Oxford: Basil Blackwell.

Schorr, A. (1992) *The Personal Social Services: an Outside View*, York: Joseph Rowntree Foundation.

Scotton, R. B. and C. R. Macdonald (1993) *The Making of Medibank*, Kensington, NSW: University of New South Wales.

Scully, A. M. (1995) 'Who owns your code of ethics?' in *Australian Nursing Journal*, 2(11), p. 30.

Segal, J. (1991) 'The professional perspective' in S. Ramon (ed.) *Beyond Community Care*, Basingstoke: Mamcillan.

Sellman, D. (1996) 'Why teach ethics to nurses?' in *Nurse Education Today*, 16(1), pp. 44–8.

Shardlow, S. (1989) 'Changing values in social work' in S. Shardlow (ed.) *The Values of Change in Social Work*, London: Routledge.

Shardlow, S. (1995) 'Confidentiality, accountability and the boundaries of client–worker relationships' in R. Hugman and D. Smith (eds) *Ethical Isues in Social Work*, London: Routledge.

Shaw, G. B. (1911) *The Doctor's Dilemma*, London: Constable.

Sheeran, P. J. (1993) *Ethics in Public Administration*, Westport, CT: Praeger.

Shera, W. (1996) 'Managed care and people with severe mental illness' in *Health and Social Work*, 21(3), pp. 196–202.

Sibeon, R. (1990) 'Social work knowledge, social actors and de-professionalization' in P. Abbott and C. Wallace (eds) *The Sociology of the Caring Professions*, Basingstoke: Falmer Press.

Siim, B. (1990) 'Women and the welfare state: between private and public dependence' in C. Ungerson (ed.) *Gender and Caring: Work and Welfare in Britain and Scandinavia*, Hemel Hempstead: Harvester Wheatsheaf.

Siiriäinen, I. (1996) 'From welfare state to knowledge society' proceedings of the IFSW/IASSW Joint Congress, *Participating in Change (Vol. 1)*, Hong Kong: Hong Kong Association of Social Workers, pp. 277–80.

Silavwe, G. (1995) 'The need for a new social work practice in an African setting' in *British Journal of Social Work*, 25(1), pp. 71–84.

Sim, J. (1989) 'Methodology and morality in physiotherapy research' in *Physiotherapy*, 75(4), pp. 237–43.

Simpkin, M. (1979) *Trapped Within Welfare*, London: Macmillan.

Sines, D. (1996a) 'Images of disability and handicap' in S. Twinn, B. Roberts and S. Andrews (eds) *Community Health Care Nursing: Principles for Practice*, Oxford: Butterworth-Heinemann.

Sines, D. (1996b) 'Advocacy' in S. Twinn, B. Roberts and S. Andrews (eds) *Community Health Care Nursing: Principles for Practice*, Oxford: Butterworth-Heinemann.

Smith, D. (1995) *Criminology for Social Work*, Basingstoke: Macmillan.

Smith, G. (1980) *Social Need*, London: George Allen and Unwin.

Smith, G. and R. Harris (1972) 'Ideologies of need and the organisation of social work departments' in *British Journal of Social Work*, 2(1), pp. 27–45.

Soares, H. H. and M. K. Rose (1994) 'Clinical aspects of case management with the elderly' in *Journal of Gerontological Social Work*, 22(3/4), pp. 143–57.

Sonntag, J. (1995) 'A case manager's perspective' in *Journal of Elder Abuse & Neglect*, 7(2/3), pp. 115–31.

Statham, D. (1978) *Radicals in Social Work*, London: Routledge & Kegan Paul.

Stathopoulos, P. and A. Amera (1992) 'Family care of the elderly in Greece' in J. I. Kosberg (ed.) *Family Care of the Elderly: Social and Cultural Change*, Newbury Park: Sage.

Stearns, P. (1977) *Old Age in European Society*, London: Croom Helm.

Stilwell, F. (1994) 'The economic context of social policy' in M. Wearing and R. Berreen (eds) *Welfare & Social Policy in Australia*, Sydney: Harcourt Brace.

Storch, J. and S. Stinson (1988) 'Concepts of deprofessionalization with application to nursing' in R. White (ed.) *Political Issues in Nursing: Past, Present and Future, vol. 3*, Chichester: J. Wiley & Sons.

Strong, P. and J. Robinson (1990) *The NHS Under New Management*, Buckingham: Open University Press.

Sullivan, M. (1992) *The Politics of Social Policy*, Hemel Hempstead: Harvetser Wheatsheaf.

Svetlik, I. (1991) 'The future of welfare pluralism in the post-communist countries' in A. Evers and I. Svetlik (eds) *New Welfare Mixes in Care for the Elderly, vol. 1*, Vienna: European Centre for Social Welfare policy and Research.

Taylor-Gooby, P. (1991) *Social Change, Social Welfare and Social Science*, Hemel Hempstead: Harvester Wheatsheaf.

Taylor-Gooby, P. and R. Lawson (eds) (1993) *Markets and Managers: New Issues in the Delivery of Welfare*, Buckingham: Open University Press.

Ten, C. L. (1993) 'Liberalism and mutliculturalism' in G. L. Clark, D.

Forbes and R. Francis (eds) *Multiculturalism, Difference and Postmodernism*, Melbourne: Longman Cheshire.

Thomas, S. and A. Ingham (1995) 'The unit based clinical practice development role' in K. Kendrick, P. Weir and E. Rosser (eds) *Innovations in Nursing Practice*, London: Edward Arnold.

Thomasma, D. C. (1994) 'Toward a new medical ethics: implications for ethics in nursing' in P. Benner (ed.) *Interpretive Phenomenology: Embodiment, Caring, and Ethics in Health and Illness*, Thousand Oaks: Sage.

Thompson, G. (1987) *Needs*, London: Routledge & Kegin Pane.

Thompson, N. (1993) *Anti-Discrimination*, Basingstoke: Macmillan.

Thorpe, R. and J. Petruchenia (1992) 'Unionism and community workers: the role of the Australian Social Welfare Union – an interview with Fran Hayes' in R. Thorpe and J. Petruchenia (eds) *Community Work or Social Change? An Australian Perspective*, Marrickville, NSW: Hale & Iremonger.

Thrift, N. (1993) 'The light fantastic: culture, postmodernism and the image' in G. L. Clark, D. Forbes and R. Francis (eds) *Multiculturalism, Difference and Postmodernism*, Melbourne: Longman Cheshire.

Thurow, L. (1996) *The Future of Capitalism*, Sydney: Allen & Unwin.

Timms, N. (1983) *Social Work Values: an Enquiry*. London: Routledge & Kegin Pane.

Timor, J. and J. Wilson (1995) 'An Aboriginal woman speaks about her practice: Aboriginal Hospital Liaison' in W. Weeks and J. Wilson (eds) *Issues Facing Australian Families: Human Services Respond*, 2nd edition, Melbourne: Longman.

Titmuss, R. (1958) *Essays on the Welfare State*, London: George Allen and Unwin.

Titmuss, R. (1970) *The Gift Relationship*, London: George Allen and Unwin.

Toren, N. (1972) *Social Work: the Case of a Semi-Profession*, London: Sage.

Torkington, N. P. K. (1983) *The Racial Politics of Health*, Liverpool; Merseyside Area Profile Group.

Touraine, A. (1981) *The Voice and the Eye: an Analysis of Social Movements*, Cambridge: Cambridge University Press.

Tschudin, V. (1994) *Deciding Ethically*, London: Ballière Tindall.

Turner, B. S. (1990) 'Outline of a theory of citizenship' in *Sociology*, 24(2), pp. 189–217.

Twigg, J. (1989) 'Models of carers: how do social care agencies conceptualize their relationship with informal carers' in *Journal of Social Policy*, 18(1), pp. 53–66.

Twinn, S. (1996) 'Nursing for community health: changing professional issues' in S. Twinn, B. Roberts and S. Andrews (eds) *Community Health Care Nursing: Principles for Practice*, Oxford: Butterworth-Heinemann.

Ungerson, C. (1987) *Policy is Personal*, London: Tavistock.

Ungerson, C. (1990) 'The language of care' in C. Ungerson (ed.) *Gender and Caring*, Hemel Hempstead: Harvetser Wheatsheaf.

Valentine, P. E. B. (1996) 'Nursing: a ghettoized profession relegated to the women's sphere' in *International Journal of Nursing Studies*, 33(1), pp. 98–106.

van Every, J. (1992) 'Who is the family? The assumptions of British social policy' in *Critical Social Policy*, 11(3), pp. 62–75.

Victor, C. (1991) *Health and Health Care in Later Life*, Milton Keynes: Open University Press.

Wagner, G. (1988) *A Positive Choice*, London: HMSO.

Walker, A. (1986) 'Pensions and the production of poverty in old age' in C. Phillipson and A. Walker (eds) *Ageing and Social Policy*, Aldershot: Gower.

Walker, A. (1993) 'Community care policy: from consensus to conflict' in J. Bornat, C. Pereira, D. Pilgrim and F. Williams (eds) *Community Care: a Reader*, Basingstoke: Macmillan.

Walker, A. (1994) 'Poverty and inequality in old age' in J. Bond, P. Coleman and S. Peace (eds) *Ageing in Society*, 2nd edition, London: Sage.

Walsh, K. (1994) 'Citizens, charters and contracts' in R. Keat, N. Whitely and N. Abercrombie (eds) *The Authority of the Consumer*, London: Routledge.

Walton, M. (1993) 'Regulation in child protection – policy failure?' in *British Journal of Social Work*, 23(2), pp. 139–56.

Walton, R. (1975) *Women in Social Work*. London: Routledge & Kegin Pane.

Ward, D. (1991) 'Gender and cost in caring' in R. M. Neil and R. Watts (eds) *Caring and Nursing: Explorations in Feminist Perspectives*, New York: National League for Nursing.

Ward, D. and A. Mullender (1991) 'Empowerment and oppression' in *Critical Social Policy*, 11(2), pp. 21–30.

Wasserman, H. (1972) 'The professional social worker in a bureaucracy' in *Social Work*, 16(1), pp. 89–95.

Wearing, M. (1994) 'Dis/claiming citizenship? Social rights, social justice and welfare in the 1990s' in M. Wearing and R. Berreen (eds) *Welfare & Social Policy in Australia*, Sydney: Harcourt Brace.

Wearing, M. and R. Berreen (1994) 'Introduction: redefining welfare' in M. Wearing and R. Berreen (eds) *Welfare & Social Policy in Australia*, Sydney: Harcourt Brace.

Webb, A. and G. Wistow (1987) *Social Work, Social Care and Social Planning: the Personal Social Services Since Seebohm*, Harlow: Longman.

Webb, D. (1991a) 'Puritans and paradigms: a speculation on the form of new moralities in social work' in *Social Work & Social Sciences Review*, 2(2), pp. 146–59.

Webb, D. (1991b) 'A stranger in the academy: a reply to Lena Dominelli' in *Social Work & Social Sciences Review*, 2(3), pp. 236–41.

Weeks, W. (1995) 'Women's work, the gendered division of labour and community services' in W. Weeks and J. Wilson (eds) *Issues Facing Australian Families: Human Services Respond*, Melbourne: Longman.

Weir, P. (1995) 'Clinical practice development role: a personal reflection' in K. Kendrick, P. Weir and E. Rosser (eds) *Innovations in Nursing Practice*, London: Edward Arnold.

Wessell, M. L. (1992) 'Said another way: an ethical issue for a profession for all seasons' in *Nursing Forum*, 27(3), pp. 29–33.

Whitaker, A. (1992) 'Post-Fordism revisited' in M. Reed and M. Hughes (eds) *Rethinking Organization*, London: Sage.

White, V. (1995) 'Commonality and diversity in feminist social work' in *British Journal of Social Work*, pp. 143–56.

Wilding, P. (1982) *Social Welfare and Professional Power*, London: Macmillan.

Williams, F. (1989) *Social Policy: a Critical Introduction*, Cambridge: Polity Press.

Williams, F. (1994) 'Social relations and welfare' in R. Burrows and B. Loader (eds) *Towards a Post-Fordist Welfare State?* London: Routledge.

Williams, S. and S. Shah (1995) 'The inroduction of casemix across Australia: implementation issues for occupational therapists' in *Australian Occuaptional Therapy Journal*, 42(4), pp. 143–50.

Williamson, C. (1992) *Whose Standards? Consumer and Professional Standards in Health Care*, Buckingham: Open University Press.

Wilson, A. G. M. (1984) 'Physiotherapy – a profession and its ethics' in *New Zealand Journal of Physiotherapy*, 12(2), p. 14.

Wise, S. (1988) *Doing Feminist Social Work*, Studies in Sexual Politics 21, Manchester: University of Manchester.

Wise, S. (1995) 'Feminist ethics in practice' in R. Hugman and D. Smith (eds) *Ethical Issues in Social Work*, London: Routledge.

Wiseman, J. (1996) 'The past and future of the Australian welfare state' in J. Wilson, J. Thomson and A. McMahon (eds) *The Australian Welfare State*, Melbourne: Macmillan.

Wisensale, S. K. (1988) 'Generational equity and intergenerational politics' in *The Gerontologist*, 28(6), pp. 773–8.

Wistow, G., M. Knapp, B. Hardy and C. Allen (1994) *Social Care in a Mixed Economy*, Buckingham: Open University Press.

Witts, P. (1992) 'Patient advocacy in nursing' in K. Soothill, C. Henry and K. Kendrick (eds) *Themes and Perspectives in Nursing*, London: Chapman & Hall.

Witz, A. (1992) *Patriarchy and the Professions*, London: Routledge.

Wolk, J. L., W. P. Sullivan and D. J. Hartmann (1994) 'The managerial nature of case management' in *Social Work*, 39(2), pp. 152–60.

Woods, C. Q. (1987) 'From individual dedication to social activism: historical develoment of nursing professionalism' in C. Maggs (ed.) *Nursing History: the State of the Art*, London: Croom Helm.

World Bank (1994) *Averting the Old Age Crisis: Policies to Protect the Old and Promote Growth*, Oxford: Oxford University Press.

Yeatman, A. (1992) 'Women's citizenship claims, labour market policy and globalisation' in *Australian Journal of Political Science*, 27(3), pp. 449–61.

Yeatman, A. (1996) 'Interpreting contemporary contractualism' in *Australian Journal of Social Issues*, 31(1), pp. 39–54.

Young, G. (Lord of Graffham) (1992) 'Enterprise regained' in P. Heelas and P. Morris (eds) *The Values of the Enterprise Culture*, London: Routledge.

Index